CW00616816

assessing reading
from theories to classrooms

An international multi-disciplinary investigation of the theory of reading assessment and its practical implications at the beginning of the 21st century

Edited by

Marian Sainsbury
Colin Harrison
Andrew Watts

CAMBRIDGE ASSESSMENT

First published in July 2006
National Foundation for
Educational Research
The Mere, Upton Park
Slough, Berkshire SL1 2DQ
www.nfer.ac.uk

The views contained in this document are
the authors' own and do not necessarily
reflect those of the NFER.

Every attempt has been made to contact
copyright holders. Please contact the NFER
if you have any concerns.

© NFER 2006
Registered Charity No. 313392
ISBN 1 905314 21 3

Design by Stuart Gordon at NFER
Layout by Helen Crawley at NFER
Index by Indexing Specialists (UK) Ltd
www.indexing.co.uk

Contents

1 **Introduction and overview**   1
   Marian Sainsbury

[Part 1]
Competing paradigms:
theories of reading and theories of assessment

2 **Validity and the construct of reading**   8
   Marian Sainsbury

3 **A psychological perspective on the diagnostic assessment of reading:**   22
   establishing priorities
   John R. Beech

4 **Cognitive psychology and reading assessment**   38
   Alastair Pollitt and Lynda Taylor

5 **Postmodernism and the assessment of literature**   50
   Colin Harrison

6 **Learning to read or learning to do tests?**   64
   Ros Fisher

[Part 2]
Historical insights as drivers of theory

7 **The assessment of reading comprehension: key historical influences**   76
   in the USA
   P. David Pearson and Diane Nicole Hamm

8 **Significant moments in the history of reading assessment in the UK**   102
   Chris Whetton

9 **Lessons of the GCSE English '100 per cent coursework' option,**   122
   1986–1993
   Paul Thompson

[Part 3]
Theory into practice: current issues

10 **Postmodern principles for responsive reading assessment:**   140
    a case study of a complex online reading task
    Colin Harrison, Nasiroh Omar and Colin Higgins

11 **Automated marking of content-based constructed responses**   158
    Claudia Leacock

12 **The role of formative assessment**   168
    Gordon Stobart

13 **Using assessment focuses to give feedback from reading**   179
    assessments
    Lorna Pepper, Rifat Siddiqui and Andrew Watts

[Part 4]
Theory into practice: national initiatives

14 **Validity challenges in a high-stakes context: National Curriculum**   196
    tests in England
    Marian Sainsbury and Andrew Watts

15 **New perspectives on accountability: statutory assessment of**   210
    reading of English in Wales
    Roger Palmer and David Watcyn Jones

16 **There is no alternative ... to trusting teachers: reading and**   222
    assessment in Scotland
    Louise Hayward and Ernie Spencer

17 **Low-stakes national assessment: national evaluations in France**   241
    Martine Rémond

18 **The National Assessment of Educational Progress in the USA**   250
    Patricia Donahue

19 **Concluding reflections: from theories to classrooms**   258
    Marian Sainsbury

    Index   260

Contributors

John R. Beech

John Beech is a senior lecturer in the School of Psychology, University of Leicester. He was Editor of *Journal of Research in Reading* for vols 24–7 and is currently a coeditor of this journal. He is author/editor of a dozen books including *Learning to Read, Cognitive Approaches to Reading and Psychological Assessment of Reading* (coedited with Chris Singleton). His research interests are in cognitive, biological and educational approaches to reading and reading development.

Patricia Donahue

Patricia Donahue is a Senior Program Administrator in the Assessment Division at Educational Testing Service, Princeton, New Jersey. She is the coordinator of the National Assessment of Educational Progress (NAEP) reading assessment and serves on the reading task force for the PIRLS study.

Ros Fisher

Ros Fisher has taught in primary schools in the north-west of England and the USA. She is now Senior Lecturer in Education at the University of Exeter. She writes widely about the teaching of literacy and has researched the role of the teacher and teacher change in current large-scale initiatives to change the teaching of literacy in England. She is currently researching the relationship between talk and writing. She has recently written *Inside the Literacy Hour* (Routledge, 2002) and edited the collection of papers from an ESRC-funded research seminar series *Raising Standards in Literacy* (Falmer, 2002).

Diane Nicole Hamm

Diane Nicole Hamm is a graduate student in Educational Psychology at Michigan State University. Her research interests include reading comprehension processes as well as the cognitive outcomes of assessment. She has co-published a number of pieces with her adviser, P. David Pearson.

Colin Harrison

Colin Harrison is Professor of Literacy Studies in Education at the University of Nottingham. He has been at various times a secondary school teacher of English, a GCSE examiner, a full-time researcher into the place of reading in school, a teacher educator and a director of national projects evaluating the place of ICT in learning. His three current research projects are in the use of digital video for teacher development, using artificial intelligence approaches in evaluating the quality of internet research, and exploring the processes of innovation and invention in the junior school.

Louise Hayward

Louise Hayward is a Senior Lecturer in the Faculty of Education, University of Glasgow. Over the past 15 years she has worked to bring research, policy and practice in assessment into closer alignment in Scotland. Currently, she chairs the Research and Development group for the National Assessment for Learning programme. Her research interests are in inclusion, assessment and transformational change.

Colin Higgins

Colin Higgins is Head of the Learning Technology Research Group in the Computer Science department at the University of Nottingham. He is interested in automatic assessment of essays, and particularly the development of the CourseMarker (formerly CEILIDH) system. His other current projects are in handwriting recognition, constructing metrics for object-oriented designs and programs, and writing programs to measure the quality of logic programs written in the Prolog language.

Claudia Leacock

Claudia Leacock is a senior member of technical staff at Pearson Knowledge Technologies. Since receiving her PhD in Linguistics at the CUNY Graduate Center, she has specialised in the automated understanding of human languages. Her primary focus during the past 10 years has been the automated assessment of constructed responses – for both content and grammar – and she has published many articles in this area. Most recently, she was a guest co-editor of the *Journal of Natural Language Engineering*'s special issue on building educational applications using natural language processing.

Nasiroh Omar

Nasiroh Omar came from a post in a technological university in Malaysia to the University of Nottingham's Learning Sciences Research Institute to work on a doctorate in the field of artificial intelligence and human learning. She has been the lead programmer and researcher on the Online Reading Internet Research Support System.

Roger Palmer

Roger Palmer was educated at Canton High School, Cardiff and University College, Cardiff where he read English and also completed a PGCE course. He taught for 20 years in schools in the Cardiff area before joining the Curriculum Council for Wales in 1989. When the Council was superseded by the Qualifications, Curriculum and Assessment Authority for Wales, Roger worked for the new body as an English Subject Officer. In September 2004, he became the Authority's Assistant Chief Executive (Curriculum and Assessment: 3–14).

P. David Pearson

P. David Pearson, a frequent writer on issues of assessment and policy, serves as Professor and Dean in the Graduate School of Education at the University of California, Berkeley. Additionally, Pearson has an active programme of research on issues of instruction and reform in high-poverty schools.

Lorna Pepper

Lorna Pepper is a Project Officer at Oxford Cambridge and RSA (OCR), developing key stage 3 English test papers for National Assessment Agency (NAA) and managing key stage 3 English test development for the Council for the Curriculum, Examinations and Assessment (CCEA). Previously, she worked in secondary education, first as an English teacher and then in various middle management roles, before taking up positions in international schools abroad and in the UK, as International Baccalaureate Coordinator and school Vice Principal.

Alastair Pollitt

Alastair Pollitt is currently a visiting fellow at the Research Centre for English and Applied Linguistics in the University of Cambridge, where he was a Senior Research Officer from 1990 to 1994. In the intervening years he was Director of the Research and Evaluation Division at the University of Cambridge Local Examinations Syndicate (now Cambridge Assessment). In 1989, while a lecturer in the University of Edinburgh, he co-directed the national survey of standards of English in Scotland's primary and secondary schools.

Martine Rémond

Martine Rémond is *Maître de conference* in Cognitive Psychology at the IUFM de Créteil, France. Her research interests[†] are devoted to reading comprehension and its assessment, to the role of metacognition, to the improvement of reading comprehension and the effects of strategy instruction training. Nationally and internationally recognised for her ability in assessment, she is reading expert for PISA (2000, 2003, 2006) and PIRLS (2001), for the French High Committee for Education Assessment (2000–05), and for the French High Committee for Reading (since 1996). She has been involved in a large number of educational and psychological researches on assessment and in large-scale studies (in France and in Europe) for her expertise in reading processes. [†](Institut National de la Recherche Pédagogique and University of Paris 8)

Marian Sainsbury

Marian Sainsbury is Head of Literacy Assessment Research in the Department of Assessment and Measurement at the NFER. She is director of the projects developing the national tests in English at key stages 1 and 2 in England and key stage 2 in Wales and international reading coordinator for the PIRLS study. Her research interests are in a variety of aspects of literacy and its assessment.

Rifat Siddiqui

Rifat Siddiqui is a freelance education consultant with a range of experience in literacy assessment. Formerly a primary teacher, she has worked for a number of education organisations including the NFER, the Qualifications and Curriculum Authority and the University of Cambridge.

Ernie Spencer

Ernie Spencer is Honorary Research Fellow in the Faculty of Education, University of Glasgow. In previous roles as Senior Research Officer at the Scottish Council for Research in Education and HMIE National Specialist in Assessment and in English he made significant contributions to the development of formative and summative assessment in Scotland.

Gordon Stobart

Gordon Stobart is Reader in Education at the University of London Institute of Education. After teaching English in secondary schools he worked as an educational psychologist in London. He then studied in the USA as a Fulbright Scholar. After working as Head of Research at London Examinations he became Principal Research Officer for the National Council for Vocational Qualifications and then for the Qualifications and Curriculum Authority. He is a member of the Assessment Reform Group, which campaigns for better use of formative assessment in teaching and learning, and has produced a series of influential pamphlets – *Assessment for Learning (1998)*; *Testing, Motivation and Learning (2002)*; *The Role of Teachers in the Assessment of Learning (2006)*. He is also editor of the international journal *Assessment in Education: Principles, Policy and Practice*.

Lynda Taylor

Lynda Taylor is currently Assistant Director of the Research and Validation Group at the University of Cambridge ESOL Examinations (part of Cambridge Assessment – a non-teaching department of the university). She is responsible for coordinating the research and validation programme to support Cambridge ESOL's wide range of language tests and teaching awards. She has extensive experience of the theoretical and practical issues involved in second language testing and assessment, and a special interest in the theory and practice of assessing reading comprehension ability.

Paul Thompson

Paul Thompson has been working as a lecturer in the School of Education at the University of Nottingham since 2001. For many years previously, he was a Head of English in City of Nottingham comprehensive schools. His main research interests centre around the relationship between oracy and literacy. He is particularly interested in theories of collaborative learning and classroom talk.

David Watcyn Jones

David Watcyn Jones became English Subject Officer (key stages 1 and 2) at ACCAC in 1998 and the following year was appointed Assistant Chief Executive (Curriculum and Assessment 5–14). This post required him to advise the Chief Executive and the Authority on curriculum and assessment policy, 3–14, and lead the development, monitoring and review of the National Curriculum and its associated statutory assessment arrangements. He also led the development of related curriculum and assessment guidance. Since his retirement from this post in 2003, he has worked as an educational consultant, primarily for ACCAC, involving himself in national initiatives and speaking at numerous conferences. He is a Welsh speaker.

Andrew Watts

Andrew Watts began his career as a teacher of English in secondary schools in Surrey, Coventry and Northampton, UK. After 11 years he moved to Singapore where he taught in a Junior College for over four years. He then worked for five years as a 'Specialist Inspector' for English in the Ministry of Education in Singapore, focusing on curriculum development in English teaching and in-service teacher development. In 1990 he returned to England and has been working with Cambridge Assessment since the summer of 1992. For most of that time he looked after teams that were developing national tests in English, Maths and Science for 14-year-olds in England, Northern Ireland and Wales. He is now working on the setting up of the Cambridge Assessment Network, whose purpose is to promote online and face-to-face professional development opportunities for assessment professionals internationally.

Chris Whetton

Chris Whetton is an Assistant Director of NFER and also Head of its Department of Assessment and Measurement. He is the author of over a dozen published tests spanning both educational and psychological uses. He has directed several large-scale national projects including the development of National Curriculum tests for seven-year-olds as these were introduced, and other National Curriculum projects including key stage 2 English development.

1 Introduction and overview

Marian Sainsbury

The nature of 'reading' is something usually taken for granted. In contemporary societies, the use of literacy for a vast range of social and personal purposes is so widespread that it is rarely questioned. Within the education system, reading becomes an explicit focus of attention, with substantial resources devoted to the teaching and learning of literacy. Even here, however, the definition of 'reading' is usually not discussed, although one can be inferred from the kinds of teaching and learning activities adopted. It is in the research community that the nature of reading becomes a defined area of study, and here, as will become apparent, there are major disagreements between different academic traditions over what is included and implied by the term 'reading'.

Essentially, this book sets out to explore some of the theories, practices and conflicts that surround the idea of reading at the beginning of the 21st century. In order to do this, it adopts a particular perspective: that of assessment. Researchers, educationalists and the population at large have questions about how well people read. Often, though not exclusively, these people are children who are still in the process of mastering reading. This need to assess leads inevitably to the question 'What exactly are the skills and understandings that we want to know about, in order to gauge reading ability?' Thus it is that a particular definition of reading becomes made concrete in an assessment. By scrutinising tests and other instruments, it is possible to study the definition of reading – the construct – specified or assumed in each one. It is the existence of this concrete evidence in the form of tests and other instruments that makes assessment a promising springboard for investigating the nature of reading.

In 2003–4, a series of seminars was held in England, supported by the research funding body the Economic and Social Research Council, with the purpose of exploring the construct of reading. The participants were selected with the deliberate intention of allowing interaction between different disciplines, and consisted of a group of specialists in assessment and reading from the United Kingdom, France and the United States. There were cognitive psychologists with research interests in reading; educationalists with a range of research backgrounds in the teaching and learning of literacy and literature; and assessment specialists. Unusually in such gatherings, there was a strong representation of test developers, whose day-to-day research activities included the practical processes of devising, trialling and refining actual reading tests.

This group set out to bring together their varying experiences of and perspectives on the construct of reading. The seminars were open-ended and built in generous time for discussion, in recognition of the complexity of the subject matter. Each individual chapter in this volume explicates its reasoning and rationale, with references that situate it within its own research background. However, some 'fault lines' in the arguments can be set out in general terms, and these apply both to ideas about reading and to ideas about assessment.

When we read, we consciously or unconsciously recognise written symbols as words with meaning. The act of reading includes deciphering, or decoding, written words and letters, transforming them into recognisable language, and understanding their meaning. Meaning is intricately tied up with communication, and communication of many kinds of meanings occupies a central role in human social intercourse. There is a fundamental divide between researchers who focus primarily on the decoding of words and those who focus primarily upon reading as an act of meaning-communication. For the former group, 'reading' proper is recognising the words; the uses of those words to communicate meaning and support social interaction are interesting, but not essential to the construct of reading. For the latter group, by contrast, it is not possible to make sense of the notion of 'reading' without communicating meanings; the communicative act is primary, and the specific skills involved in decoding written words cannot logically be separated from this.

These two perspectives can be thought of as competing paradigms: theory-systems that shape experience. The paradigm determines what counts as evidence, what observations are relevant, and even what is observed. Because the difference between them is logical, definitional rather than empirical, no observation can prove that one is right rather than the other. But this rather bleak view of paradigm competition does not rule out an understanding of both, nor a rapprochement between them in practice. In the real world of a literate society and an education system preparing children to participate in it, the stark differences outlined above are masked. All agree that children need to acquire the ability to recognise words fluently and to use this ability to facilitate and enrich their everyday lives.

At the same time, there are equally fundamental disagreements about what – and whom – assessment is for, and once again these can be seen as competing paradigms. One kind of assessment purpose is to pinpoint strengths and weaknesses in reading development and to diagnose barriers to that development. Such assessments give rise to indications that guide teaching or prescribe remedial action. These formative and diagnostic assessments can be seen as broadly for the benefit of the learner, but also of teachers and other professionals, whose effectiveness is enhanced by this information.

Formative assessment stresses the value of informative feedback in the course of ongoing teaching. The information obtained from informal, day-to-day assessment is used by the teacher to provide better-focused teaching. It can also be used by the learner as a powerful tool for improvement. If pupils are able to monitor their own learning in this way, rather than relying on the teacher and other outsiders, they can play an active part in planning their own learning experiences. In this classroom use, the assessment is very informal. The evidence can be entirely ephemeral, such as a pupil's answer to a teacher's question, or take the form of feedback comments on a pupil's written work. It is also possible to use more formal assessments in this formative way. Rather than focus on the numerical score obtained in a test, it is possible to make an analysis of the strengths and weaknesses demonstrated at individual, group or class level, and to use this information to plan the curriculum.

Diagnostic assessment is used when a child is experiencing difficulties in learning to read, in order to pinpoint the perceptual or cognitive problems that underlie the lack of progress. For this purpose, carefully designed batteries of subtests are devised, and are administered on an individual basis by an educational psychologist.

An entirely different purpose for assessment is certification. Final examinations and tests assess the reading curriculum covered in the course of schooling. The certificates awarded on the basis of these assessments serve to attest to the competence and under-standing of the student. They thus benefit the student, in providing a recognised measure of attainment, but also society, where they fulfil the purpose of selecting candi-dates for further study or for employment. They are high-stakes assessments, because the individual student's life chances are affected by them.

In some countries in recent years, however, notably the UK and the USA, the pre-dominant purpose for assessment is political accountability. Governments have a legitimate interest in improving educational standards. Better national attainment in lit-eracy benefits individuals as well as enhancing the economic performance of a country. In this context, tests have the role of providing the performance outcomes that are used by government and the public to evaluate progress towards defined targets. As a result, the tests acquire high stakes for the local authorities, schools and teachers who are being held to account for their pupils' performance.

The participants in the seminars represented a range of interests in and allegiances to these differing views on the nature of reading and on the purpose of assessment. They were brought together with the aim of understanding more about one another's perspec-tives, and perhaps finding an overarching position that brought them closer. In the latter aspiration, it is fair to say that the seminars had only limited success, as the incompatibility of the underpinning theories became if anything more evident. This will be discussed in more detail in the concluding comments of the book. But in the aim of fostering mutual understanding and respect, the seminar series can be counted a success.

This book is the outcome of those seminars, and the themes outlined above are worked out in a variety of cross-cutting ways in the following chapters. Part 1 is devot-ed to explicating in more depth some of the theoretical underpinnings of reading and of assessment. Each of the authors in this section sets out a single perspective; it is only later in the book that the links between them become apparent.

Marian Sainsbury starts this process by outlining the evolving theory of construct validity in assessment and suggesting an overall shape for the construct of reading that attempts to integrate competing points of view.

In John Beech's chapter, a psychological perspective is advanced that can broadly be situated in the tradition focusing primarily on the decoding of the written word. In highlighting the contribution of psychology to the study of reading, he stresses the value of soundly researched psychological theories, arguing that these are rarely if ever embodied in reading tests. His stance on assessment is to highlight its diagnostic and theory-building potential, with tests contributing to research and to remediation of difficulties.

Alastair Pollitt and Lynda Taylor also adopt the perspective of cognitive psychology, and agree with Beech's argument that reading test design fails to reflect psychological research and theory. Their particular focus is upon the processes that characterise reading comprehension and they use research findings and practical illustration to build a picture of the process of constructing meaning from text. In this way, their chapter directly contributes to the delineation of the construct of reading that runs through the book.

In the fourth chapter of theoretical exploration, Colin Harrison takes a radically different perspective, situated firmly within socio-cultural and literary traditions. His starting point is the challenge posed to the definition of reading by postmodernism. On this view, meaning itself is shifting and ephemeral and texts are susceptible to a variety of readings, none of which is privileged over others. He draws from this position a demanding set of requirements for any valid assessment of reading. Harrison's chapter adds a new dimension to the emerging outline of the construct of reading and raises fundamental questions about assessment itself.

Ros Fisher adopts yet another stance, this time looking at reading and its assessment from the perspective of teachers and children. Her chapter argues strongly for the centrality of these stakeholders in the assessment of reading. For Fisher, purposes for assessment must be evaluated according to how well they support the enterprise of teaching and learning, and the construct of reading in tests is contrasted unfavourably with school literacy, which itself is narrower than the broader, richer and more subtle nature of literacy as social practice.

These introductory chapters highlight the assumptions and demands of several of the most influential paradigms that compete in the definition of reading and its assessment. By their very nature, these chapters present incommensurable theories; the arguments of one cannot be translated into the terms of another. However, any serious attempt to investigate the construct of reading must take account of this bewildering complexity, reflecting as it does the variety of viewpoints attracted by this important human activity. There is no attempt here to build bridges. Instead, these opening chapters raise and illuminate the issues that arise in different forms in the remainder of the book.

Any test or assessment can be seen as a concrete embodiment of a construct of reading and of an assessment purpose. In designing a test, in espousing an assessment system at any level from individual to class to nation, decisions are made about reading and about purpose which define a specific form in the context of a specific use. This book is about actual assessments just as much as the theories that underlie them. By examining reading tests and other less formal assessment approaches, the abstract notions set out in the first part of the book can be investigated in practice. The later chapters take on this task, sometimes focusing closely on a single test, sometimes more than one, sometimes following up practical implications of particular ideas.

In the second section, three chapters cast a historical light upon the assessment of reading, revealing patterns of change over time and discovering reasons and causes in the historical context. P David Pearson surveys some key moments in the history of reading tests in the USA, pointing up the evolution in underlying theory that gave rise to each new development. Similarly, Chris Whetton highlights significant points in reading testing in the UK, but argues that political and social influences are at least as important as theoretical developments in determining key outcomes. Paul Thompson's chapter chronicles the course of one influential innovation in the UK, demonstrating in its own way the jostling of literary and educational theories with political imperatives in determining the shape of reading assessment at one moment in time.

Leading on from these historical insights, the third section of the book looks at the cutting edge of current work and finds two apparently contradictory ideas occupying equally prominent positions. On the one hand, developments in information and communication technology have led to a burgeoning interest in computer-based assessment. Colin Harrison introduces some fundamental issues and principles for consideration. Once again juxtaposing theory with practice, Claudia Leacock's chapter describes an innovative computer program, already operational, that makes possible the assessment of open written responses, releasing computer-based reading tests from the limitations of the multiple-choice question.

On the other hand, a contrasting area of interest and innovation that can be discerned in current thought is the use of informal assessment by both teacher and pupils to support learning – known broadly as the 'assessment for learning' movement. Gordon Stobart sets out the principles of formative classroom assessment and applies them to reading. To complement this, Lorna Pepper, Rifat Siddiqui and Andrew Watts describe a research project investigating the value of giving feedback in a specific form to students who have taken a reading test.

In implementing national assessment systems, governments make decisions about the nature of reading and the purpose of assessment that set the agenda for national discourse. The seminar group included participants who were directly involved in devising the national assessments in England, Wales, Scotland, France and the USA. The insights from these very different systems make up the fourth and final part of the book.

Marian Sainsbury and Andrew Watts describe a system of national testing in England that attempts to combine a complex, meaning-centred, literary construct of reading with the constraints of a high-stakes testing regime. Roger Palmer and David Watcyn Jones describe a similar construct of reading operating in Wales, but their chapter traces the evolution of a similar high-stakes accountability assessment system into one that supports teachers in assessing for formative and diagnostic purposes. This perspective is further amplified by Louise Hayward and Ernie Spencer, writing about Scotland. Here, there is an established commitment to formative assessment that is worked out in all aspects of the national assessment system.

The national evaluations in France take a distinctive view of both the construct of reading and of the nature and purpose of national assessment. Martine Rémond describes a set of formal national tests that are entirely formative in purpose, and that embody a definition of reading which accords more importance to grammatical knowledge than is usual in the Anglo-Saxon world. Finally, Patricia Donahue sets out yet another different national response to the set of questions posed by the definition and purpose of reading assessment. The National Assessment of Educational Progress in the USA is a national survey of reading attainment that yields indications of performance that are crucial to political decision-making but low stakes for individual students. The construct of reading can broadly be situated within a 'responsive reading' paradigm. These five national assessment systems therefore represent a variety of ways in which contemporary societies obtain their evidence about reading, and demonstrate how these governmental decisions are both reflections and determinants of national values.

Each of these chapters is capable of standing alone, giving a summary and overview of a particular perspective. The book can be used for reference, bringing together a collection of theoretical and practical information about the assessment of reading in its political, educational, geographical, historical and contemporary contexts. Reading the entire book brings out the interaction between these factors, as principles are juxtaposed with concrete examples, political demands with academic, social influences with individual, theories with classrooms.

[Part 1]

Competing paradigms:
theories of reading and theories of assessment

2 Validity and the construct of reading

Marian Sainsbury

This book sets out to examine the nature of reading by way of its assessment. The central question running through it is the apparently simple one of how *reading* should be defined. The question can be investigated in many different ways, but in this book the main focus is upon the constructs embodied in different reading tests and assessments. The need for careful definition of constructs is a central element of validity theory, the branch of psychometrics that raises philosophical questions about what is assessed and how. This chapter will lay some foundations for later discussions by exploring the concept of validity itself, its recent evolution into a more flexible and powerful form and the implications of this for the assessment of reading.

Validation evidence

In most cases, a test user wishes to generalise beyond the scope of test items themselves, to draw inferences about valued attributes that go beyond the test. As Haertel (1985) puts it:

> *Tests are settings for structured observations designed to provide an efficient source of information about attributes of examinees. Often, these are attributes that cannot be observed directly. The necessity of making inferences to a broader domain than the test directly samples brings a need for some deeper theoretical basis for linking test and criterion. This is a need for construct validation.*
> (Haertel, 1985, p.25)

The validation of a test consists of defining the underlying construct of interest and establishing the theoretical and empirical links between this and test performance.

A complex but clear theory of validity emerges from the mainstream of recent scholarship. Of particular note in articulating this broadly accepted view are Messick's (1989) comprehensive overview of the field and the latest version of the *Standards for Educational and Psychological Testing* (AERA/APA/NCME, 1999). On this account, the validation of an assessment consists of establishing lines of argument that demonstrate that inferences about the construct can validly be drawn from performances on the test. This process of validation is not related abstractly to the test in itself, but is specific to the purposes for which the test is used. The test developer has a responsibility to work from a definition of the information the test is intended to provide and the purposes for which it is required to provide it. From these definitions, appropriate lines of argument can be determined and the evidence to support the validation argument collected and reported.

Any discussion of the validation of an assessment requires consideration of the purposes of its use and the kinds of evidence that can support its appropriateness for that purpose. A reading test may be intended for the diagnosis and remediation of difficulties for individual students; examinations in reading aim to certify competence in relation to employment or further study; national and international tests and surveys in reading are designed for the evaluation of the overall functioning of schools and education systems within or between countries. These purposes for assessment form an essential part of the foundations upon which validation arguments are built.

Five broad types of evidential argument are identified in the *Standards* (AERA/APA/NCME, 1999), and validation for specific purposes takes the form of collecting evidence and building arguments of one or more of these types. The first type of evidence listed is that based on test content. The definition of the construct will set out a range of knowledge, skills and understandings. Content evidence is a consideration of how well the range of performance elicited by the test represents the range described in the construct. On Messick's (1989) analysis, construct under-representation is one of the major threats to test validity. As an example, it is important for a curriculum-based assessment to represent adequately the range of knowledge and understanding included in the curriculum guidelines. Only with such adequate representation can test scores be taken as a valid indication of how well the student has mastered the curriculum taught. Validation evidence for test content representation is largely judgemental. Test items may be mapped on to elements of the construct in a systematic way and the strength of the relationship between the two reviewed by experts. In the case of many types of reading tests, this evaluation of content must be applied both to passages of text and to the questions asked.

A second type of validation evidence is that based on response processes and this too relates to the adequate representation of the construct. In answering a test question, the thought processes engaged in by candidates should replicate as closely as possible the ways of thinking described in the construct. For example, if a test of reading is based on reading and understanding an extract which is intended to be unseen, candidates with prior knowledge of the text from which the extract is drawn are likely to give answers based on that prior knowledge, rather than their abilities to read and understand a passage presented unseen. Any rote learning of model answers would also fail to elicit the desired thought processes in test takers. In this case, the aim is to provide evidence of the students' mental processes. These are by their very nature invisible, but can be accessed to some extent through words or actions. For example, an open response question in a reading test may ask a pupil to draw an inference about character or motivation in a literary reading passage and present some textual evidence for the answer. Analysis of written answers can yield a range of indications of students' reasoning. Test development processes may also include a trial stage, where test-takers are asked to think aloud as they read, or to explain how they obtain their answers to comprehension questions, and this evidence can also be presented in a validation argument.

In both of the above lines of validation argument, the differential performance of different groups – boys and girls, for example, or different ethnic groups – may also provide evidence. Alongside construct under-representation, the second threat to validity identified by Messick (1989) is construct-irrelevant variance. For example, if a reading passage contains subject matter that is more familiar to one group than others, the responses to test items could reflect that familiarity, rather than the knowledge and thought processes defined by the construct. Correspondingly, scores on the test would provide information about cultural familiarity rather than about the construct of interest and inferences about the construct would be invalid.

A third type of validation evidence is provided by statistical analyses of the internal structure of the test. The definition of the construct should indicate whether the domain being assessed is homogeneous or consists of a variety of distinguishable but related elements. A curriculum-related reading test, for example, could address aspects such as: literal understanding of content; grammatical analysis of sentence structures and authorial techniques such as the use of imagery. Validation evidence might look for greater consistency between items within each of these elements, rather than across different ones. Other reading tests, for example those devised to assess word recognition, might have a more unidimensional structure.

There is a strong tradition of validation studies based on correlation with other variables and this type of evidence constitutes a further potential line of argument. The scores on a given test should relate strongly to variables that represent the same or similar construct, providing 'convergent' evidence and should relate weakly to variables defined as irrelevant to the construct – 'discriminant' evidence. In these investigations, new tests under development may be correlated with a criterion measure. In the development of standardised reading tests, evidence is often obtained from a sample who take the new test together with an established test of the same construct; a high correlation is desirable in these cases. In curriculum-based test development, a strong correlation between test scores and teachers' ratings of the attainment of the same pupils would stand as validation evidence.

The final category of validation evidence listed in the *Standards* (AERA/APA/NCME, 1999) relates to the consequences of test use. This area has been the subject of lively debate in recent years, for example filling an entire issue of the journal *Educational Measurement: Issues and Practice* in 1997 (Volume 16, number 2). Since the validation of a test provides evidence that it is suitable to be used for a specific purpose, the consequences that ensue when it is used for that purpose become relevant to its validity. A clear example of this is found in high-stakes curriculum related tests. Where there are important consequences of test scores in terms of targets or penalties, teachers and others are likely to find ways of maximising performance on the specific content and format of the test's items. An over-emphasis on this could lead to a distortion of the curriculum, where only what is tested is taught. The consequences of testing are therefore a legitimate part of validation evidence. However, test results can be used for many different purposes, some of them unintended and unforeseeable and the debate has raged over the scope of the concept of validity and the extent of the test developer's responsibilities in these cases. In the example, it is evident that a test can only have this effect of narrowing the curriculum if it under-represents the construct in significant ways. The mainstream view of consequential evidence, as expressed in the current *Standards* (AERA/APA/NCME, 1999), is that it is only relevant to validity where it can be traced back to construct under-representation or construct-irrelevant variance. Broader consequences may be investigated and are of interest in informing policy decisions, but are not strictly a part of validity.

Thus contemporary theorists regard validity as a unitary concept in which the test's relationship to the construct is central. Different lines of argument and different types of evidence can be brought to bear in validating a test, but in all cases these arguments and evidence serve to illuminate and justify the relationship between test and construct. This can be depicted in a simple diagram, shown in Figure 2.1, where the lines of argument provide evidence about the relationship between concrete performances on a specific test instrument and the abstract ideas that make up the construct of interest.

This unitary concept differs from earlier accounts of validity in the psychometric literature (for example, AERA/APA/NCME, 1966). Previously, distinctly different types of validity were identified. 'Content validity' corresponded to the first type of evidence described above. Then, 'criterion-related validity' looked at the relationship between the test and an external criterion. This was divided into 'concurrent validity' where the criterion measure was administered or collected at the same time as the administration of the test and 'predictive validity', where a criterion measure was collected later, in the form, for example, of subsequent examination success. Correlational studies were prominent in the validation literature as a result. Finally on this traditional account, 'construct validity' was evaluated by investigating the qualities measured by the test and relating this to theoretical constructs.

The contemporary conception of validity is more complex and flexible and correspondingly more powerful, including all the ideas covered by the previous subdivisions but going beyond them and uniting them. It is the responsibility of the test developer, in conjunction (where appropriate) with the test user, to define the purpose and circumstances

Figure 2.1 Diagrammatic representation of construct validation

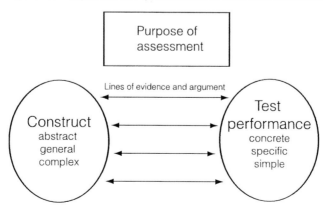

of the use of the test or assessment and to delineate the construct being addressed. In the light of this, appropriate lines of validation argument must be identified and relevant evidence collected. This unified concept means that a very broad range of types of assessment can be encompassed, going beyond traditional paper-based short-item tests to include assessments of extended performances, practical skills, computer-based interactions and portfolios of performance, for example. The types of evidence relevant to a diagnostic individual test for use by educational psychologists are likely to be very different from those for a high-stakes curriculum related test and different again from an observational checklist of the behaviours of young children. Yet this over-arching analysis of construct validity can be applied to all of these.

Published writing on validity in the UK, the location of the seminars on which this book is based, is generally more variable and lacks the spirit of lively debate found in the USA, where all the writing described above took place. There is some work investigating particular instances of validity argument (see, for example, Stobart, 2001) and definitions of validity can sometimes be found in the literature. However, there is little discussion addressing the definition itself, or developing it beyond what has already been established. Gipps (1994) gives a good overview of validity as a unified concept and of the debate over consequences. A recognition of recent ideas about validity is also apparent in the work of Wiliam (see, for example, 1993, 1996). Other authors, however, show little acknowledgement of the recent evolution of ideas. Harlen (2004) gives a supposedly authoritative review of research into the validity of assessment by teachers for summative purposes. Yet her introductory definition largely relies on traditional concepts of different types of validity: 'content', 'face', 'concurrent' and 'construct' validity. Messick's ideas are mentioned briefly in this review, in the context of consequential validity, but the mainstream of scholarship on the unified concept of construct validity is referred to in just half a sentence as 'a view held by many' (Harlen, 2004, p.13). Similarly, Stuart and Stainthorp (2004) offer a review of 17 currently available British reading tests, but refer only to the traditional notions of 'construct validity' and 'content validity' and to correlational studies in their discussion. It is clear that thinking on validity elsewhere in the world offers a more comprehensive and dynamic background than that in the UK, both in respect to reading and more widely.

The challenge of the interpretative tradition

Recent work in the USA does not represent a complete consensus, however. For some commentators, the range of lines of argument and types of evidence within this mainstream definition of validation remains too narrow. This challenge is part of the far-reaching debate about the nature of social science: the psychometric tradition with its emphasis on quantifiable evidence versus the interpretative tradition in which human meaning takes on central importance. Although this debate may seem abstruse, it has important implications for the range of reading assessments covered by this book.

A key exponent of the case for the broadening of validity theory is Moss (1992, 1994, 1995, 1996, 1998, 2003), who argues strongly for the inclusion of evidence based in interpretative research. Essentially, this approach recognises human individual and social interpretation of contextualised meaning as a central and valid source of research evidence, rather than relying on a notion of scientific objectivity. She does not wish to reject the mainstream account of validation evidence, but argues that, in ignoring human meaning and judgement, it is too narrow.

One consequence of this view is to place Moss amongst those arguing for a stronger role for consequential evidence in validation. When test scores are communicated to different stakeholders – teachers, students, parents – mainstream theories assume a neutral, authoritative, shared understanding of their meaning. But when this communication is analysed in terms of the interpretative theories of discourse analysis and social psychology, the actual ways in which scores are interpreted by different people become relevant. Moss's argument is that these individual meanings should be regarded as part of the consequences of test use and part of the validation evidence (Moss, 1995, 1998).

Moss explains how research in the hermeneutic tradition can lead to the inclusion of a wider range of judgements in arriving at an evaluation of validity. She characterises this hermeneutic approach as follows:

> … a holistic and integrative approach to interpretation of human phenomena that seeks to understand the whole in the light of its parts, repeatedly testing interpretations against the available evidence until each of the parts can be accounted for in a coherent interpretation of the whole.

(Moss, 1994, p.7)

Included in this evidence might be a teacher's specialised knowledge of the context in which a portfolio of work was produced, personal acquaintance with the student and expert knowledge of the subject matter. The expert dialogue that takes place between referees for academic journals, or examiners of doctoral theses, is better characterised in this way than by drawing upon the standardised and de-personalised approach of mainstream psychometric theories. Moss argues, not for an abandonment of these theories, but for an open-minded examination of various lines of evidence, from a variety of theoretical perspectives, in order better to account for the complexity of the validation process.

Moss's constructive questioning of established approaches to validation is particularly important for the consideration of assessments that do not take the form of traditional tests. These ideas have found an application in the area of formative classroom assessment (for example, Black and Wiliam, 1998; Moss, 2003; Stiggins, 2001). This refers to the ongoing judgements made by teachers, with stress on the value of informative feedback in the course of ongoing teaching. The information obtained from informal, day-to-day assessment is used by the teacher to provide better-focused teaching. It can also be used by the learner as a powerful tool for improvement. If pupils are able to monitor their own learning in this way, rather than relying on the teacher and other outsiders, they can play an active part in planning their own learning experiences. Black

(2003) argues that significant learning gains arise when pupils become autonomous, self-monitoring learners in this way. In this classroom use, the assessment is very informal. The evidence can be entirely ephemeral, such as a pupil's answer to a teacher's question, or take the form of feedback comments on a pupil's written work.

Moss's argument is that mainstream validation studies are inadequate for the analysis of such assessment, for a number of reasons. Unlike a formal test, classroom assessment is not a discrete activity; it is integral to the continuing interaction within the learning environment, so that it is difficult to isolate a 'performance' that can be related to the construct. Similarly, there are problems when one attempts to define a given set of inferences that should be derived from the test performance; instead, interpretations are fleeting and provisional and not always recorded. Classroom assessment is individual rather than standardised across groups and the contextual factors make each individual's response different. Consequences of assessment in this fluid context take on central importance; both intended and unintended effects result from individual interpretations and shape future learning. She argues that little sense can be made of the idea of aggregating these individual judgements into an overarching 'score' to summarise attainment; rather, the informal judgements and comments themselves constitute the validity of this assessment approach. In these circumstances, Moss argues, the hermeneutic approach demonstrates its worth, whereas the mainstream approach fails. Similar arguments are developed by Wiliam (2004) and Stiggins (2004).

These ideas apply to the assessment of reading in many different ways, some of which are worked out in more detail in other chapters of this book. Reading itself is an act of interpretation and individuals may make different but valid interpretations of what they read. Assessments of reading include some item-based tests that fit quite comfortably into the mainstream of validation argument. But in other cases, there is an evident tension between the openness necessary for recognising individual interpretations and the standardisation required by the mainstream tradition. In the study of literature by older students, postmodernism rules out any single correct interpretation. And much reading assessment is informal, taking place from day to day in the classroom in spontaneous exchanges between teacher and pupil. In all of these contexts, the interpretative tradition of research may have more to contribute than mainstream psychometrics.

Shifting the focus

It is not currently clear whether these challenges to the mainstream view of validity in the USA will result in a consensus on a broader definition or lead to fragmentation within the field. For the purposes of this chapter, however, it is possible to see how the differing perspectives can be brought together into a unified, though multifaceted, view of the issue.

For this book is mainly concerned with a construct – the construct of reading – and its reflection in different assessments. Because the focus is on the construct rather than the assessment, no approach should be arbitrarily excluded and this book includes chapters on computer-based assessment and formative classroom assessment alongside more traditional item-based tests. Centring the discussion on the construct itself, however, makes it possible to see how the two sides of the debate described above can be integrated.

Many chapters of this book describe reading tests on a fairly traditional model: whether the focus is on word recognition, comprehension or literary understanding, the test consists of a standard set of requirements, with marks and scores awarded for performance. For all of these instruments, the mainstream account of validity can be brought to bear. A construct can be delineated and lines of evidence established to support the use of the test in giving information about that construct. These constructs exist as complex, abstract and general notions in answer to the question 'What does it mean to be a reader?' Sometimes they are described exhaustively in words; in other cases they are inferred from curriculum documents or from briefer descriptions in the test documentation. But constructs exist only as ideas and it is this quality that makes possible a rapprochement between formal and informal assessments.

The construct embodied in a test is an idea frozen in time, set out in written form as a fixed point. But ideas can also be viewed as reflected in human consciousness, in a more dynamic, interactive form. And in this form, a construct of reading can be found in the consciousness of every teacher. It is this individual, personal construct that allows teachers to plan literacy lessons. It is also the teacher's personal construct that gauges questioning and feedback to make the ephemeral judgements that constitute classroom assessment. When teachers help students to understand the criteria for successful performance in their work for formative purposes, they are attempting to make available in the learner's consciousness a fuller, more specific and detailed version of that same construct. Wiliam (2004) and Marshall (2004) make a similar point when both identify a need for a community of practice to underpin a shared construct of quality in a subject, as a necessary requirement for formative assessment.

The arguments of the validity debate can be seen as two sides of a single coin. The relationship between the static construct of reading in a test and dynamic constructs of reading in people's heads is a two-way one, in which neither could logically exist without the other. The construct of a test has itself been derived interactively, through reviewing related research and discussion with colleagues and experts. The individual teacher's construct has been built up through contact with established, published, theories. Indeed, the entire world of human understanding must be seen in this way, both contributing to and derived from individual instances of interaction (Sainsbury, 1992).

The construct of reading

This review of validity theory reinforces the importance of defining the relevant construct, whether embodied in a formal test or informing an exchange between teacher and pupil. It is this centrality of the need for construct definition that gave rise to a seminar series focused entirely on the construct of reading. All of the chapters of this book explore aspects of this topic in depth, but it is possible to sketch out here some of the broad features that can be distinguished in the construct of reading. Haertel (1985) gives a helpful analysis of what he calls 'achievement constructs', which he distinguishes from the constructs of psychology. Achievement constructs are grounded in curricular theory on the one hand, and educational psychology on the other.

Assessments, in an educational context, aim to give information about valued educational outcomes. They aim to tell us how well the pupils have learned what they have been taught. They are typically about cognitive outcomes, with understanding, knowledge and skill as central elements. Defining an educational construct is likely to involve, at the very minimum, ideas about the nature of the subject itself, *what the pupils have been taught* and what is known about *how children learn* in that curriculum area. Educational constructs, as Haertel pointed out, will inevitably be complex constructs, with both logical and psychological aspects.

Reading is a fundamental educational construct and it is unsurprising that its definition is difficult. It is a flexible skill rather than a body of knowledge. In outline, it can be seen to involve, at least, knowledge of language, knowledge of the written code, the ways in which children learn to read and the difficulties they may encounter. A consideration of the purposes that are intrinsic to the act of reading brings in aesthetic and emotional as well as pragmatic factors for the individual. The social, philosophical and political context can be seen in the functions fulfilled by reading in society and the role of literature in cultural life. Like much knowledge, skill and understanding, the act of reading itself is mostly invisible, consisting of mental changes that cannot be directly observed, so that evidence about reading has to be evinced through observable performances of one kind or another.

The diagram in Figure 2.2 depicts a schematic structure for conceptualising this valued educational attribute – an overall construct of reading as it emerges from a variety of reading tests and assessments.

This envisages four main reading processes: decoding, comprehending, responding and analysing. The four are nested in the diagram, as there is a substantial overlap between them. Each of the four 'layers' of the construct manifests itself in research, in teaching and in assessment.

The outer ring, 'decoding', recognises that the ability to translate written words into their spoken form underlies all other reading processes, which are therefore represented within it. In the outer ring alone are theories addressing the ways in which children learn to decode text, investigating such areas as phonological awareness, visual memory and the use of analogy (for example, Adams, 1990; Goswami and Bryant, 1990; Garrod and Pickering, 1999). The teaching implications of these theories find their form in phonics, the systematic teaching of phoneme-grapheme correspondences, which forms a part of most early literacy programmes. In assessment terms, the area of decoding is represented by numerous specialist tests such as the Phonological Assessment Battery (Fredrickson, 1996) and also general word-reading tests such as Schonell (1945).

Figure 2.2 Diagram of the construct of reading

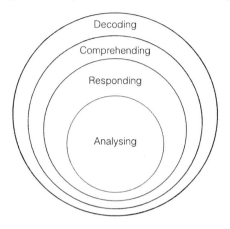

Within the outer ring is the second layer, 'comprehending'. The area that lies within this ring alone has a relatively small representation in recent research. Here, lexical and grammatical knowledge is combined with recognising the written form of the word, so that meaning is attached to the word, sentence or passage. In teaching terms, too, it is difficult to point to many relevant practices, although the teaching of word and sentence recognition to beginner readers and the old-fashioned 'comprehension exercise' can be seen as examples. Assessment, by contrast, is strongly represented in this area. There are many tests of sentence completion and straightforward literal comprehension, for example the Suffolk Reading Scale (Hagley, 1987) or the Neale Analysis of Reading Ability (Neale, 1997).

The third of the rings is labelled 'responding'. This is the process by which the reader engages purposefully with the text to make meaning and it underpins most recent theories of comprehension in cognitive psychology as well as literary theories. The discourse comprehension theory of Kintsch (1988), the reader response theories of Iser (1978) and Rosenblatt (1978) and the constructively responsive reading of Pressley and Afflerbach (1995) all envisage an active reader, bringing individual world knowledge to build a personal understanding of the text. Literary theory offers many elaborations of this process and the postmodern view set out in Harrison's chapter (chapter 5) in this book makes it clear that the interpretation of texts is an infinitely varied and flexible process. In current teaching terms, this is text-level and literary knowledge. The early stages are taught by shared and guided reading, in which the teacher models the processes of making sense of ideas, themes, plot and character. Later, in secondary school and beyond, it becomes the study of literature.

The fourth ring, 'analysing', is related to the same research and theories as responding. In analysing, the reader steps back from the meaning of the text, and considers it in relation to the authorial techniques adopted and the literary traditions within which it was produced. In this activity, by contrast with responding, the literary theories are explicit and a conscious part of the reader's understanding.

The reading tests that attempt to assess responsive reading are those that present in their entirety texts that were written for real purposes and ask thought-provoking questions for which more than one answer may be acceptable. The key stage reading tests in England and Wales (QCA, 2004; ACCAC, 2004) and the tests used in the PIRLS (Campbell *et al.*, 2001) and PISA (OECD, 2003) international surveys are examples of this approach. For older students, public examinations, coursework and essays assess this understanding. These assessments also include the ability to analyse, though this is much more fully worked out for older students than younger ones.

The diagram in Figure 2.2, while representing the overall shape of the construct in simplified form, also illuminates the differing emphases in the ways reading is taught and tested. One way of seeing the rings is cumulative, with decoding preceding comprehension and response and analysis following. The alternative view is a holistic one, with teaching and testing addressing all four layers at once, and it is this latter view that is embodied in the England National Curriculum and Literacy Strategy. Considering reading tests for young children, the Suffolk Reading Scale addresses decoding and simple comprehension, whereas the national reading tests for children of the same age ask questions requiring some response to text and the recognition of some obvious authorial devices.

Informal classroom assessment is not located within one section of the diagram, but may focus upon any of the skills and understandings in any of its rings. Because it is dynamic and responsive, teachers may shift their attention from moment to moment: a teacher of young children is likely to be supporting and assessing decoding skills one minute and response to literature the next. With older students, as well as checking basic understanding, there may be open-ended discussions exploring different interpretations and analysing techniques.

Reading by an experienced adult is an activity that is normally characterised by the 'responding' category. Word recognition and understanding of vocabulary and grammar are taken for granted, as the experienced reader reads for a purpose. This may be practical, as in following a recipe, for interest and enjoyment, or in engaging in any number of professional and social functions. The reader brings knowledge and experience to the text and this interaction brings about the meaning that the reader is seeking. These varied meanings are embedded in the personal and cultural experiences of the individual, so that reading is woven into the very fabric of social life. It is because of the variety of meanings and purposes that the construct is so complex: reading a bus timetable is different from appreciating *War and Peace*, but the scope of the construct of reading encompasses them both.

Purposes for reading and purposes for assessment

The assessment of reading unites two intertwined strands of human activity, each of which has purpose and meaning for individuals and for society. Reading itself is not (or, at most, not for long) the purely mechanical activity of decoding written signs into spoken words. Its nature is essentially bound up with the fulfilment of purposes, relationships and actions. The construct of reading is defined by these purposes as much as by the related skills and understandings.

From validity theory it is clear that assessment, too, has the notion of purpose at its heart. Validation consists of gathering evidence that an assessment provides the information necessary for a purpose, within the classroom, the education system or in society more broadly. An individual assessment of reading is based on decisions about the range of reading skills and purposes, drawn from within the overall construct, that it should include in order to fulfil its assessment purpose.

In the other chapters of this book, the issues surrounding the definition of the construct of reading are worked out in many different ways. At first sight, it may seem that there is little commonality between them and it is for this reason that an appreciation of the complexity of the theoretical background is so important. The last quarter-century has seen a dynamic evolution of the theory of validity, from its positivist roots into a broad and flexible approach that can be adapted to apply to all forms of assessment, however formal or informal. Over the same period, discussion of the nature of reading has not stood still, as cognitive, social, linguistic and literary theories have continued to challenge one another. Defining the construct of reading draws upon the full range of ideas from both of these well-developed theoretical contexts.

References

Adams, M.J. (1990). *Beginning to Read: Thinking and Learning about Print*. Cambridge, MA: MIT Press.

American Educational Research Association, American Psychological Association and National Council on Measurement in Education (1966). *Standards for Educational and Psychological Testing*. Washington, DC: AERA.

American Educational Research Association, American Psychological Association and National Council on Measurement in Education (1999). *Standards for Educational and Psychological Testing*. Washington, DC: AERA.

Black, P. and Wiliam, D. (1998). *Inside the Black Box: Raising Standards through Classroom Assessment*. London: School of Education, King's College.

Black, P. (2003). 'The nature and value of formative assessment for learning', *Improving Schools*, **6**, 3, 7–22.

Campbell, J., Kelly, D., Mullis, I., Martin, M. and Sainsbury, M. (2001). *Framework and Specifications for PIRLS Assessment. 2nd Edition*. Boston: International Study Center.

Frederickson, N. (1996). *Phonological Assessment Battery*. Windsor: nferNelson.

Garrod, S. and Pickering, M. (Eds) (1999). *Language Processing*. Hove: Psychological Press.

Gipps, C. (1994). *Beyond Testing: Towards a Theory of Educational Assessment*. London: The Falmer Press.

Goswami, U. and Bryant, P. (1990). *Phonological Skills and Learning to Read*. Hove: Lawrence Erlbaum Associates.

Haertel, E. (1985). 'Construct validity and criterion-referenced testing', *Review of Educational Research*, **55**, 1, 23–46.

Hagley, F. (1987). *Suffolk Reading Scale*. Windsor: nferNelson.

Harlen, W. (2004). *A Systematic Review of the Evidence of Reliability and Validity of Assessment by Teachers used for Summative Purposes*. London: EPPI-Centre.

Iser, W. (1978). *The Act of Reading*. Baltimore: Johns Hopkins University Press.

Kintsch, W. (1988). 'The role of knowledge in discourse comprehension: a construction-integration model', *Psychological Review*, **95**, 163–182.

Marshall, B. (2004). 'Goals or horizons – the conundrum of progression in English: or a possible way of understanding formative assessment in English', *Curriculum Journal*, **15**, 2, 101–113.

Messick, S. (1989). 'Validity.' In: Linn, R.L. (Ed) *Educational Measurement. Third Edition*. London: Collier Macmillan.

Moss, P.A. (1992) 'Shifting conceptions of validity in educational measurement: implications for performance assessment', *Review of Educational Research*, **62**, 3, 229–58.

Moss, P.A. (1994). 'Can there be validity without reliability?', *Educational Researcher*, **23**, 2, 5–12.

Moss, P.A. (1995). 'Themes and variations in validity theory', *Educational Measurement: Issues and Practice*, **14**, 2, 5–13.

Moss, P.A. (1996). 'Enlarging the dialogue in educational measurement: voices from interpretive research traditions', *Educational Researcher*, **25**, 1, 20–28.

Moss, P.A. (1998). 'The role of consequences in validity theory', *Educational Measurement: Issues and Practice*, **17**, 2, 5–12.

Moss, P.A. (2003). 'Reconceptualizing validity for classroom assessment, *Educational Measurement: Issues and Practice*, **22**, 4, 13–25.

Neale, M. (1997). *Neale Analysis of Reading Ability. Second Revised British Edition*. Windsor: nferNelson.

Organisation for Economic Co-operation and Development (2003). *The PISA 2003 Assessment Framework: Mathematics, Reading, Science and Problem Solving Knowledge and Skills*. Paris: OECD.

Pressley, M. and Afflerbach, P. (1995). *Verbal Protocols of Reading: The Nature of Constructively Responsive Reading*. Hillsdale, NJ: Lawrence Erlbaum Associates.

Qualifications and Curriculum Authority (2004). *Reading Tests for Key Stages 1, 2 and 3*. London: QCA.

Qualifications, Curriculum and Assessment Authority for Wales (ACCAC) (2004). *Reading Tests for Key Stages 2 and 3*. Cardiff: ACCAC.

Rosenblatt, L.M. (1978). *The Reader, the Text, the Poem: The Transactional Theory of the Literary Work*. Carbondale: Southern Illinois University Press.

Sainsbury, M. (1992). *Meaning, Communication and Understanding in the Classroom*. Aldershot: Avebury.

Schonell, F. (1945). *The Psychology and Teaching of Reading*. Edinburgh: Oliver and Boyd.

Stiggins, R. (2001). *Student-involved Classroom Assessment. 3rd Edition*. Upper Saddle River, NJ: Merrill Prentice Hall.

Stiggins, R. (2004). 'Overcoming a legacy of mistaken assessment beliefs.' Paper presented at the Annual Meeting of the National Council on Measurement in Education.

Stobart, G. (2001). 'The validity of National Curriculum assessment', *British Journal of Educational Studies*, **49**, 1, 26–39.

Stuart, M. and Stainthorp, R. (2004). 'The assessment of reading: A theoretically motivated review of currently available tests', *Viewpoint No. 16*. London: University of London Institute of Education.

Wiliam, D. (1993). 'Validity, dependability and reliability in National Curriculum assessment', *Curriculum Journal*, **4**, 3, 335–50.

Wiliam, D. (1996). 'Meanings and consequences in standard setting', *Assessment in Education*, **3**, 3, 287–307.

Wiliam, D. (2004). 'Assessment and the regulation of learning'. Paper presented at the Annual Meeting of the National Council on Measurement in Education.

3 A psychological perspective on the diagnostic assessment of reading: establishing priorities

John R. Beech

The psychological assessment of reading is one of several perspectives on the assessment of reading in children and adults. We will briefly look at the position of psychology within its wider context before examining the problems confronting psychologists. Of course, some of these problems will be common to other approaches as well, but there are some aspects that are distinctive to psychology. The principles of good assessment will be considered and it will be argued that these should include the involvement of reading theory with reading assessment, the involvement of training studies, the importance of sound research and the appropriate use of measurement theory.

The context of psychology

Psychologists are not the only professionals concerned with reading assessment, so let us first look at the bigger picture. Figure 3.1 illustrates many of the potential influences that affect a young person's development in reading. The outer part illustrates the interests of different disciplines, professionals, parents and others, with some much more connected to reading than others. The inclusion of some professions, such as politicians, may raise eyebrows, but politicians are involved at some level because they ultimately control resources for assessment and have to make choices based on the evidence given to them.

The relationship between assessment and how to allocate resources is an interesting one. It could be argued that if a particular assessment is conceivably not going to produce much overall improvement then it is not worth consuming resources to undertake it. For example, there appear to be relatively few readers with surface dyslexia, but if an assessment of this results in the improvement of a minority of readers, it would be worth it for the quality of their life. This problem is very much like a medical issue in which a relatively large amount of money might be spent on expensive surgery for the benefit of a relative few. Effect size is an important consideration when looking at the potential advantages of an assessment. This, too, is an important factor in medicine when the effect size of a medication can be relatively small. Take for example aspirin, which has an effect size of a low 0.3 standard deviation in its effects in reducing myocardial infarction; but although small this can translate into the savings of thousands, if not hundreds of thousands of lives within a nation (Steering Committee of the Physicians' Health Study Research Group, 1989). Psychologists can sometimes be critical of studies showing small effect sizes, but in the assessment and educational contexts these can still be very important.

Figure 3.1 could conceivably be much larger and detailed than shown, but the generic terms represent in broad terms most influences. The relative weightings of these are likely to be very variable. The inner part is a selection of factors that could potentially influence a child's reading and therefore might be usefully assessed. (There is not an intended connection between inner and outer parts – think of two independent wheels.) The vast majority of research has been on cognitive influences on reading, which would include language processing characteristics (for example phonology). But other aspects also have some role to play.

One summarising formula for most of the inner wheel would be the well-known formula of Kurt Lewin (1936):

$$B = f(P, E)$$

Whereby behaviour (in this case reading performance) is a function of the interaction of P and E. P stands for all the individual's inner determinants (such as attitude, intelligence)

Figure 3.1 A schematic representation of two spheres of influence on the child learning to read. The outer circle represents various agencies, professionals and other influences who have different degrees of effect on reading and the inner part represents internal and external influences on reading. The relative positions of items in the inner and outer circles are not intended to be connected.

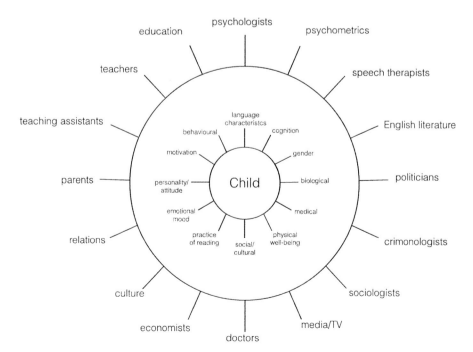

while E represents environmental factors (such as the influence of the teacher). This may not get us much further on, but it is at least a summarising principle that implies that if we know one element we can predict the unknown variable.

One example illustrating the interaction of some of these elements would be the gender of a child, which does have an influence on reading performance. Girls are more positive in their beliefs about reading in Grades 1 to 4 (Eccles *et al.*, 1993). In addition, Smart *et al.* (1996) found a much stronger connection between reading problems and behavioural problems in boys compared to girls in Grades 2 and 4 in Australia. Gender illustrates that several possibilities could be operating, such as the interplay between sex role and culture, the biological or hormonal basis for sex differences, effects on personality and even the over-preponderance of female teachers of reading in the classroom.

Despite all these potential influences, psychologists might be forgiven for believing that psychological influences are the most pervasive, especially when the variance that can be accounted for in predicting reading development appears mainly to derive from psychological factors. To give just one example, Awaida and Beech (1995), in a cross-sectional longitudinal study, tested children and then examined their performance one year later. Mainly cognitive tests of 5- and 6-year-olds accounted for 79 per cent and 78 per cent of the variance one year later in predicting reading quotient (reading age as a proportion of chronological age). It was interesting that reading performance itself one year earlier accounted for most of the variance. A case of the better readers getting better, which we will return to later.

Principles of good assessment

We shall now look at what in my view should be good principles of reading assessment from the perspective of a psychologist. No particular principle is to be recommended in isolation; it helps if an assessment can satisfy most if not all of the following points. Without getting too far ahead, it is all very well having an assessment based on a solid theoretical basis, but if that assessment does not ultimately lead to an improvement of some aspect of reading skill, then it may be good for 'blue skies' research, but not much use for helping children to improve their reading.

Integrating theory with assessment

Good assessment should be integrated with a good theoretical basis. However, many if not most reading assessments can be regarded as atheoretical (for example, Lipson and Wixson, 1991; Schwartz, 1984). Schwartz believed that most reading tests are of questionable scientific value and Lipson and Wixson noted the mismatch between most formal reading tests and current reading definitions and yet professional educators are currently using them. Englehard (2001) proposed that we need to work backwards from existing reading tests to find out if there is any underlying theory behind these tests. He wrote:

I predict that in most cases it will be found that the construction of many reading tests was not guided by an explicit translation of reading theory into testing practice, but in fact the instruments will have more of an atheoretical, craft-like feel.

(Englehard, 2001, p.13)

So why is it so necessary to construct theories? The problem with just collecting substantial quantities of data is that these data in themselves do not provide a complete picture. We need theories to integrate this information and to give it meaning. Theories should serve the function of filling gaps in our knowledge and should enable us to make predictions. A key purpose of an assessment should be to provide an instrument that can adequately test participants to examine their position within this theoretical framework. For example, Eysenck (1947) found the orthogonal dimensions of extraversion-introversion and neuroticism. Individuals can take his subsequent questionnaire (for example the Eysenck Personality Questionnaire) and it provides a measure of their relative position within a plot of these axes.

As a brief illustration of how a reading theory can be the basis for an assessment, one might be interested in constructing an assessment based on traditional reading stage models (for example, Frith, 1985; Marsh *et al.*, 1981). This illustration should not be seen as an endorsement of the model, which has its critics (for example, Goswami, 1998; Stuart and Coltheart, 1988). Frith's well-known model divides reading development into three main stages of logographic, alphabetic and orthographic processing. One could develop a test instrument that measures the level of attainment in each of these stages. The result might be that in a group of early readers the instrument would show that the great majority of children were at the logographic stage, and a few were already within the alphabetic stage. As one moves through increasingly older groups of readers these proportions should change, so that in a much older group the majority were at the orthographic stage with a possible few still predominantly in a alphabetic or even a logographic phase. This is a hypothetical example, but serves to illustrate how assessment could be integrated with theory.

Some might point to dyslexia as an example of an integration of theory and assessment. The term 'dyslexia', although it has variations in its definition, is basically a deficit in reading taking into account underlying intelligence. The model relies on the intelligence test, which can measure general intelligence, or 'g' as Spearman (1904) called it. General intelligence is significantly correlated with reading vocabulary level, such that bright children generally are better readers (for example Rutter and Yule, 1975). The argument runs that because of individual differences in the development of g, a better way of assessing reading is to look at reading development as a function of general ability rather than by chronological age.

At present the Wechsler Objective Reading Dimensions (WORD) (Rust *et al.*, 1993) test in conjunction with the WISC-IV can be used to provide not only age-related norms but to assess reading (and spelling) performance in relation to general intelligence. The WISC-IV comprises four subcomponents: verbal comprehension, perceptual reasoning, working memory and processing speed, from which a full scale IQ measure can be computed. The WORD test provides statistical tests to allow the assessor to find out if a child is reading at a level that is significantly below that predicted from IQ. The same test can be undertaken for reading comprehension. This reading comprehension test involves the child silently reading a passage. (Although the instructions allow children to read aloud if they wish, in my experience they read silently.) They are asked a single question after each passage which is scored according to a template of correct possibilities.

One of the major justifications of using the IQ test is that it is an important component of determining dyslexia. Children with dyslexia are reading at a level below that expected based on their IQ. By contrast, some children will be poor readers but reading at a level that would be expected on the basis of their IQ. This is because there is considered to be a level of low intelligence below which most children will perform below average reading level. Such children have general learning difficulties and would be described as reading backward, compared to those above this benchmark level. This is referred to by Yule and colleagues as having specific reading retardation (Yule *et al.*, 1974), and by using the criterion of 2 standard errors below expected reading scores found that 3.1 per cent of 10-year-olds in the Isle of Wight were in this category.

Unfortunately there are some problems with this particular approach. One problem is that it seems that when defining boundaries for dyslexia there is a certain degree of instability. Shaywitz *et al.* (1992) used the criterion of 1.5 standard errors and found that by third grade, of those who had been defined as having dyslexia at the end of their first grade, only 28 per cent were left. This sort of figure does not inspire confidence in using dyslexia for the purposes of assessment. Another problem is that it takes a long time to test children (each one is tested individually) using these tasks. Also, it can lead to apparently bizarre outcomes, such as a very intelligent child being found to be significantly impaired in reading, but having the equivalent level of reading as a child of average IQ and average level of reading. Using these criteria the very intelligent child qualifies for extra training in reading. Because of the difficulties in measuring intelligence (for example, the length of time involved in testing, the historical controversies connected with IQ testing, conceptual difficulties defining intelligence, and so on) this is not something that is normally undertaken in the classroom. Nevertheless, the assessment of general ability is an important tool currently used by educational psychologists. But is it justified? I would suggest that it does not add much that is useful and might be considered to be low in terms of information gained for the amount of time spent in assessment, at least in the context of reading assessment. This is because current experimental work indicates little justification for arguing that dyslexia (defined as looking at the discrepancy between reading level and reading predicted by full scale IQ) is a special condition (for example, Share *et al.*, 1987; Fletcher *et al.*, 1994; Stanovich and Siegel, 1994).

Perhaps a more useful model of reading is dual route theory (for example, Castles and Coltheart, 1993; Coltheart, 1978). This is not exactly a developmental model of reading, but proposes that we have a lexical and a phonological route for reading. The lexical route is a direct visual route and evokes a dictionary entry of the word, whereas the phonological route involves coding letters (or graphemes) that correspond to phonemes. These phonemes are blended to provide a pronunciation. This phonological route enables decoding of nonwords and regularly spelled words, but irregularly spelled words are more likely to be decoded by the lexical route. Dual route theory is particularly useful in providing a basis for the interpretation of acquired dyslexias (for example, Patterson *et al.*, 1985).

Dual route theory affords a means of assessing developmental phonological and surface dyslexia. For example, Bailey *et al.* (2004) tested 5th Grade dyslexic readers and split them into subgroups of surface and phonological dyslexics, based on their performance reading nonwords and exception words. These scores were converted to z scores and non-word scores were subtracted from exception word scores. For example, suppose a child was better at reading non-words than exception words, this would be a profile of a surface dyslexic. Thus this child has greater proficiency in using the phonological route. This formula provided a gradation in performance from extreme surface dyslexia at one end of the scale to extreme phonological dyslexia at the other. Bailey *et al.* then chose children above and below the top and bottom 25th percentiles, respectively, to produce a group of surface dyslexics and a group of phonological dyslexics. The children in these two groups were matched on their level of word identification. The children then undertook a training study to examine how well they learned nonwords with either regular pronunciations or irregular pronunciations. Bailey *et al.* found that phonological dyslexics have a specific phonological deficit. Such children develop differently from normal younger readers of equivalent reading age.

Conversely, surface dyslexics were much more similar to normal younger readers and seem to have a different type of deficit. Studies such as these are valuable in showing that it is not useful to assume that those with dyslexia are within an homogenous group. But we must be clear that although this study shows important differences between the two types of reading deficit and that although it helps us to understand the underlying mechanisms better, it does not as yet illuminate how these two groups might benefit from differential training programmes. We will examine one study that attempts to undertake a specific programme for surface dyslexics in the next section.

Integrating assessment with later training

Having examined the importance of a theoretical basis for the purposes of diagnostic assessment, we next look at the connection with subsequent training methods after the assessment results are known. An important part of assessment should be whether the assessment instrument allows one to select a sub-population that is particularly going to benefit from some kind of intervention or training. There are instances where just training at the critical time is crucially important, without prior assessment. For instance, Gorey (2001) in a meta-analysis of 35 preschool studies found that preschool training programmes (defined as between 2 and 5 years) had large significant effects on both intelligence and cognition, even 5–10 years later and 70–80 per cent did better than their control groups. The evidence also shows that over 10 to 25 years there is a substantial beneficial impact on personal and social problems.

The Perry Preschool Project in the USA – later called High/Scope – was an early intervention study that included heavy parental participation. Key features were that it tracked from pre-school to nearly 30 years later and it had random allocation to treatment and control groups. It has been shown from this particular project that for every $1000 invested in such an intervention, $7160 (after inflation) is returned in terms of fewer arrests, higher earnings (and hence taxed income), reduced involvement with social services and so on (Schweinhart and Weikart, 1993). The impact of training is clear, not just economically, but in terms of children fulfilling their potential (we included the involvement of criminologists, sociologists, politicians and economists in Figure 3.1.) The economic costs of assessment of aspects of reading and then targeted subsequent training may well have a similar abundant return not only for the children involved but for society as well. This would be much more a 'magic bullet' approach than blunderbuss and just might put arguments across in a way that politicians can appreciate.

So where in particular can we point to an assessment followed by training making an impact? Bradley and Bryant (1983) published what has become a classic well-known study, in which pre-reading children were assessed and selected on the basis of their poor phonological skills. These children were put into various types of training programmes and they found that training phonological awareness, and training in letter-sound connections in particular, had a significant impact on future reading performance relative to controls who had been given the same amount of attention, dealt with the same materials, but had a semantic type of task. According to Bradley (1987), the relative differences in reading ability between their different training groups persisted even when the children were ready for secondary school. The implication here is that assessing poor phonological skills with a view to subsequent training can be an aid to improved reading. Subsequent studies have refined and built on this work (for example, Wagner and Torgesen, 1987).

It turns out that training phonological awareness can be relatively rewarding in relation to the resources expended. Wagner *et al.* (1993) in a meta-analysis, showed an effect size of 1.23 on phonological awareness after nine hours of training and Foster *et al.* (1994) in a computerised training study of phonological awareness took only 4.5 hours to achieve an effect size of 1.05 standard deviations. Several studies have shown that training phonemic awareness significantly improves subsequent reading (Ball and Blackman, 1991; Barker and Torgesen, 1995; Cunningham, 1990; Kjeldsen and Abo Akademi, 2003; Lundberg *et al.*, 1988; Torgesen *et al.*, 1992).

Such programmes of training should normally be useful for phonological dyslexics (although some find it very difficult to improve their phonological skills, for example Torgesen and Burgess, 1998), but what about surface dyslexics? A recent Italian study (Judica *et al.*, 2002) compared two groups of surface dyslexics one of which was trained in simply reading briefly presented words, the idea being to force processing away from the serial processing of graphemes. This training had the desired effect in that eye fixations on words were shorter and word naming times were faster. However, there was no improvement in comprehension relative to controls. This is perhaps a crude approach for the treatment of surface dyslexia, but there do not seem to be many training programmes available for them at the moment and although we can assess the surface dyslexic fairly accurately, this does not get us much further on.

Although there is now strong evidence for the efficacy of training phonology and its effectiveness in improving reading there are still many sceptics who believe that it is important that children need to discover for themselves the magic experience of getting lost and totally engrossed in reading. These are advocates of what is sometimes known as a 'top-down' approach to reading. Here they emphasise the importance of comprehension rather than concentrating on learning how to decode words. A whole-language theorist such as Reid (1993) is critical of instruction on how to decode words that is taken out of context. It is fair to say that there has been a paradigm war between an emphasis on decoding skills on the one hand and an emphasis on whole language (see Stanovich and Stanovich, 1995 and Pressley, 1998 for further discussion).

Both paradigms would be able to explain evidence that children who read a lot tend to be better readers. Stanovich (1986) attracted a lot of citations by coining the phrase 'the Matthew effect' to describe this. He and Cunningham (Cunningham and Stanovich, 1991; Stanovich and Cunningham, 1992) used recognition tests of authors and book titles to show that better readers recognised more book authors, presumably because they had read more books. Such tests could be useful as indicators of the extent to which children are immersing themselves in reading.

It might be (mistakenly) believed from this that one step forward is to encourage children to use context in reading to help them progress through a passage of text. It might help them identify difficult words as well as encourage semantic processing. However, context is not actually all that useful as the probability of guessing the correct word on the basis of context is quite low (for example, Perfetti *et al.*, 1979). Furthermore, good readers do not use word context more than poor readers to help with their word recognition. In reaction time word recognition studies where participants are primed with context beforehand poor readers actually show greater context effects (for example, Briggs *et al.*, 1984; West and Stanovich, 1978). Stanovich and Stanovich (1995) argue that these and other findings pose a problem for top-down theorists. Good readers have achieved automaticity in their word recognition skills to the extent that they do not need context. By contrast, poor readers try to use contextual information due to weak decoding skills, but this does little to help their plight. An assessment test evaluating children's skill in the use of context while reading under these circumstances is not likely to be useful.

To conclude this section, it can be argued that designing a particular assessment for reading in the absence of knowledge about what kinds of training are going to work after these results are known, is putting the cart before the horse. It would be better to start with finding a type of training that works particularly well for a selected group and then developing an assessment instrument that could be employed for larger-scale usage, to find children from the general population who would benefit from this intervention. Spear-Swerling and Sternberg (1998) have much useful and pragmatic advice for those constructing intervention programmes. This includes first giving priority to the child's immediate success in reading and then building on this; second, the professionals involved must have the conviction that all children can learn reading if they are instructed appropriately and third, there needs to be strong support for the teachers involved in the programme and they should have plenty of opportunity for giving feedback. As far as the phonological awareness programmes are concerned, however, Spear-Swerling and Sternberg note that a significant number of children do not respond to such training (for example, 30 per cent in the Torgesen *et al.* study) and that there is a need to explore the effects of training other types of related skill.

Assessment based on sound research

So far we have seen that a good starting point for diagnostic assessment is to start with training methods that have been found to be effective for particular groups of children and develop the assessment from there. We have also seen that it is important to have a good theoretical basis in order to explain the processes or skills that are being assessed and subsequently improved. The third important principle is that good experimental research is based on sound research designs and research that is connected with the assessment of reading is no exception. Taking the perspective that assessment is justified where one knows that subsequent intervention actually works one needs to look at good intervention studies. One starting point is look at studies in which the allocation of participants into experimental and control groups was randomised. Thus one can examine more accurately the potency of an intervention. Torgerson *et al.* (2003), carrying out a review and meta-analysis, identified 4555 potential papers on interventions in literacy or numeracy in adults, and adapting various criteria for quality rejected a staggering 96.3 per cent of these. There were further exclusions, leaving just 59 papers. They found evidence of probable publication bias with a significant difference in effect size between published versus unpublished studies (0.49 v. 0.26). There were still substantial problems even with these studies; for example, the control participants did not receive an intervention. The experimental group could have improved due to a Hawthorne effect. Clearly a great deal of effort has been expended in collecting data if one takes the sum total of effort to create these 4555 papers, but not enough care is going into using an appropriate design. In the end Torgerson *et al.* could not make any conclusions about any specific intervention on the papers that they looked at in detail.

In the UK it is quite difficult (but not impossible) to arrange a properly randomised control design due to sensitivities about having control participants within a paradigm that at that point is not designed to help them. Some experimenters, to circumvent this, do train the controls with the same materials as the experimental group at a later point, but in doing so this unfortunately rules out looking at potential effect sizes of the intervention in the longer term.

Clarity in the relationship between measurement theory and reading theory

The fourth principle is to do with the relationship between a theory of reading and measurement theory. Measurement theory is about theoretical models that have an underlying statistical basis for making measurements or analysing data. Messick provides a more detailed definition: 'Theories of measurement broadly conceived may be viewed as loosely integrated conceptual frameworks within which are imbedded rigorously formulated statistical models of estimation and inferences about the properties of measurements or scores' (Messick, 1983, p.498). Engelhard (2001) proposes a relationship between measurement theory and reading theory, which is partly represented by Figure 3.2. In an ideal world he believes that reading tests are affected by measurement theory and reading theory and in turn, measurement theory and reading theory should interact with each other for mutual development. In this section we are going to explore his ideas further.

Charles Spearman (1904) – in the same paper referred to earlier – began test theory or classical test theory with the basic idea that an obtained score (X) is equal to a true score (Xt) and a variable error (e), which can be positive of negative, shown thus:

$$X = Xt + e$$

The error component can be derived from problems with the actual test, the participant's physical condition, error in scoring, error due to time of day and so on. Subsequent statistical derivations are based on this simple beginning. Estimating this error has led to many different formulations of reliability, such as the Kuder-Richardson method. Further information on test construction for reading using classical test theory, such as the use of reliability (internal consistency, test-retest, etc), can be found in Beech and Singleton (1997).

Unfortunately there are many problems with this approach (as outlined by Englehard). One difficulty is the 'attenuation paradox' (Loevinger, 1954) in which, contrary to what one might expect, increasing test reliability eventually decreases test validity (Tucker, 1946). One way a tester can achieve higher reliability is by maximising test variance. Schumacker (2003) taking this to its extreme (and with tongue firmly in cheek) notes that maximum test variance is produced when half the participants score zero and the other half are at ceiling. Perhaps a more understandable situation is where

Figure 3.2 Part of Englehard's conceptual framework (2001) for the assessment of reading

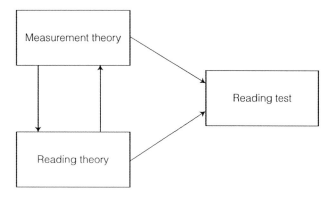

one has run a new test, which produces a certain level of reliability on the Kuder-Richardson (KR21). One can then experiment by eliminating items to increase the inter-item correlations. But the problem with this process as one proceeds is that one potentially ends up with items so well correlated that in effect they reduce to one item. This process is obviously reducing the validity of the test. Kuhn (1970) proposed that when confronted with a paradox this is the beginning of the downfall of that theory to make way for another paradigm. The paradigm that should be used in the place of classical measurement theory in the view of Schumacker (2003), Englehard (2001) and others should be the Rasch measurement model. Without going into the detail of the rationale of the Rasch model, this particular method maximises both reliability and validity by taking out the extreme positively and negatively discriminating items, so that the same problem does not arise. Item elimination should be accompanied by careful qualitative scrutiny.

Englehard in his argument goes on to note the strong reliance of traditional tests of reading on reliability and on norm-referencing rather than examining validity. One might conceivably have a highly reliable measure of reading, but it may be of doubtful validity. There are some Rasch calibrated reading tests, such as the Woodstock Reading Mastery Test (1973, 1998), which Englehard believes was the first diagnostic reading test to make use of Rasch measurement. He notes that Rasch measurement can provide extra information on construct validity and hopes that future reading test developers will make use of these advantages. One of his conclusions is that so far reading theories have not usually determined the construction of reading tests and that to improve quality we need to ensure a much closer association between the two. He also notes that, from an historical perspective, in the early days of the developments in measurement theory reading theorists had a very close involvement. One outstanding example of this was the work of E.L. Thorndike who was innovative both in measurement theory and reading theory. However, since then the two fields seem to have drifted away from each other. But this is not to say that teams of experts from each domain might well cooperate with each other in the future.

Conclusion

A huge amount of world-wide effort goes into the creation of reading assessments and even more effort into the subsequent testing and evaluation of children and adults. But is it all worth it? At this stage in the development of research in reading we have some well-developed theories and have collected a great deal of experimental evidence. It seems that there is a gap between this work and the development of properly constructed assessment tests. Furthermore, despite all this effort, there does not seem to be enough energy being put into undertaking well-constructed studies that select particular individuals according to their profiles and then giving them specialised training to improve their skills. This selection would be based on psychometric assessments that are well constructed. The final figure (Figure 3.3) attempts to put this idealised process together.

Figure 3.3 An idealised conceptual framework in which the assessment of reading leads to selection of a sub-population followed by training of that group. The results inform further development or refinement of the theory in a continuous cycle.

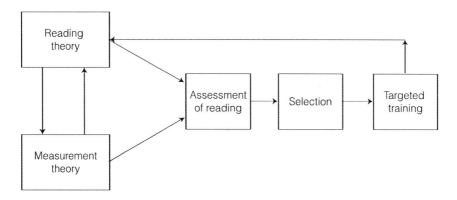

This shows how reading theory and measurement theory produce an instrument for assessment. Once the instrument is appropriately constructed it is used to select individuals for specialised training. This training is monitored and the outcomes can be used to inform theory leading to further refinements in a continuous process. It can be seen from this view that assessment without the close involvement of theory and some kind of training procedure for putative readers is considered to be less than useful.

We started with the role of the psychologist in reading research and its assessment. Psychologists have a role in terms of their involvement in properly controlled experimental studies in reading, in the construction of appropriate assessment tests, in helping to conduct experimental studies of training and in the evaluation of outcomes. Psychologists are part of a wider community of professionals all concerned with helping children to progress in reading and it is only by closely collaborating with this community that real progress can be made.

References

Awaida, M. and Beech, J.R. (1995). 'Children's lexical and sublexical development while learning to read', *Journal of Experimental Education*, **63**, 97–113.

Bailey, C.E., Manis, F.R., Pedersen, W.C. and Seidenberg, M.S. (2004). 'Variation among developmental dyslexics: Evidence from a printed-word-learning task', *Journal of Experimental Child Psychology*, **87**, 125–54.

Ball E. and Blachman, B. (1991). 'Does phoneme awareness training in kindergarten make a difference in early word recognition and developmental spelling?' *Reading Research Quarterly*, **26**, 49–66.

Barker, T. and Torgesen, J. (1995). 'An evaluation of computer-assisted instruction in phonological awareness with below average readers', *Journal of Educational Computing Research*, **13**, 89–103.

Beech, J. and Singleton, C. (Eds) (1997). *The Psychological Assessment of Reading*. London: Routledge.

Bradley, L. (1987). 'Categorising sounds, early intervention and learning to read: A follow-up study'. Paper presented to British Psychological Society London Conference, December.

Bradley, L., and Bryant, P. (1983). 'Categorizing sounds and learning to read – a causal connection,' *Nature*, **301**, 419–21.

Briggs, P., Austin, S. and Underwood, G. (1984). 'The effects of sentence context in good and poor readers: a test of Stanovich's interactive-compensatory model', *Reading Research Quarterly*, **20**, 54–61.

Castles, A. and Coltheart, M. (1993). 'Varieties of developmental dyslexia', *Cognition*, **47**, 149–80.

Coltheart, M. (1978). 'Lexical access in simple reading tasks.' In: Underwood, G. (Ed) *Strategies of Information Processing*. London: Academic Press.

Cunningham, A. (1990). 'Explicit versus implicit instruction in phonemic awareness', *Journal of Experimental Child Psychology*, **50**, 429–44.

Cunningham, A. and Stanovich, K. (1991). 'Tracking the unique effects of print exposure in children: associations with vocabulary, general knowledge, and spelling.' *Journal of Educational Psychology*, **83**, 264–74.

Eccles, J., Wigfield, A., Harold, R.D. and Blumenfeld, P. (1993). 'Age and gender differences in children's self- and task perceptions during elementary school', *Child Development*, **64**, 830–47.

Englehard, G. (2001). 'Historical view of the influences of measurement and reading theories on the assessment of reading', *Journal of Applied Measurement*, **2**, 1–26.

Eysenck, H. (1947). *Dimensions of Personality*. London: Routledge and Kegan Paul.

Fletcher, J. *et al*. (1994). 'Cognitive profiles of reading disability: Comparisons of discrepancy and low achievement definitions', *Journal of Educational Psychology*, **86**, 6–23.

Foster, K. *et al*. (1994). 'Computer administered instruction in phonological awareness: evaluation of the *DaisyQuest* program', *Journal of Research and Development in Education*, **27**, 126–37.

Frith, U. (1985). 'Beneath the surface of developmental dyslexia.' In: Patterson, K.E., Marshall, J.C. and Coltheart, M. (Eds) *Surface Dyslexia: Neuropsychological and Cognitive Studies of Phonological Reading*. London: Erlbaum.

Gorey, K. (2001). 'Early childhood education: A meta-analytic affirmation of the short- and long-term benefits of educational opportunity', *School Psychology Quarterly*, **16**, 9–30.

Goswami, U. (1998). 'The role of analogies in the development of word recognition.' In: Metsala, J.L. and Ehri, L.C. (Eds) *Word Recognition in Beginning Literacy*. Hillsdale, NJ: Lawrence Erlbaum Associates.

Judica, A. *et al*. (2002). 'Training of developmental surface dyslexia improves reading performance and shortens eye fixation duration in reading', *Neuropsychological Rehabilitation*, **12**, 177–98.

Kjeldsen, A.-C. and Abo Akademi, U. (2003). 'Training phonological awareness in kindergarten level children: consistency is more important than quantity', *Learning and Instruction*, **13**, 349–65

Kuhn, T. (1970). *The Structure of Scientific Revolutions*. (Second edn). Chicago: University of Chicago Press.

Lewin, K. (1936). *The Principles of Topological Psychology*. New York: McGraw-Hill.

Lipson, M. and Wixon, K. (1991). *Assessment and Instruction of Reading Disability: An Interactive Approach*. New York: HarperCollins.

Loevinger, J. (1954). 'The attenuation paradox in test theory', *Psychological Bulletin*, **51**, 493–554.

Lundberg, I., Frost, J., and Petersen, O. (1988). 'Effects of an extensive program for stimulating phonological awareness in preschool children', *Reading Research Quarterly*, **23**, 264–84.

Marsh, G. *et al*. (1981). 'A cognitive-developmental theory of reading acquisition, reading research: advances in theory and practice.' In: MacKinnon, G.E. and Waller, T.G. (Eds) *Reading Research: Advances in Theory and Practice, Vol. 3*. New York: Academic Press.

Messick, S. (1983). 'Assessment of children.' In: Mussen, P.H. (Ed) *Handbook of Child Psychology, Vol. 1: History, Theory and Methods*. New York: John Wiley.

Patterson, K., Marshall, J. and Coltheart, M. (1985). *Surface Dyslexia: Neuropsychological and Cognitive Studies of Phonological Reading*. Hillsdale, NJ: Lawrence Erlbaum Associates.

Perfetti, C.A., Goldman, S. and Hogaboam, T.W. (1979). 'Reading skill and the identification of words in discourse context', *Memory and Cognition*, **7**, 273–82.

Pressley, M. (1998). *Reading Instruction that Works: The Case for Balanced Teaching*. New York: The Guildford Press.

Reid, D. (1993). 'Another vision of "Visions and Revisions"', *Remedial and Special Education*, **14**, 14–6, 25.

Rust, J., Golombok, S. and Trickey, G. (1993). *Manual of the Wechsler Objective Reading Dimensions*. London: The Psychological Corporation.

Rutter, M. and Yule, W. (1975). 'The concept of specific reading retardation', *Journal of Child Psychology and Psychiatry*, **16**, 181–97.

Schumacker, R. (2003). 'Reliability in Rasch measurement: Avoiding the rubber ruler.' Paper presented at the annual meeting of the American Educational Research Association, April.

Schwartz, S. (1984). *Measuring Reading Competence: A Theoretical-Prescriptive Approach*. New York: Plenum Press.

Schweinhart, L. and Weikart, D.P. (1993). *Significant Benefits: The High/Scope Perry Preschool Curriculum Comparison through Age 23*. Ypsilanti, MI: High/Scope Press.

Share, D.L., McGee, R., McKenzie, D., Williams, S. and Silva, P.A. (1987). 'Further evidence relating to the distinction between specific reading retardation and general reading backwardness', *British Journal of Developmental Psychology*, **5**, 35–44.

Shaywitz, S. *et al*. (1992). 'Evidence that dyslexia may represent the lower tail of a normal distribution of reading ability', *New England Journal of Medicine*, **326**, 145–50.

Smart, D., Sanson, A. and Prior, M. (1996). 'Connections between reading disability and behaviour problems: testing temporal and causal hypotheses', *Journal of Abnormal Child Psychology*, **24**, 363–83.

Spearman, C. (1904). 'General intelligence objectively determined and measured', *American Journal of Psychology*, **15**, 201–93.

Spear-Swerling, L. and Sternberg, R.J. (1998). *Off Track: When Poor Readers Become 'Learning Disabled'*. Boulder, CO: Westview.

Stanovich, K. (1986). 'Matthew effects in reading: some consequences of individual differences in the acquisition of literacy', *Reading Research Quarterly*, **21**, 360–407.

Stanovich, K. and Cunningham, A. (1992). 'Studying the consequences of literacy within a literate society: the cognitive correlates of print exposure', *Memory and Cognition*, **20**, 51–68.

Stanovich, K. and Siegel, L. (1994). 'Phenotypic performance profile of children with reading disabilities: a regression-based test of the phonological-core variable-difference model', *Journal of Educational Psychology*, **86**, 24–53.

Stanovich, K. and Stanovich, P. (1995). 'How research might inform the debate about early reading acquisition', *Journal of Research in Reading*, **18**, 87–105.

Stuart, M. and Coltheart, M. (1988). 'Does reading develop in a sequence of stages?' *Cognition*, **30**, 139–81.

Steering Committee of the Physicians' Health Study Research Group (1989). 'Final report on the aspirin component of the ongoing physicians' health study', *New England Journal of Medicine*, **32**, 129–35.

Torgerson, C.J., Porthouse, and Brooks, G. (2003). 'A systematic review and meta-analysis of randomized controlled trials evaluating interventions in adult literacy and numeracy', *Journal of Research in Reading*, **26**, 234–55.

Torgesen, J. and Burgess, S. (1998). 'Consistency of reading-related phonological processes throughout early childhood: evidence from longitudinal-correlational and instructional studies.' In: Metsala, J.L. and Ehri, L.C. (Eds) *Word Recognition in Beginning Literacy*. Mahwah, NJ: Erlbaum.

Torgesen, J.K, Morgan, S. and Davis, C. (1992). 'The effects of two types of phonological awareness training on word learning in kindergarten children', *Journal of Educational Psychology*, **84**, 364–70.

Tucker, L. (1946). 'Maximum validity of a test with equivalent items', *Psychometrica*, **11**, 1–13.

Wagner, R. and Torgesen, J. (1987). 'The nature of phonological processing and its causal role in the acquisition of reading skills', *Psychological Bulletin*, **101**, 192–212.

Wagner, R., Torgesen, J. and Rashotte, C. (1993). 'The efficacy of phonological awareness training for early reading development: A meta-analysis.' Symposium presented
at annual meeting of the American Educational Research Association, Atlanta, GA,
April.

West, R. and Stanovich, K. (1978). 'Automatic contextual facilitation in readers of three
ages', *Child Developmental Psychology*, **49**, 717–27.

WISC-IV. (2000). *Weschler Intelligence Scale for Children*. Fourth edition. Texas, San
Antonio: Harcourt Assessment Inc.

Woodstock, R. (1973). *Woodstock Reading Mastery Tests – Revised*. Circle Pines, MN:
American Guidance Service.

Woodstock, R. (1998). *Woodstock Reading Mastery Tests – Revised*. Circle Pines, MN:
American Guidance Service.

Yule, W., Rutter, M., Berger, M. and Thompson, J. (1974). 'Over and under achievement in reading: distribution in the general population', *British Journal of
Educational Psychology*, **44**, 1–12.

4 Cognitive psychology and reading assessment

Alastair Pollitt and Lynda Taylor

Theory and practice

The past forty years have seen a great expansion in the amount of empirical research carried out in the field of reading assessment. Many of the various question formats commonly used have been the subject of intense investigation with regard to issues of reliability and validity; multiple-choice and cloze, in particular, have been the focus of considerable attention with large numbers of studies devoted to analysing the efficiency of multiple-choice items or the relative merits of one cloze format over another. Others have studied the strategies adopted by test-takers during a reading test, the role of cultural or background knowledge, or the relationship between reading and other language skills.

There has been rapid expansion in all areas of both L1 and L2 reading research. The late 1960s and the 1970s saw extensive advances in the development of theories and models of reading, a trend which continues to this day. Considerable attention has been directed towards trying to identify and describe the component processes of reading at a level beyond basic decoding (the so-called higher order reading skills) and towards finding an appropriate model to describe and explain the nature of comprehension. Recent models for text comprehension have stressed the active and constructive nature of the process in which meaning is generated by the cognitive processes of the reader; using text together with pre-existing knowledge, the reader apparently builds a personal mental representation which may be modified by personal attitudinal characteristics and intentions; this mental representation may be visual, or verbal, or both.

It is surely reasonable to suggest that reading comprehension theory and reading assessment theory must overlap and that research developments in one field are likely to be of relevance and value to the other. One might therefore expect there to exist between these two fields a strong and reciprocal relationship, as a result of which advances in our understanding of reading processes and products are directly reflected in developments in reading assessment theory and practice. This has not always been the case and it is easy to see a considerable gap between current theories of reading comprehension and current practice in the testing of reading comprehension ability. The result of this mismatch is that much of what is currently done in reading comprehension assessment is undertaken without sufficient regard to what we now understand about the process of reading comprehension.

Most researchers and practitioners working in the field of reading test design and use probably assume that an underlying relationship automatically exists between, on the one hand their own theory and practice and on the other, a theory of reading; various comments in the literature, however, suggest that some researchers perceive a gap between current theories of reading and current reading test design. Farr and Carey (1986) and Anderson *et al.* (1991) conclude that reading tests have not changed significantly in the last fifty years and have not therefore responded to changes in how comprehension is understood:

> *While models of reading have evolved, changing our thinking about how the printed word is understood, the tests that we use to measure that understanding have not changed significantly.*
>
> *It would thus appear that an examination of the construct validity of current reading theories, is in order.*

(Anderson *et al.*, 1991, p.41)

Changes in the approach to construct validity

Considerable changes have taken place in the treatment of validity in educational assessment over the past 10 years, partly inspired by Samuel Messick's seminal article in 1988. Interest in the purely empirical forms, such as predictive or content validity, has declined in favour of a growing concern for the more theoretical *construct* validity (Weir, 2005), in parallel with an insistence that educational tests should support some kind of criterion reference. This is especially true for formative assessments, which generally do not lead to serious and irreversible decisions about students. Language teachers, amongst others, have come to expect that the tests they use measure how well students use language, rather than just look right and make accurate predictions.

This shift can also be seen as a move from concern for *product*, or test scores, to a concern for *process*, or what the student is doing during the test. According to this view, if we want to find out how good a student is at 'reading' we should make sure that what they are doing during the test is indeed 'reading'. Pollitt and Ahmed (2000) expressed this in their 'cognitive psychology approach to construct validity': it is a prerequisite for valid assessment that 'the students' minds are doing the things we want them to show us they can do'.

A modern view of cognition

We use Anderson's (1983, 1993) ACT theories of cognition to analyse the reading process, but most of what we say would differ very little if we chose a different approach. Recent theories of cognitive processing argue that there is little real distinction to be made between the three familiar terms learning, remembering and thinking. When a student reads a text and constructs a meaning representation because of it, this is thinking, but it operates on structures recalled from memory and the resulting representation is returned to memory, at least for some time; if it remains long enough in memory we say that the understanding of the text has been learned. The close relationships between these terms were first described by Anderson (1976) and later developments are outlined in Anderson (2000).

The active brain

One of the most startling findings from recent cognitive and neurological research is just how active and busy our brains are. A quick arithmetical calculation offers a simple way of demonstrating this. Any neurology textbook will confirm that the brain of a normal adult has about 10^{11} neurons and that each of these makes, on average, a thousand connections, or synapses. Since a baby's brain at birth has only about 10^{11} synapses, it is clear that nearly all of the adult complement of synapses – more or less 10^{14} of them – must be formed in the few years of early childhood. For simplicity let us assume that 'childhood' takes ten years.

The implications are dramatic:

Now, this means that:

The developing brain must add:

In 10 years		10^{14}	synapses
In 1 year		10^{13}	synapses
In 1 day	÷365	2.5×10^{10}	synapses
In 1 hour	÷24	10^{9}	synapses
In 1 minute	÷60	1.5×10^{7}	synapses
In 1 second	÷60	2.5×10^{5}	synapses

That is, at least 250,000 new connections every second.

Following these very conservative calculations we can see that a child's brain must be adding at least a quarter of a million new connections *every second* of its life, whether the child is studying, playing, or even just sleeping. Recent research suggests that the full complement of synapses is completed in just the first two years of life and that brain development thereafter is largely a matter of selective reinforcement of useful connections from the vast numbers that have been formed, with loss of many of the rest. At the peak of this period about two million new synapses are being formed every second.

The exact numbers are not important. What matters is to understand just how busy the brain is. A synapse is a physical structure that can be seen through a microscope (though not, of course, in a living brain) and the amount of both physical and chemical activity involved in creating so many changes to the brain is enormous.

There is no reason to think this level of activity ceases in adulthood; although it weighs only 2 per cent of body weight, the brain uses about 25 per cent of the body's fuel supply. Rather we should understand that the adult brain is still capable of modifying itself – that is, of learning – an enormous number of times every second: 'The brain performs billions of neural computations every second that we are alive' (Bear *et al.*, 2001, p.119). To understand what happens during reading we should keep in mind the vast amount of activity that is going on inside the child's brain.

The nature of reading comprehension

To construct a valid assessment of reading, we must begin by asking what is meant by 'reading comprehension' in the particular contexts we are interested in. The basic problem is that, at least after the early stages of developing the skill, reading is an unobservable process; to understand what is happening inside a student's mind needs careful investigation and we will begin by summarising the areas of agreement amongst researchers of the comprehension process.

The key is that reading comprehension is seen as a process of *constructing* meaning. Bartlett (1932) proposed the idea that prior knowledge is organised into *schemas* that a reader will recall, whenever appropriate. Anderson (1977, pp.415–31) describes these schemas as providing 'the ideational scaffolding' that helps the reader access the information in the text. Johnson-Laird (1977) emphasised how active the reading process is and how much the reader brings to comprehending the text. His sentence 'Words are cues to build a familiar mental model' expresses the fact that reading is an intensely personal construction of meaning, mostly using as its elements structures (schemas) that have already been built by the reader during earlier linguistic and cognitive experiences.

Gernsbacher's 'Structure Building Framework' (Gernsbacher, 1990; Gernsbacher and Foertsch, 1999) proposes that comprehension begins when some of a reader's 'memory nodes' are activated by incoming perceptual stimuli as words are read. These form the foundation of a mental structure which develops as reading continues. In line with Grice's (1975, pp.225–42) well-known maxim 'Be relevant', readers assume that new information can be added to this structure and they will only break off and start a new structure, or sub-structure, when they are unable to see the relevance of and integrate the incoming data. The advertisement below, designed to encourage young men to join the Singapore Defence Force, cleverly exploits this process. If you read it slowly, you can almost feel how your mind is constructing mental representations in real time.

A huge fireball engulfed the enemy
fighter as Sgt Hong's missiles hit. Anticipating
a further wave of fighters, he quickly
discharged the spent cartridge and
reloaded *fresh toner into the printer.*
Don't just dream about it: join the SDF

At the start, you began building a representation using schemas your mind already contained about warfare, modern high technology military aircraft and the thrill of combat. As you read on, more details were added to that initial representation – until you reached the italicised phrase. Its meaning – something to do with maintaining office equipment – cannot immediately be fitted into the existing representation, so a new structure is begun to accommodate it. Finally, when you reached the word 'dream' (if not before then) and driven by the maxim of relevance to integrate everything in the text, you created a new super-structure that resolved the conflict by representing 'Mr' Hong as a young man rather bored by his everyday duties and fantasising about a more exciting life. And then you added extra layers or facets to the structure as you noted the humour, the fact that it was an advertisement, your feelings about militarism and so on. That's an awful lot of brain activity provoked by just 39 words.

Many experiments could be chosen to illustrate some of the unconscious processing that is part of the reading process. Consider this sentence:

The king died and the queen died of grief.

This seems an easy sentence stating two simple propositions, but in fact we must make several crucial *inferences* in order to 'understand' it. Ask yourself the following questions:

- Who died first?

- Why did the queen die?

- Were the king and the queen related?

That we can readily answer these questions shows that our brains spontaneously make many inferences, going beyond what is explicitly stated in the text in order to build a coherent and satisfactory representation of the meanings this text seems to contain.

Lessons for assessing reading

For our purpose of understanding how children read text, and so how we ought to try to assess their reading ability, there are several lessons to be taken from this psychological view of cognition and the reading process. The importance of schemas in the current view should make us realise that meaning does not reside in the text, but in the interaction between text and reader. We cannot ignore the importance of the reader's pre-existing schemas, since these are the very stuff with which the meaning structures are built. To the extent that the past experiences of different readers vary, so the meanings they construct will be different. At the very least, each student's representation of (i.e. provoked by) the text will reflect differences in their interests and their purposes for reading it: their structure of meaning will represent what the test means *for them*. This leads to a problem: if understanding is necessarily idiosyncratic, how can we ever hope to measure it? Spolsky (1994) argues that we cannot and that we would do better to seek rich descriptions of students' understanding than to claim we are measuring it. We will suggest a solution to this problem later.

Schemas are pre-fabricated structures that are activated in their entirety when provoked, even though much of what each one contains will not necessarily be needed for the text in question. They prepare us for whatever is likely to arise in a subsequent text, in terms of what we would expect to encounter in a context capable of provoking them. Their influence is both subtle and strong; we enhance our imagined representations with stereotypic people, objects and events to fill out the 'slots' in the schema that are not explicitly specified by the author, stereotypes that may not be consistent with the author's own imagination. A simple proof of this is the lack of surprise we feel if, in a narrative about a crime or road accident, reference is made to *the* policeman, even though no policeman has yet been mentioned, apparently contravening the general rule that characters must first be introduced to an English narrative with the indefinite article. It can be argued (Brown and Yule, 1983) that the policeman was introduced along with the schema and had been present implicitly from that point.

Children, especially in the unnatural and rather stressful conditions of a test or examination, will be less able to distinguish what is their own idiosyncratic knowledge and expectation from the meanings intended by the author and less able to avoid the pitfalls of stereotypic thinking as they read. We must take care to ensure that the test does not unfairly depend on our adult consensus of what ought to be in a reader's schemas. Taylor (1996) observed marked differences between the schemas of younger and older teenagers (13–14-year-olds and 17–18-year-olds) which no doubt resulted from their varying degrees of life experience.

We should recognise that the meaning of a text is not constructed in a simple linear fashion. As the Sergeant Hong example showed, we can modify our meaning structures retrospectively in the light of new information. Later parts of the text may change our understanding of earlier parts; this is obvious when you consider that almost every modern novel begins *in media res*, leaving the setting, the characters and even the scene to be set as the narrative progresses. The study of literature assumes our ability to alter our understanding of a text through study and reflection. Most pertinent to our concern is the effect of comprehension test questions. Gordon and Hanauer (1993) reported empirical evidence that multiple-choice questions can cause some readers to over-elaborate their mental representations, incorporating misleading 'information' from the distractors, but a cognitive model of reading implies that any question will at least provoke re-consideration and so cause changes in the meaning structure. We face a rather serious 'Heisenberg' problem: we need to use questions to find out about the representation the student has made while reading the text but the questions are bound to change that representation. Perhaps some kinds of questions may cause less change than others?

Finally, for the moment, we should question the distinction commonly made between *understanding* and *remembering*. Is it reasonable to claim that you have understood a text if you cannot remember the important things about it? In most current theories of cognition, thinking operates on memory and what we think of as new information from a text is actually a new structure in memory built from elements that were already present in memory. There is no separate 'place' where thinking takes place, for thinking consists of changes in memory and the only question is whether or not the new structures will persist after the reading is finished. Barring some sort of short term memory pathology, it seems that a coherent and meaningful representation that has no unresolved inconsistencies will remain accessible in memory, at least for as long as it takes for us to test it.

How should we assess reading?

If 'reading' equals 'building models of meaning', how can we test the quality of a child's comprehension quality? The first step seems obvious: we must investigate the models that readers build. It has long been accepted that asking a reader to produce a summary – oral or written – of what they have read is a reasonable way of accessing the mental representation which they have built for themselves. Summary tasks enjoy a natural appeal among English teachers, since a summary is an attempt by the student to express their mental representation in words. What we know from empirical research into the cognitive operations involved in the summarisation process suggests that they include skills such as identifying relevant information, distinguishing superordinate from subordinate material and eliminating trivial or redundant material; such operations are key to constructing a mental model and can thus provide insights into comprehension (Kintsch and van Dijk, 1978; Johnston, 1984).

We need to recognise, however, that summary production can be a very difficult and cognitively demanding task for children and even for college students (Brown and Day, 1983); after all, the child's mental representation is a multi-modal model of a *world* rather than a literal one of the text (Garnham, 1987). A traditional summary production task usually involves a set of questions to which the reader must give written answers after reading a particular text or set of texts. But there is a significant danger associated with the testing method we usually use. If it is difficult to turn the multi-modal mental structures into a string of words and the original text presents just that simple string of words, children are far more likely to draw directly on the text to answer questions rather than to try to answer from their mental representations. What will happen if we remove the text following reading but before asking them the questions?

The effect of removing the text

If the direct route from text to test is blocked, the result will be that the child is obliged to refer to the mental representation and we are therefore much more likely to be assessing the real result of reading (see Figure 4.1).

Taylor explored this possibility experimentally, using a test format called 'summary completion'. Her results 'suggest that it is possible to design text-removed summary completion tasks which will function as highly reliable and valid measures of reading comprehension ability' (Taylor, 1996, p.236).

Why might different people find different features salient?

We believe that a valid test of text comprehension should consist of asking the reader to provide some sort of summary of the text, because a summary will be the closest approximation we can get to a description of the mental representation they have built while reading. Even so, we must remember that there are several reasons why different readers will, quite validly, construct different representations from reading the same text. We have already noted that they will approach the task with different prior knowledge and experiences and so will start their construction of meaning with different schemas. We should also remember that there is more involved than just information. Schemas contain affective components too, including memories of the emotions felt in the experiences from which they derive; the meaning structures readers build will incorporate all the feelings of interest or boredom, pleasure or distaste that they feel while reading. How they feel about the author, both in the sense of evaluating the quality of the writing and in the sense of agreement (or not) with the author's attitudes and assumptions, may profoundly affect the meaning they make of the text.

All of these factors will cause readers to prioritise the content of the text differently, leading to Spolsky's problem with 'measuring comprehension' we referred to earlier.

There is one way that we can reduce the problem. In one sense measuring reading is no more problematic than measuring writing or science or running. We don't actually want to measure 'reading' at all; we want to measure 'the ability to read'. Just as in sport or in any educational test, the results of a reading test are of no value – they are not generalisable to other contexts of interest – unless the reader agreed to 'play by the rules'. To measure children's ability to read we need to ensure (a) that what they are doing is what we mean by reading, (b) that they know what we are expecting of them and (c) that they agree to try their best.

Figure 4.1 The effect of removing the text

There is one final feature of 'real' language use that we have not yet discussed which is crucial to our success in achieving these demands and it is that real language use is purposeful. In real life we read for a purpose. We may read a poem to appreciate the poet's feelings, or a novel for enjoyment, or a reference source for information. We may study a journal article to grasp the writer's opinions and argument, or a specialist book to deepen our understanding of a topic we already know quite well. These five categories of purpose for using language, with their mnemonic Affect, Enjoyment, Information, Opinion, Understanding, were developed for the AAP, the Scottish national survey of standards in English (Pollitt and Hutchinson, 1990). In each case the purpose precedes the reading and guides it. The different kinds of reading which are sometimes tested – gist, skimming or scanning, criticism – have developed to serve these different purposes.

The best way to make reading purposeful in a test is not to try to explain to students what purpose you would like them to adopt, but to make the purpose arise naturally from the context in which the reading takes place. For example, if a student knows that they are reading a text in order to judge the suitability of the story for a younger audience (as in Taylor, 1996) or to explain the argument to fellow students, or to write a detailed critique, or to find the best way to travel to Timbuktu, they will approach the task appropriately without needing specific detailed instructions. Purpose is much easier to understand through context than through instructions which can place an extra set of linguistic demands on readers.

Conclusions: some principles for testing reading comprehension

These considerations lead us to make six recommendations to anyone trying to assess students' ability to read.

1 Contextualise the reading test

It is not difficult to create simple contexts for reading tasks. Usually they will involve reading in order to do some other task – reading in order to write, or reading in order to discuss, for example. Context is an essential part of real world reading and is the easiest way to convey to students the precise purpose for which they are being asked to read the text. Remember that a test may cause or increase stress for students and it is unwise to risk overloading them with instructions.

2 Give the reading task a purpose

The most fundamental problem is that the construction of meaning from a text is a personal, idiosyncratic process and there is often no single meaning which is better than any other. However, we can reduce this problem to a manageable level by constraining comprehension through purpose. If it is clear that the reading is meant to achieve a certain purpose and that the student is expected to show that they can achieve it, then they will at least know the rules of the game. Of course, we cannot guarantee that all of them will be motivated enough to play the game to the best of their ability.

3 Remove the text

Some kinds of reading properly require detailed and repeated reading of the text. For other kinds of reading, however, if we leave the text in place and then ask questions that refer to particular parts of it, it is a near certainty that the students will answer by referring to the text and not by referring to their mental representations. In the worst cases the result will involve nothing but a simple matching of words in the question to words in the text that tells us little of real value about the student's understanding.

4 Ask the students to summarise the text

Ensure that the task they are asked to carry out as a result of the reading is to summarise the text in a way that is appropriate to the given purpose. Once you have expressed a purpose to the students it would be dishonest to ask them questions that are not related to that purpose. Thus, for instance, it will usually be inappropriate to use a reading task as an opportunity to test the students' knowledge of vocabulary or of details of syntax. If the text expresses a point of view and the purpose is to evaluate the argument, the questions should amount to a critical summary of the logic and its assumptions and the test should not dwell on aspects of style.

5 Minimise the questions

Remember that questions will change the student's mental representation of meaning. Asking for a summary is one, albeit cognitively demanding, way of avoiding this problem entirely and it may be that you can devise, in a contextualised test, a form of response that is so natural that it has little or no backwards influence on the process of comprehension. Students might be asked to write notes for a discussion, or to chart or tabulate the information they need for their purpose. Any questions that do not relate to the student's perceived purpose for reading will necessarily interfere with our desire to 'see' the mental model they have built.

6 Give the students room to tell you what the text means for them

Remember that many different meaning structures can be defended as interpretations of a single text. If possible, give the students an opportunity to tell you what they remember most, what struck them as most interesting, in the text – even if their answers are not to be scored in the usual way. We are encouraged to include a few questions of this open kind in a survey questionnaire, to show that we respect the respondents' right to hold personal and unpredictable opinions, so perhaps we should adopt a similar approach in reading tests. After all, the students are human beings too.

References

Anderson, J.R. (1976). *Language, Memory and Thought*. Hillsdale, NJ: Lawrence Erlbaum Associates.

Anderson, J.R. (1983). *The Architecture of Cognition*. Cambridge, MA: Harvard University Press.

Anderson, J.R. (1993). *Rules of the Mind*. Hillsdale, NJ: Lawrence Erlbaum Associates.

Anderson, J.R. (2000). *Learning and Memory: An Integrated Approach*. New York: Wiley.

Anderson, N., Bachman, L., Perkins, K. and Cohen, A. (1991). 'An exploratory study into the construct validity of a reading comprehension test: triangulation of data sources', *Language Testing*, **8**, 41–66.

Anderson, R.C. (1977). 'The notion of schemata and the educational enterprise.' In: Anderson R.C., Spiro, R.J. and Montague, W.E. (1977). *Schooling and the Acquisition of Knowledge*. Hillsdale, NJ: Lawrence Erlbaum Associates.

Bartlett, F.C. (1932). *Remembering: A Study in Experimental and Social Psychology*. Cambridge: Cambridge University Press.

Bear, M.F., Connors, B.W. and Paradiso, M.A. (2001). *Neuroscience: Exploring the Brain*. Baltimore, MD and Philadelphia, PA: Lippincott Williams and Wilkins.

Brown, A. and Day, J. (1983). 'Macrorules for summarizing texts: The development of expertise', *Journal of Verbal Learning and Verbal Behavior*, **22**, 1–14.

Brown, G. and Yule, G. (1983). *Discourse Analysis*. Cambridge: Cambridge University Press.

Farr, R. and Carey, R.F. (1986). *Reading: What Can be Measured?* Newark, DE: International Reading Association.

Garnham, A. (1987). *Mental Models as Representations of Discourse and Text*. Chichester: Ellis Horwood.

Gernsbacher, M.A. (1990). *Language Comprehension as Structure Building*. Hillsdale, NJ: Lawrence Erlbaum Associates.

Gernsbacher, M.A. and Foertsch, J.A. (1999). 'Three models of discourse comprehension.' In: Garrod, S. and Pickering, M. *Language Processing*. Hove: Psychological Press.

Gordon, C. and Hanauer, D. (1993). 'Test answers as indicators of mental model construction.' Paper presented at the 1993 Language Testing Research Colloquium, Cambridge/Arnhem.

Grice, P. (1975). 'Logic and Conversation.' In: Cole, P. and Morgan, J. (Eds) *Syntax and Semantics, Vol. 3: Speech Acts*. New York: Academic Press.

Johnson-Laird, P.N. (1977). *Mental Models*. Cambridge: Cambridge University Press.

Johnston, P. (1984). 'Prior knowledge and reading comprehension test bias', *Reading Research Quarterly*, **19**, 219–39.

Kintsch, W. and van Dijk, T.A. (1978). 'Toward a model of text comprehension and production', *Psychological Review*, **85**, 363–94.

Messick, S. (1988). 'Validity.' In: Linn, R.L. (Ed) *Educational Measurement*. Third edn. New York: Macmillan.

Pollitt, A. and Ahmed, A. (2000). 'Comprehension Failures in Educational Assessment.' Paper presented at the European Conference for Educational Research, Edinburgh.

Pollitt, A. and Hutchinson, C. (1990). *The English Language Monitoring Project. Report of the Assessment of Achievement Programme, Second Round, 1989*. Edinburgh: Scottish Education Department.

Spolsky, B. (1994). 'Comprehension testing, or can understanding be measured?' In: Brown, G., Malmkjaer, K., Pollitt, A. and Williams, J. (Eds) *Language and Understanding*. Oxford, OUP.

Taylor, L.B. (1996). An investigation of text-removed summary completion as a means of assessing reading comprehension ability. Unpublished PhD thesis, University of Cambridge.

Weir, C.J. (2005). *Language Testing and Validation*. Basingstoke: Palgrave Macmillan.

5 Postmodernism and the assessment of literature

Colin Harrison

Introduction – the plate tectonics of assessment

How should we assess response to literature? It is worth considering this issue, since to do so raises many of the problems that traditionally accompany assessment in the arts, or indeed assessment in any area in which it is difficult to say whether a student's response is unequivocally right or wrong. I also want to argue that we need to take a postmodern perspective on assessing response to literature and to suggest that although postmodernism poses some major challenges for traditional assessment, such problems are inescapable, but they are also soluble.

Assessment systems are by their nature conservative. This is hardly surprising: as guardians of standards, arbiters of achievement and gatekeepers whose role is to determine in significant ways the life course of both students and their teachers, those in control of assessment systems bear a heavy responsibility and it is understandable that they should in general adopt a historical model of definition and an incremental (or even plate tectonic) model of change.

To anyone who works in an examinations board in the UK, however, the suggestion that changes proceeds at a lithospheric pace would seem risible, since – even if it is structurally conservative – the examination system in all UK countries has been through a period of unprecedented and unceasing change for the past thirty-five years. The main precipitating agents of these changes have been external to the boards themselves: external forces in the shape of government interventions have speeded up the rate of change in the lithosphere of assessment and these changes in turn have led to the production of new assessment life forms (not all of which have had a healthy long-term prognosis).

When the context of assessment changes, everything changes and in the UK the context began to change in the late 1970s. Interestingly, up to that point, gradual systemic change had been taking place in the examination system of the UK and it had been initiated in partnership with teachers, teachers' organisations and teacher educators. If teacher autonomy in curriculum and assessment is gold, then yes, in England and Wales there was once a golden age and that age was in the 1960s and 1970s, when teachers, teachers' groups and unions held sway within the Schools Council. Innovation in curriculum and assessment was encouraged through university departments of education and was led at the grass roots by school-based consortia, answerable to locally responsive examination boards (see Paul Thompson, chapter 9, for an account of many of these innovations).

But by 1981, the mood had changed. Sir Keith Joseph was Secretary of State for Education, Margaret Thatcher was Prime Minister, planning for a National Curriculum and examination system was well under way and the Schools Council was three years from closure. None of this centralisation of control over assessment and curriculum was wholly a Conservative idea, however. In a speech given in 1976 at Ruskin College Oxford, James Callaghan, the Labour Prime Minister, sketched out what was to become the agenda for governments of both complexions for the next thirty years: Callaghan argued that there was a '... strong case for the so-called "core curriculum" of basic knowledge'; and alongside that, it was important '... to maintain a proper national standard of performance' (Callaghan, 1976). Callaghan felt that governments should accept a moral imperative to take responsibility in the field of education and he quoted the words of R.H. Tawney, that 'what a wise parent would wish for their children, so the state must wish for all its children' to endorse his point. The same sentiment, quoted nearly thirty years later by the Labour peer Lord Adonis in his maiden speech, seems unexceptionable, but the question now, just as it was in 1976, is whether the state should act as a coercive parent or as a trusting one; whether the government should control curriculum and assessment, or manage it, leaving the control in the hands of education professionals (Hansard, HL, 2005).

In the 1990s, during what was for many teachers who had been in the vanguard of teacher-led and student-centred assessment in the 1970s a very depressing era (see Paul Thompson's account in his chapter in this book), many of those who had been involved in the assessment process began to take stock and to give more careful consideration to the principles that underpinned their approaches. Some of this thinking appeared in two books on assessment that came out towards the end of the 1990s (Harrison and Salinger, 1998; Coles and Jenkins, 1998) and these books, in part at least, attempted to clarify the theoretical undergirding that supported the case for radical and student-centred approaches to assessment. These two collections of papers by leading assessment theorists and practitioners reviewed national and international progress in assessment, particularly literacy assessment and included a paper that attempted to identify a philosphical and theoretical basis for reading assessment (Harrison and Salinger, 1998).

What was argued in the Harrison (1998) chapter was that the most appropriate theoretical position to adopt in seeking a principled basis for the assessment of response to literature was that of postmodernism. Nearly a decade later, this analysis seems no less relevant: if anything, there appears to be an even broader acceptance of the central argument of Jean-François Lyotard, that postmodernism is not so much a theoretical option as the condition of our society and that a key feature of that condition is an 'incredulity towards metanarrative' (Lyotard, 1984, p.xxiv).

A postmodern view of assessment – incredulity towards metanarrative

Broadly speaking, in relation to the concept of assessing response to literature, Lyotard's position can be understood from two related perspectives: one scientific and one literary. From a scientific perspective, an incredulity toward metanarrative would suggest a mistrust of traditional 'scientific' approaches to assessment. By the word 'metanarrative', Lyotard was referring to the grand socio-historical narratives, which, for example, would portray science as a dispassionate march towards objectivity and it is such grand narratives which postmodernism calls into question. A postmodern account of science would note the many ways in which science has had to reinvent its own rules; in quantum theory, for example – as a result of which many scientists have become much more cautious in using concepts such as 'truth', 'scientific accuracy' and 'objectivity'. These new systems of thinking have replaced a single notion of 'science' with a more flexible one: the single metanarrative has been replaced by a series of locally applicable discourses and the scientist's role is to select from these as appropriate.

From a literary perspective, too, postmodernism implies some fundamental changes to the ground rules. Following Wittgenstein (1953) and using his theory of 'language games', Lyotard argues that in arts as well as sciences we must accept multivalent solutions to philosophical problems: we will find ourselves using a range of language games, each of which has its own discourse rules. Each language game produces its own strand of narrative, which is locally coherent and which generates new understandings. A postmodern view would call into question the validity and authority of national testing programmes, for example. It would question the extent to which it is even possible to validly test reading attainment on a national scale and it would question the assumption that test data can present an 'objective' picture of reading standards, given that so many subjective decisions have to be made to produce national test results.

In a general sense, therefore, a postmodern approach to assessing response to literature would seem to pose a major threat to the validity of large-scale assessment structures. Lyotard's theories challenge the overall approach to assessment, but within literary theory, other perspectives also destabilise the lithosphere. There is only space in this chapter to briefly summarise some of these, but it is important to at least mention three of the most influential – Bakhtin, Iser and Derrida – because their analyses each pose different problems for a traditional view of response.

Clearly it is fundamental to any notion of examining in a formal system that a student's response to an examination question is to be regarded as correct in so far as it approximates to a template provided by an expert and accepted by the examiners and such a template would need to be based upon an agreed meaning. Mikhail Bakhtin (Medvedev and Bakhtin, 1978; Bakhtin, 1973), however, challenged the notion of a 'monologic' concept of meaning. Instead, Bakhtin emphasised a text's 'dialogic' nature and argued that language was a series of acts of communication, each of which takes place in a unique social, cultural and ideological context. The 'meaning' of a word is not fixed, because 'meaning' is a social as well as a linguistic phenomenon. Bakhtin argued that not just words but whole texts were 'dialogic'. Dostoyevsky's novels, for example, are not 'monologic'; they introduce a 'polyphonic' range of points of view, expressed through the various characters and between which the author does not adjudicate. Instead, the reader is faced with the difficult task of struggling to come to an active, personal and individual interpretation of meaning and to engage in a personal search for unification.

This emphasis on the reader as determiner of meaning was also attractive to Wolfgang Iser (1978), who argued that the process of reading is a dynamic one, to which readers bring personal experiences and social and cognitive schemata, and in which predictions, assumptions and inferences are constantly made, developed, challenged and negated. Iser's reception theory positions the reader as a central and active collaborator in making meaning; whose habits of interpretation are challenged and disconfirmed by reading, a process which leads to new insights and understandings, not only of the text, but also of themselves. Iser's theory goes further than Bakhtin's in suggesting that the text is unfinished without the reader's contribution to making meaning: it is the reader who, in partnership with the author, fills the 'hermeneutic gap' in the text, bringing to it his or her own experience and understanding and resolving the conflicts and indeterminacies which the author has left unresolved.

An even more extreme challenge to any notion of stability in meaning and interpretation – a notion which is essential if we are to retain any hope that it is possible to assess response to reading with any notion of certainty – is that posed by the literary theories of Jacques Derrida. Derrida's *Of Grammatology* (1976) proposed a theory of 'deconstruction' of texts which was so radical that it seemed to imply not only the 'death of the author' as determiner of meaning, but to threaten the death of meaning itself. According to Derrida, the reader's role is not to discover meaning, but to produce it: to dismantle (*déconstruire*) the text and rebuild it another way. Derrida uses the metaphor of bricoleur to describe the reader's role. He denied that the search for meaning could be so banal as a simple 'logocentric' transfer of consciousness from the 'transcendental subject' (the author) to the 'subject' (the reader). For Derrida, written texts are the site of an endless series of possibilities, oppositions and indeterminacies. Deciding on a text's meaning under these circumstances is not possible – the reader can do no more than look for traces of meaning and contemplate the text's geological strata during the unending fall into the abyss of possible deferred meanings.

Here, then, are three formal challenges to traditional assessment of response to literature:

From Bakhtin (1973): *the meaning of individual words and whole texts is unstable.*

From Iser (1978): *it is the reader (not the literary critic, or the chief examiner) who brings meaning to the text.*

From Derrida (1976): *any search for an agreed meaning is doomed to failure, since a text is not so much an IKEA flat pack that the reader assembles (what we might think of as the archetypal do-it-yourself task) as a set of power tools that can perform an infinite number of jobs.*

At this point, one might expect to encounter a complete philosophical stalemate, since these postmodern perspectives appear to be fundamentally incompatible with the value system that produced traditional English Literature examinations for GCSE and A-level and more recently, end-of-key-stage tests in England and Wales. But in fact this has not happened. Where there have been plate tectonic collisions, these have been over government policy, rather than over incompatible theories and the reason for this has been a general acceptance, if not of postmodernism, then of some of the implications of a postmodern position. As I have argued elsewhere (Harrison and Salinger, 1998; Harrison, 2004), agreeing to adopt a postmodern view is not what is crucial; what is important is to consider the practical implications of postmodernism and to determine whether or not these can be accommodated.

The following are the six implications of a postmodern perspective that I have suggested need to be considered and which could form a principled basis for assessment. What is interesting is that these six implications (and I have presented them elsewhere as moral imperatives) are in many respects far less contentious than the theories from which they derive (Harrison, 2004).

The imperatives for responsive assessment (the first three derived from a scientific perspective on postmodernism, the second three from a literary perspective), were these:

1. that we acknowledge the potential of local system solutions if global system solutions are difficult or impossible to achieve

2. that we acknowledge the importance of the individual subject, given that the concept of 'objectivity' has to be recognised as problematic

3. that we acknowledge the importance of accepting as valid a range of methodologies

4. that we acknowledge that we need to recognise a polysemic concept of meaning

5. that we acknowledge a privileging of the role of the reader

6. that we acknowledge a diminution of the authority of the author and of the text.

How should these imperatives drive a practical model of assessment of literature? Let's consider some examples, if only briefly.

1 We acknowledge the potential of local system solutions if global system solutions are difficult or impossible to achieve

The term 'local system solutions' could be interpreted in a number of ways, but I want to apply it to the examination industry as a whole, but with a comparison in mind between the present national boards and the more locally-responsive boards that preceded them. The local and regional consortia that connected classroom teachers to examination boards in the 1970s and 1980s served a number of purposes: they broke down national structures into regional chunks that had local autonomy and the freedom to innovate; they provided a mechanism for enabling individual teachers to develop an understanding of how marks, levels and boundaries were applied in the coursework of hundreds of students, including their own and the consortia provided a forum within which there was mutual respect for each others' expertise and a shared sense of purpose. The advantages of these arrangements were bidirectional – certainly most teachers felt that they gained immeasurably: from participating in the construction of new courses; from seeing students, many of whom hated exams, put heart and soul into their coursework and they gained from being treated as professionals, with unique expertise and a distinctive role to play in setting standards, rather than as technicians whose job was simply to 'deliver' a curriculum. But the exam boards gained, too: teachers, particularly newer teachers, were inducted into the craft knowledge of assessment; they came to understand not only what grades and levels meant in reality, they also learned how validation at whole school level worked, what excellent (and shoddy) coursework looked like, they learned that unreliable marking would be identified and where necessary regraded by experts.

2 We acknowledge the importance of the individual subject, given that the concept of 'objectivity' has to be recognised as problematic

The second imperative, acknowledging the importance of the individual subject, derives from an acknowledgement that 'objectivity' is always difficult to achieve and potentially uncertain and to recognise that acknowledging subjectivity can in some ways be more honest and no less valid. In assessment, this leads to a consideration to three types of more subjective assessment that during the 1990s were marginalised within national assessment programmes, namely teacher-assessment, self-assessment and peer-assessment. A postmodern perspective implies a rethinking of the assumptions and power relations underpinning assessment. Lather (1986) puts it this way: 'Emancipatory knowledge increases awareness of the contradictions hidden or distorted by everyday understandings and in doing so it directs attention to the possibilities for the social transformation inherent in the present configuration of social processes.' Putting an increased emphasis on teacher-assessment is important because it offers the possibility of making much better use of assessment information to guide instruction and assist the development of individuals, as the Scottish 'Diagnostic Procedures' and 'Next Steps' projects, for example developed by Louise Hayward and Ernie Spencer make clear (chapter 16). One serious problem for assessment in the UK is that decades of externally-administered tests of reading have made many teachers feel deskilled, but I would argue that teachers are the professionals who are potentially in the best position to make a contribution to assessment processes and are well positioned to put the information which comes from assessment to good use. Quality assurance is important if teachers' assessments are to be trusted and given due weight, but there is no reason why teachers should not be trained, accredited and awarded professional certification in this important area.

Giving serious attention to self- and peer-assessment, however, is potentially even more powerful than teacher-assessment, since it implies a shift of perspective from the student as the object to the subject of assessment, to the controlling agent in the assessment process. Denny Taylor's 'student advocacy model' of assessment (1993) was one of the approaches which attempted to recognise, theorise and exemplify this radical shift, but, as with many innovations, it is not without its precedents. Over thirty years ago, Terry Phillips (1971) was filming teacherless small groups of nine-year-olds discussing children's literature and recording their conversations as part of a student self- and peer-assessment approach. We would certainly want to suggest that it will be enormously important to develop a wide body of information on self- and peer-assessment in the near future and to put in place mechanisms for sharing the information. To attempt this is not without risk, however; children's self-assessments are social practices that can be negative as well as positive, constraining as well as emancipatory (Johnson, 1994). Students, like teachers, will need support if their own contribution to assessment is to be truly emancipatory, but studies such as that of Almasi (1995) into peer-led discussion of literature suggest that this can be done, and that information can be obtained which captures much of the richness and complexity of decentralised participation structures.

3 We acknowledge the importance of accepting as valid a range of methodologies

Within a postmodern approach to the assessment of response to literature, extending the range of methodologies can take us in a number of directions that support some of the points already made. The modes of examining can be extended: if it is agreed that there is no fundamental superiority of formal over informal examination modes, of written examinations over oral, of national over local, then the floodgates are opened to a much wider range of assessment opportunities. These would have the potential to not only increase teacher and student motivation, but also to create much clearer alignment between curriculum and assessment than is generally possible. But a radical approach to assessment would also envisage the principles of assessment being negotiated with the all the participants. Such negotiated decisions might relate to the contexts within which assessments occur, the nature of the assessment procedures, the format and structure of assessment reports, the nature of what is to be considered as evidence and the final content of any report which is to be shared with a wider audience. This is not at all unusual in higher education: masters level students on many courses can have a say over how they are assessed; it would be a challenge, but a perfectly feasible challenge, to extend the range of such opportunities to school students.

The issue of evidence is a crucial one. Understandably, it is usually teachers and other assessment specialists who decide what is to be counted as evidence; it is relatively unusual for students to participate in making those decisions. I would argue both that students should be involved in deciding what evidence of their response to literature is to be recorded and that the range of evidence should be broadened. In the past, evaluation of response to literature has been based on an assessment of a student's critique of a work of literature, a template-matching exercise that invites an essay or similar response and compares it to a model produce by an examiner. I have no fundamental problem with this, but I would want to suggest that playscripts, role-playing, PowerPoint presentations, response logs, narratives, web pages, annotated maps, interviews, set designs, storyboards, annotated graphs, collages, photographs, videos and displays are also, in principle, admissible as evidence of responses to literature and are capable of being assessed.

A postmodern analysis would not judge a PowerPoint presentation on a Wilfred Owen poem for example, as inherently any more difficult to assess than an essay written in 40 minutes in an examination, and in many respects such a presentation might go beyond what could be conveyed in an essay. The presentations on the Converse site (Converse, 2005) use animation, colour, diagrams and paintings to make points about the lexis, alliteration, hyperbole, structure and themes of Owen's poem 'Exposure' and does so in ways that are novel and powerful. Figure 5.1 (shown here in black and white) shows some of these effects: colour and arrows clarify emphasis and add dynamism to the points being made; the inclusion of John Nash's painting 'Over the Top' is a inter-textual leap that offers evidence of the students' sensitivity not only to the historical context of the poem, but also to its evocation of the coldness of the night, the terrible losses sustained in unprotected attacks and the absurdity of war.

Figure 5.1 Slide from a PowerPoint presentation on Wilfred Owen's poem 'Exposure'
(Adapted in black and white from Converse, 2005)

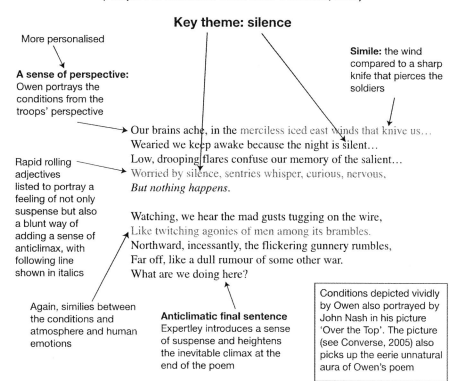

To be open to alternative methodologies is not to say that anything goes, however: The wider range of response modes has to be open to the same critique as the traditional modes. A postmodern perspective may problematise objectivity, but it also adopts a consensual and principled framework of values and while it approves multivalent solutions, there is no reason why it would not also reject what was agreed to be shoddy or false. One of the criteria for an effective metaphor is that it should be both just and complete and we might apply the same criterion for judging the worth of intertextual or multimodal responses to literature. In the case of the PowerPoint presentation cited above, for example, the introduction of the Nash painting produces associations and resonances that reverberate in a number of dimensions – historical, aesthetic, thematic and moral. We might contrast this with a different task taken from the internet: a suggested activity within a Scholastic unit which has the title: 'Be a Theme Park Designer!' (Scholastic, 2005). In this unit, which it is suggested is conducted over seven days of classroom activity, students are invited to work 'in cooperative learning groups' to research settings, textiles, food and entertainment 'related to a literature selection and its time period' and to 'design costumes, menus and theme park rides from that literature's time period'. When I first located this unit, using the search term 'response to literature', I assumed it was a spoof, but it is offered as a serious curriculum activity, with Romeo and Juliet as a text. We can imagine students having fun creating 'Juliet's Spooktakular Creepy Crypt Freak Fest' for example, but working on these theme park units might ultimately insulate the students from any serious engagement with the text and might have absolutely nothing to do with response to literature. Only a close examination of the products produced by the theme park ride activity and any commentary that might accompany then would permit an external evaluator or assessor to judge whether were was indeed any deep, thoughtful or penetrating 'response to literature' stimulated by the unit.

4 We acknowledge that we need to recognise a polysemic concept of meaning

Literary criticism has existed as long as literature has existed and Plato's stern moral tone in *The Republic* reminds us that there is nothing new in challenging the author, nor in accusing a poet of failing to tell the truth. But Plato was not postmodern – he did believe passionately in the truth and believed that the truth could be found. Assessing response to literature from a postmodern perspective brings us up against two problems simultaneously: a polysemic concept of meaning and a contextualised theory of truth. As we have already suggested, however, neither problem is irresoluble. In most assessment of literature, response comes down to one of three forms: reproduction (quotation or 'close reference' to the text), transformation (putting the text into one's own words) or juxtaposition (an intertextual response that demonstrates understanding through offering textual connections that have associational linkages that extend our understanding of the original). Reproduction and transformation are the two forms of response that are most congruent with a monosemic concept of meaning, but their place in assessment may be diminishing.

In assessing response, exam boards prefer not to put too much emphasis on reproduction, since it may be independent of comprehension: a student could simply parrot an answer, or give direct quotation without any paraphrase or commentary and this gives very little evidence of understanding. Similarly, exam boards prefer not to put too much emphasis on transformation, which may betoken comprehension, but may also be independent of the reader's having integrated meaning at the whole text level, or of that reader's having a rich associational response. However, while juxtaposition can offer evidence of comprehension and creative response, here the problem is the opposite: the more creative and original the intertextual links suggested by the reader, the more risky for the student and the more problematic for the exam board in terms of interpretability and inter-rater reliability (see any issue of *The London Review of Books* letters page for evidence of this in the context of contemporary literary criticism).

But juxtaposition is the route that must be travelled: not only postmodern literary theorists but also cognitive psychologists now accept that texts are best understood as arrangements of propositions made up of complex semantic vectors that exist in loosely structured relationships and that knowledge is best understood in the same way (Kintsch, 1998). For Kintsch, comprehension does not involve the application of precise semantic and syntactic rules, but is rather a process of spreading activation, in which fuzzy mental representations are created in response to text, which yield understandings that are approximate solutions, full, initially at least, of irrelevancies and redundancies. The challenge of comprehension is to integrate those networks of propositions into coherent mental representations and the challenge of assessment is to offer opportunities for readers to give evidence of that integration through sharing those representations and constructing others that use juxtaposition to forge new associations that give evidence of understanding, but are also novel, just and complex.

5 We acknowledge a privileging of the role of the reader

What are the implications of this imperative? Again, we could do worse than to begin with a quotation from Kintsch, who noted that asking comprehension questions was 'an unnatural act', in that a person's answers do not generally show what they have learned, but rather what they already know (Kintsch, 1998). To privilege the role of the reader, therefore, we might begin by letting the reader choose an area of the text for focus, putting the reader more in the role of literary critic than examinee. Offering the reader the choice of text and offering the reader a chance to define a self-generated text activity on the basis of which the quality of their response will be judged would be challenging, but it might have a number of benefits. First, such a task would open up the possibility of many more types of response and the less formulaic the task, the less easy for the student to locate an off-the-shelf plagiarised answer. Second, a self-generated text activity would help to shift the balance of assessment away from content knowledge to skill

development, which in turn helps to avoid the problem that in less exam-oriented
assessment approaches, content knowledge is harder to test, because the text is not with-
held from the student. Finally, if new approaches to assessment are to be worthwhile,
one criterion they should meet is that of greater alignment with post-school and real-
world tasks and self-generated text activity, with text focus and task determined at least
in part by the student, would tend to approximate more closely to real world reading
than would formulaic exam questions on a set task judged against a common answer
template.

As Pearson and Hamm make clear (chapter 7), in the USA portfolio-based and student-centred approaches to assessment gained currency and even began to become
fashionable during the 1990s, but their population began to wane as the calls for high-
stakes testing became more insistent. This drop in popularity occurred in relation to two
problems – authenticity and generalisability. 'Whose work is it anyway?' was the cry
that went up and the answer was 'we don't know': in portfolio-based work the student
clearly had plenty of input, but teacher also certainly had some input and so had peers.
The generalisability issue was related to the fact that student performance is more variable in portfolio-based work than it is within the narrower boundaries of traditional
examinations. This should hardly surprise us, because reliability goes down whenever
the range of item types, content and media goes up, but if the impact on measured reliability is negative, there certainly are problems in acceptability for employers and
others who would wish to use literature exam results as an indicator of overall competence in reading and writing at a high level. However, this is not an insurmountable
problem. If, as Pearson and Hamm report, in order to obtain a reliability score above .9,
an open-book portfolio-type exam needed 13 hours of task activity, compared with 1.25
hours for some traditional exams, then teachers simply need to build exam tasks into the
regular curriculum. As Richard Kimbell found in a recent e-assessment project on
Design and Technology for the Qualifications and Curriculum Authority in England, it
proved possible to set a reliable open-ended six-hour design task that was executed over
two days by 500 students, using hand-held PDAs, with students uploading to the web an
e-portfolio containing diagrams, text, photographs and even audio files (Kenny, 2005).
Under the classroom exam conditions of this examination, the teacher withdrew from
the role of mentor and guide and peer support was minimal; each student produced an
individual portfolio and the fact that there were opportunities to discuss ongoing work
during breaks was not regarded as a problem, since it was the skills exhibited during the
class time that were being assessed, rather than content knowledge.

6 We acknowledge a diminution of the authority of the author and of the text

There is a certain irony about the harmony between the pedagogical goals and theoretical
positions implicit in the teacher-led movements that supported 100 per cent coursework
examinations in the 1970s and that are currently supporting calls for e-portfolios in the

2000s. They developed for reasons that were largely or even wholly independent of the theoretical earthquakes that were erupting in science and the world of critical theory. Teachers have not embraced coursework and student-centred approaches to assessment because they questioned the grand narratives of science, or because they had been reading contemporary French philosophy. Broadly speaking, English teachers of the 1970s still held to Enlightenment theories of knowledge and hierarchical, canonical, Leavisite theories of literary criticism, which placed Shakespeare, Milton and Dickens at the top of the Great Chain of Literary Being. The rationale for developing new approaches to assessing response to literature had much more to do with the comprehensive school movement and a pragmatic determination to offer an experience of great literature to a broader range of pupils than any postmodern theoretical position.

There is, nevertheless, a powerful alignment between postmodernism and these newer approaches: when student engagement has to be courted rather than assumed, motivation, choice and extensions to the concept of the role of the reader move up the teacher's agenda and these most certainly harmonise with postmodern principles. More recently, technologies have also played a significant part in extending the concept of literature and of response: new technologies have spawned multiliteracies and these have contributed to a major change in the authority of knowledge in relation to literature. Postmodernism redefines the authority of the text and redistributes it, with a new and much greater share in this zero sum game being won by the reader. But the internet has also redefined authority: the author, the text and the teacher are no longer the only sources in the quest for meaning or knowledge. The search term 'Hamlet' evoked 14 million results in November 2005 and the term 'Shakespeare' 46 million. The internet has truly opened up the possibility of changing the authority structure of literary enquiry and although concerns over plagiarism and authentication have led to a questioning of open-ended approaches to assessment, these flood gates cannot now be closed.

The question 'who is the author?' no longer applies only to issues of response to literature – it applies to the works themselves. Fan fiction sites (featuring full-length novels based on the same characters as those from celebrated works of fiction) on the internet offer many hundreds of novels echoing Jane Austen, and over two hundred thousand (at least half of which are on a continuum from mild sexual fantasy to outright pornography) based on the characters from the Harry Potter novels (FanFiction.net is the most visited and best organised source). What is more, these novels are reviewed by their readers: many Harry Potter fan fiction novels are more than 50,000 words in length and many have over 100 reviews. No author receives royalties and no student receives a grade for their review, but not only are hundreds of thousands of fan fiction novels, there are tens of millions of fan fiction reviews, which have generated their own discourse and abbreviations ('A/U' = 'alternative universe'; 'UST' = 'unresolved sexual tension'; 'PWP' 'plot – what plot?', usually referring to a story in which there is a conspicuous absence of UST).

What one would want to emphasise here is that our notions of what counts as literature are evolving and our notions of what counts as response to literature are transmuting as new technologies and new literacies also evolve. To most teachers, it would seem absurd to classify fan fiction as literature and to regard internet reviews of fan fiction as response to literature that might in principle be assessed, but I would want to suggest that to compose good fan fiction does require sensitivity to character, historical and social context, tone, diction and figurative language and so on and to review that fiction calls in principle upon the same skill set that is used by professional literary critics.

Conclusion

It may be some time before exam boards include fan fiction as an assessed element in A-level English Literature, but it is already the case that exam boards are dramatically changing how they view electronic assessment, and are encouraging much greater alignment between curriculum and assessment, at a time when the curriculum is evolving at a rapid pace and that evolution is being accelerated by new technologies (see, for example, DiDA, the Diploma in Digital Applications, Edexcel, 2005). Maintaining trust in national examination systems is a delicate challenge and in England as recently as 2002 (Tomlinson, 2002) the Qualifications and Curriculum Authority had its fingers seriously burned when public confidence wavered for reasons that were more attributable to a press feeding frenzy than any fundamental instability. But behind a public discourse that emphasises steady and responsible development, the exam boards are changing and in my view these changes, seeking local solutions, valuing the individual, extending the range of examination modes, attempting to take account of multiple perspectives on meaning, bringing back portfolio approaches and redefining authority, are essential. To attempt to ignore the calls for such changes, or to attempt to hold them back, would be fruitless and ultimately catastrophic, because these changes are fundamentally linked to movements in the plate tectonics of our civilisation. Postmodernism is not a choice, it is the condition of our society and represents the state of our somewhat unstable cultural lithosphere; what is needed therefore are design solutions that can cope with stress, uncertainty and change; solutions that are flexible, responsive and adaptable. Fortunately, there is emerging evidence of that responsiveness in our assessment system, and it will be interesting in the coming years to observe the ways in which the postmodern continues to impinge upon assessment in general and the assessment of response to literature in particular.

References

Almasi, J.F. (1995). 'The Nature of Fourth Graders' Sociocognitive Conflicts in Peer-Led and Teacher-Led Discussions of Literature', *Reading Research Quarterly*, **29**, 4 304–6.

Bakhtin, M.M. (1973). *Problems of Dostoevsky's Poetics*. Ann Arbor, MI: Ardis.

Callaghan, J. (1976). 'Education: towards a national debate.' Speech given at Ruskin College, Oxford, 18 October.

Coles, M. and Jenkins, R. (Eds) (1998). *Assessing Reading: Changing Practice in Classrooms, International Perspectives on Reading Assessment*. London: Routledge.

Converse (2005). PowerPoint presentation by 'Richard' and 'James' on Wilfred Owen's poem 'Exposure' [online]. Available: http://aspirations.english.cam.ac.uk/converse/studentwork/OwenExposure.ppt#1 [4 November, 2005].

Derrida, J. (1976). *Of Grammatology*. Trans. Spivac, G.C. Baltimore: Johns Hopkins University Press.

EDEXCEL (2005). What is DiDA? (the Diploma in Digital Applications) [online]. Available: http://dida.edexcel.org.uk/home/aboutdida/ [7 November 2005].

Ellis Ryann, K. (2005). E-Learning Standards Update [online]. Available: http://www.learningcircuits.org/2005/jul2005/ellis.htm [7 November 2005].

Hansard. House of Lords (2005). Lord Adonis: maiden speech. Lords Hansard, 25 May 2005: C 470. [online]. Available: http://www.publications.parliament.uk/pa/ld199900/ldhansrd/pdvn/lds05/text/50525-04.htm [28 September, 2005].

Harrison, C. (2004). *Understanding Reading Development*. London: Sage.

Harrison, C. and Salinger, T. (Eds) (1998). *Reading Assessment: Theory and Practice*. New York: Routledge.

Iser, W. (1978). Wolfgang Iser, Der Akt des Lesens: Theorie ästhetischer Wirkung (1976, *The Act of Reading: A Theory of Aesthetic Response*. Trans. Iser, 1978).

Johnson, J. (1994). 'The National Oracy Project'. In: Brindley, S. (Ed) *Teaching English*. London: Routledge.

Kenny, J. (2005). 'The great e-scape.' *Times Educational Supplement TES Online*, 4 November 2005, 11.

Kintsch, W. (1998). *Comprehension: A Paradigm for Cognition*. Cambridge: Cambridge University Press.

Lather, P. (1986). 'Research as Praxis', *Harvard Educational Review*, **56**, 3, 257–77.

Lyotard, J.-F. (1984). *The Postmodern Condition: A Report on Knowledge*. Trans. Bennington, G. and Massumi, B. Manchester: Manchester University Press.

Medvedev, P.N. and Bakhtin, M. (1978). *The Formal Method in Literary Scholarship*. Trans. Wehrle, A.J. Baltimore: Johns Hopkins University Press.

Phillips, T. (1971). 'Poetry in the Primary School', *English in Education*, **5**/3, 15–62.

Scholastic (2005). 'Responses to Literature: Be a Theme Park Designer!' [online]. Available: http://teacher.scholastic.com/lessonplans/unit_themeparkdesign.htm [7 November, 2005].

Taylor, D. (1993). 'Assessing the complexity of students' learning: A student advocacy model of instructional assessment.' In: *From the Child's Point of View*. London: Heinemann.

Tomlinson, M. (2002). *Inquiry into A-level Standards*. (The Tomlinson Report) [online]. Available: http://image.guardian.co.uk/sys-files/Education/documents/2002/12/03/alevelinquiry.pdf [25 October, 2005].

Wittgenstein, L. (1953). *Philosophical Investigations*. Trans. Anscombe, G. Oxford: Blackwell.

6 Learning to read or learning to do tests?

Ros Fisher

Introduction

In this chapter I intend to consider the position of teachers and children amidst this discussion about the assessment of reading. Paul Black and Dylan Wiliam thoughtfully entitled their booklet on assessment *Inside the Black Box* (Black and Wiliam, 1998). They argue:

> [P]*resent policy seems to treat the classroom as a black box. Certain inputs from the outside are fed in or make demands – pupils, teachers, other resources, management rules and requirements, parental anxieties, tests with pressure to score highly and so on. Some outputs follow: hopefully pupils who are more knowledgeable and competent, better test results, teachers who are more or less satisfied and more or less exhausted. But what is happening inside? How can anyone be sure that a particular set of new inputs will produce better outputs if we don't at least study what is happening inside?'*

(Black and Wiliam, 1998, p.1)

Teachers and pupils are centrally involved in assessment. They are involved not only as people to whom the assessment is administered but those who are the agents of the assessment. In addition, regardless of the intentions of those who design the assessment and judge its outcomes, it is the teachers and pupils who ultimately interpret the nature of the construct.

This chapter is essentially a personal reflection of someone who is not an expert in assessment as are others in this book. I write here as someone who has worked as and with teachers of language and literacy over many years. And as someone who is as concerned with the minutiae of seemingly inconsequential outcomes as with the big picture of raised scores. It is these minutiae that represent individual children and individual lives. I start with a reflection on my own position as a primary school teacher in the 70s and 80s and then move on to how I see the changes in relation to assessment in classrooms today. I shall then reflect, with the perspective of distance, on what teachers and pupils may require from assessment. Finally I want to consider how these points could relate to the construct of reading. Much of what I have to say relates to many subjects in the curriculum. However, I shall argue that the case of reading may be significantly different from other subjects in some ways.

Teaching and learning of reading

Retrospective

When I started teaching, at my first school, the main form of reading assessment was how many books from the reading scheme a child had read. The headteacher kept a chart in her study and each time a child took a new book, she or he had to take it to the office and have a square coloured in. Woe betide any teacher whose pupils had not made the requisite progress in any month. Progress was measured purely on a basis of the number of books from the reading scheme: regardless of the length of the book, any other book read or any activities around the text that we might have undertaken. The construct here was clearly that reading was about reading ever more words and finishing the book. This practice also impacted on my teaching. The pressure to ensure those squares were coloured in regularly resulted in getting books finished having a high priority – we were all complicit in this: myself, my colleagues and, by no means least, the children. I wonder if those children, now as adults, have the sense of disappointment that I sometimes feel on coming to the end of a book that I have really enjoyed.

Later, at a different school, reading tests that gave a particular reading age were important. The Schonell reading test (Schonell, n.d.) was time consuming – each individual child had to read the list of words. Only when they got 10 consecutive words wrong could we stop – oh the disappointment when they got the fifth one right and we had to move on to the next line. The construct was interesting here. Words got harder in that they got more uncommon and usually longer. But, as is the way with English words, as they got more uncommon they also got more phonically regular. The last line including 'metamorphosis, somnambulist, bibliography, idiosyncrasy' could be 'sounded out' painfully and with a quizzical and uncomprehending expression to achieve maximum score. Administering this test was the first occasion I can remember being explicitly aware of reading being closely associated with life and the child's world. There was one line in that test at which I could predict with a fair amount of accuracy whether a child would falter or proceed. The line read:

> *university   orchestra   knowledge   audience   situated*

Success here was not to do with phonics, it was closely related to home context and the sort of things that were talked about in the family. Although at that time I did not know the term 'cultural capital' (Bourdieu, 1990), I was acutely aware that this line advantaged children from some homes more than others.

Later, at the same school, in order to make the task of testing children's reading ability less time consuming, Schonell was changed to the Young's Group Reading Test. Now testing could be done much more quickly. 'We are going to do some puzzles in the hall – just a bit of fun' the headteacher would say and it was all over in half an hour. One of the main purposes for this test was to identify those pupils who were in need of extra help with their reading. Any child with a standardised score of 80 or less was visited by the educational psychologist and a programme to support their learning was developed.

Therefore, as the teacher I wanted those children who I felt needed help to score 80 or less.

The other outcome from the test was the assignment of a reading age to each child. In the absence of any other norm referenced measure, these were important to parents – comparing reading books at the school gate was the only other way they had of knowing how their child was doing. Here again, as a teacher, the narrowness of the construct was frustrating. It was so hard to explain to parents without appearing to have low expectations of their child that the fact that Nicola at five had a reading age of 11.6 years did not mean she should be reading books for eleven-year-olds. Trying to explain the gap between a child's ability to read individual words or short sentences and their ability to follow a complicated plot or tackle conceptual complexity seemed to sound as though I wanted to hold their child back. Both Schonnel and Young advantaged slow careful word by word reading. Yet fluency seemed important.

Fortunately, I had also read about miscue analysis (Goodman, 1967). This was a revelation to me. The way I suddenly was able to judge what a child knew and could use and what they didn't know or couldn't use was fantastic. All of a sudden I was able to do something specific with individuals. The reading tests had told me what I knew already – that someone was not making good progress in their reading or was doing really well. Now I had something I could do about it. Not only did miscue give me a way of judging what help my pupils needed, it also taught me about the small parts of decoding and to recognise them in any reading context, not just when specifically assessing reading. The construct with miscue is clearly mostly about decoding and early comprehension. In fact, it gave me little help with more able readers. However, as an enthusiastic and critical reader who enjoyed all kinds of texts, I feel miscue helped me develop my own understanding of the process of reading rather than limit my own definition of the construct.

Inside today's black box

Assessment today exerts far greater pressure on teachers and children than it did twenty years ago. However, it is not just the weight of that pressure that is significant, it is the two-way pull of the different purposes for which assessment is used. There were two pressures on me as a young teacher: assessing how the children in my class were *learning* to read, particularly with the intention of helping them do it better and getting some information about children's *performance* in comparison to others to tell headteacher, LEA and parents. But now the stakes are higher, much higher. Children's performance is used to judge how well schools are doing. Teachers are paid according to how successful they are in increasing children's scores on tests. Whereas I sometimes wanted children to perform below their potential on a test as it triggered more help, now good scores are all important. The clear result of this is that making sure children do well on the test may be seen as more important than making sure children are successful at learning.

The move to raise standards of literacy in various parts of the world have led to initiatives designed for this purpose (National Literacy Strategy (NLS) in England (DfEE,

1998); Literacy Block in Australia (DEET, Vic, 1997, 1998, 1999); Success for All (now Roots and Wings) (Slavin, 1996). The success of these programmes is judged by the assessments that children take. Often for political reasons as much as educational ones, there is considerable pressure for children to do well on the assessments. Where teachers' status and even pay are determined by these results there is considerable pressure for children to do well on the assessments. Where government ministers' political ambition is also involved the pressure becomes greater. When learning becomes a political issue more than an educational one, there is danger that learning loses out to attainment.

The team for Ontario Institute for Studies in Education (OISE) in Canada that was charged with the evaluation of the implementation of the NLS, in the final report, comment favourably on the success of the programme. However, they go on to warn,

Targets or standards and high stakes testing are among the most contentious elements of large-scale reform. Most would agree that the move toward higher standards is necessary and important. There is less agreement, however, about the way that tests and targets are used in the process. ... [We] see some evidence that the high political profile of the 2002 national targets skewed efforts in the direction of activities that would lead to increases in the one highly publicised score.

(Earl *et al.*, 2003)

This importance afforded to national test results places a strong emphasis on performance as opposed to learning: on what children can do as opposed to what they can't do; on the product of the reading rather than the process.

But what is the product of reading? As Sainsbury (this volume) argues, the product of reading for a test does not represent the full scope of the construct. Rather the test should allow the tester to 'draw inferences about valued attributes that go beyond the test' (p. 8). While this may be the case, these 'valued attributes' are unlikely to include indicators for reading attitudes and practice in the long term. If the teaching of reading is to go beyond teaching the performance of certain skills, application of the skills to a range of purposes and attitudes to reading must be important.

A further consequence of the focus on performance is the concern for what children can do as opposed to what they cannot do. Many classrooms now use records in which children record what they can do. For example, 'I can divide a word into syllables', 'I can find the main character in a story'. Hall and Myers (1998) argue that criterion referencing and 'can do' statements accord status to the *what* rather than the *how* of learning. Hall and Myers report on a study by O'Sullivan and Joy (1994), which showed that children, when talking about reading problems, attributed these to lack of effort as opposed to ability. O'Sullivan and Joy conclude that teachers' emphasis on practice and working hard allows children to retain a naïve understanding of the reading process. Teachers' practice of focusing on *what* is to be achieved rather than *how* it is achieved can only reinforce this. Dweck (1989) proposes two kinds of achievement goals (learning goals and performance goals) and describes the sort of learners who favour these types of goals. Learners who set themselves learning goals try to increase their competence. They choose challenging tasks, persist despite the challenge and work out strategies for gaining proficiency. On the other hand, learners who set themselves performance goals, in which they strive to gain favourable judgements from others, tend to avoid challenge, attribute difficulty to low ability and give up in the face of problems.

This proposition is interesting in the light of Moss' (2000) study on gender and reading. She explored the place of reading in the curriculum and children's responses to this. She found that boys and girls reacted differently to the judgements made about their proficiency as readers and that this impacted on their progress in reading. Whereas girls were likely to respond to unfavourable judgements about their reading by trying harder, boys were more likely to avoid the challenge. She speculates that boys, contrary to popular belief, choose information texts not because they prefer them but because when 'reading' information books they are better able to conceal any difficulty with decoding and enhance their status by showing expertise in the topic.

> *Non-fiction texts allowed weaker boy readers to escape others' judgements about how well they read, how competent they were. At the same time, they enabled them to maintain self-esteem in the combative environment of their peer group relationships. … They bought self-esteem at the expense of spending much time practising their reading skills.*

(Moss, 2000, p.103)

The climate in education at the moment is all about performance, about trying to do better, to achieve better results, to be judged to be a level higher than last year. Teachers under pressure to show increased performance, both on their own part and on the part of their pupils, are not well placed to focus on learning itself and to encourage children to seek difficulty and ways of overcoming it. The emphasis on performance over learning makes quick fix solutions attractive. Yet there is a danger that concentrating on helping children to perform well in the short term, may not provide the foundations for a lifetime of thinking and achievement.

What teachers and children require from reading assessment

Dweck (1989) argues that prioritising performance goals will not help the learner learn how to learn. Metacognition is the consciousness of your own cognitive processes – in other words an awareness of what's going on in your mind while you are doing something. Quicke and Winter (1994) argued that, if children are to become better learners, teachers need to make them aware of the psychological processes entailed in learning. Although such learning may be subconscious at first (Richmond, 1990), children can be helped to think and talk about how they are learning. Indeed, Hall and Myers claim there is 'fairly robust evidence that an awareness of one's own understanding, is strongly linked to success' (Hall and Myers, 1998, p.8). Williams (2000) hypothesises that understanding the processes involved in learning will help pupils make conscious decisions about how to tackle tasks in the future. She concludes that, 'enabling them to acquire metacognitive understanding is both emancipatory and empowering' (Williams, 2000, p.3).

For this to happen, teachers need to know a lot about what is involved in reading and children have to be confident to accept challenges and be open about difficulties. Reading is a complex process in which a range of knowledge and skills are orchestrated to make meaning from text. We have long been aware that children who fail to make progress in reading and writing find the putting together of the component parts more difficult than learning each separately. For example, Clay (1979) found that the poorest readers tended to do exactly and only what they had been taught and appeared to have become instruction dependent, with the result that, although they knew letter sound correspondences, they did not use them efficiently because they used them exclusively. Similarly, Garner (1987) showed that whereas good readers monitor their comprehension of a text, poor or less experienced readers do not seem to recognise when the text does not make sense. In both these cases an awareness, first, of the need to select an appropriate decoding strategy before applying it and, in the second case, that readers should continuously check on their understanding of the text would help these readers. This strategic knowledge is important to learners but difficult to test.

In reading assessment that examines the product of the reading, the strategic activity will be largely unobservable. Teachers need to develop pupils' strategic repertoires so they can make conscious choices and take control over their reading. This implies a construct of reading that is complex and not fixed. It also implies a model of teaching and learning that values uncertainty and challenge over correctness and simplicity. Miscue analysis recognised that a great deal of insight could be gained into how readers were processing text from the errors or 'miscues' that they made. We need to encourage children to face challenge and welcome less than perfect outcomes as a way of helping them develop their own strategies and for the insight those errors give the teacher into how children are tackling an activity that involves reading.

The question of what teachers and children require from reading assessment is inextricably bound up with the socio-cultural context of the assessment. In a climate where success is judged by test scores, performance outweighs learning in importance. However, the performance is surely meant to act as a marker for learning? Therefore in response to the question 'what do teachers and children want from reading assessment?' I would propose:

Teachers want reading assessment to:

- tell them if their teaching is successful

- tell others that their teaching is successful

- tell them what children can already do

  because performance does matter. But also to:

- tell them what children still need to learn

- tell them how to get Johnny to read better.

In all of these they want the assessment to be manageable and convincing. It is likely that teachers cannot get all this from one form of assessment. Nisbet (1993) in a report on assessment for the Organisation for Economic Co-operation and Development (OECD) proposes that 'there is an ideological divide between those who hope to raise standards by more extensive testing and those who hope to improve the quality of learning by changing assessment methods' (p.28). It is arguable whether these two purposes of assessment can operate together or whether they are mutually incompatible. Gipps (1994) argues 'assessment to support learning, offering detailed feedback to the teacher and pupil, is necessarily different from assessment for monitoring and accountability purposes' (p.3).

In response to the question of what children require from reading assessment, I would argue that they want to know:

- that they are doing OK

- that what they are trying to do is achievable for them

- that what they can do (or are trying to do) matters

- how they can do better.

If I am right about these points, perhaps we have more indication about what assessment should do and what it can do. If these points matter, then reading has to be seen as something that others like them *can* do and *do* do. Thus reading is not just a construct of school and school-based literacy purposes but a part of lives before, during and after school. It is not just something difficult that other people can do well, it is something that all of us do to some extent or other as part of our everyday lives. They need to understand that the best readers can be uncertain about interpretation of texts; confident readers happily tackle difficult texts to find out something that they need.

How this contributes to the teaching of reading

I have argued above for more focus on learning than on performance, but teachers need to know what it is that is to be learned. Their own expectations and understandings of reading behaviour, their interpretation of the curriculum and their assessment practices influence the decisions they make about their teaching. I envisage the current impact of assessment for accountability on learning to read as a funnel in which the broad spectrum of literacy practices found in society today is gradually narrowed (see Figure 6.1). Some narrowing is unavoidable. A curriculum is necessarily a selection of practices that are judged by the curriculum developer to matter. In the same way, a test is the test developer's best way of gaining information about a learner's performance on tasks selected from the curriculum acting as a 'proxy' for that curriculum. This only becomes a problem when external influences cause a funnel effect in which the narrowing squeezes out everything but the test practices. In my model, school literacy practices can be informed both by the social practices and by test practices – it is when one has more influence than the other that problems arise.

Children, as well as teachers, need to know what and why they are learning. Black *et al*. (2002) are emphatic about the importance of learning goals. 'Pupils can only achieve a learning goal if they understand that goal and can assess what they need to do to reach

Figure 6.1 The funnel effect

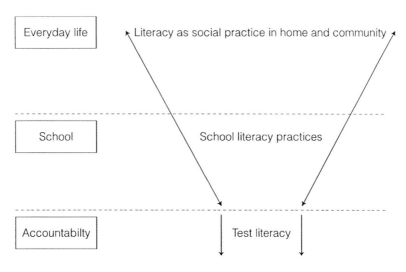

it' (p.10). However, in a subject such as reading, in which the overall aims relate to fluid and complex outcomes such as interpreting text and developing critical judgement, identifying learning goals can be problematic. The NLS 'Framework of Objectives' gives a clear menu of teaching objectives. It is when these teaching objectives are translated into learning outcomes that there is a danger of narrowing children's (and teachers') perception of what being a reader means. Marshall (2004) argues that teachers do need a clear idea of progression in English, but that this should be related to 'horizons not goals'.

Peer- and self-assessment can help here by encouraging learners to focus on the process and the learning; not just the performance. Sadler (1989) argued that criteria alone are not enough to ensure progression. He argues that it is important to know how to interpret the criteria in specific cases by developing 'guild knowledge'. In being involved in self- and peer-assessment, learners can engage in discussion about reading practices – about pleasures and difficulties as well as achievements. It seems to me that in order to learn about reading, children should engage in writing and vice versa. When readers assess other readers and writers, they are helped in identifying the goals of learning to read. Here we are not talking about how many words that can be read or which comprehension questions can be answered, but what sort of enjoyment can pupils derive from a text? How able are they to judge the validity of an information text? How good are they at seeing through the rhetoric of a newspaper editorial? By working with authentic texts from the child's world there is a greater likelihood of engagement as opposed to disaffection. For teachers too, being involved in open-ended discussion around texts and writers will help develop their own guild knowledge – related perhaps to their own understanding of being a reader rather than an understanding derived from expected test outcomes.

What has to be accepted is that, if we agree that different assessments are needed for differing purposes, then we must also agree that one form of assessment must not outweigh the other in the value that is attributed to it. Earl *et al*. (2003) report that the high-stakes assessment has had a narrowing function on the curriculum. Others go further and argue that the curriculum has had a narrowing function on the model of literacy taught. Street (1984) argued that many schools adopt what he terms an 'autonomous' model of literacy in which literacy itself is an object to be studied and learned rather than social practice which is shaped by those who use it. It is also argued that this 'autonomous' view of literacy disadvantages some children for whom the relationship between literacy practice at home and school literacy is not evident. As Luke (2003) argues:

> *the classroom is one of the few places where formal taxonomic categories (e.g. the curriculum) and the official partitioning of time and space (e.g. the timetable) often are used to discourage children from blending, mixing and matching knowledge drawn from diverse textual sources and communications media.*

(Luke, 2003, p.398)

Street and Luke's criticisms of school versions of literacy are valid. Literacy as social practice stands at one end of a continuum of reading practices of which the practices tested by most reading tests stand at a distant other end. Teachers need to keep the broad view of reading in their mind as an end point and make sure that children too keep the big picture in mind. In this way children can be helped to see why they are learning to read and how worthwhile and relevant it is to their lives. It is possible to retain the big picture while smaller skills and strategies are taught while working on authentic tasks, discussing reading practice and behaviours, accepting different view points. Assessment of what children are doing when talking about their reading can provide teachers with a greater understanding of what is involved in reading (in the way that miscue analysis enabled me to identify how children were decoding). This then will enable them to design teaching tasks that are sufficiently structured to scaffold learning but not so tightly defined to limit thinking.

The solution is to widen the narrow end of the funnel. As a society we do need feedback on the outcomes of our education system but we should not expect this monitoring to do everything else as well. Analysis of national assessment results show that there is not a blanket problem with attainment in literacy. There are specific problems in particular aspects of literacy or particular groups of learners. Specific problems require specific solutions. Torrance and Pryor (1998) describe two types of assessment: convergent and divergent. Convergent assessment is a closed system which judges *if* learners know, understand or can do something. Whereas divergent assessment is more open and assesses *what* a learner knows, understands or can do. It seems that what is needed now, as well as a national assessment system that gives a broad picture, is a bank of formative assessments for particular purposes that are related to particular children's needs. These would allow the teacher to adapt their teaching to the needs of the learner – not to the demands of the text.

It is not enough to say that formative and summative assessment are mutually incompatible. In the current climate, summative assessment will necessarily drive the formative. Society needs to monitor the outcome of what happens in school, but this should not result in the distorting of what happens in the classroom. It may well be that these instruments are not the same. In summative assessment teachers and children need a test that values what children are learning to do and that is valued by those who see and use the results. They also want formative assessment procedures that can help them judge what children can do, what they are trying to do and what they can't yet do. From their own life experience, teachers and children already have a picture of reading that encompasses literacy as social practice as well as literacy for school purposes. They need to be confident that the procedures for assessment and uses to which the assessment is put do not value one type of reading over another.

References

Black, P., Harrison, C., Lee, L., Marshall and Wiliam, D. (2002). *Working inside the Black Box: Assessment for Learning in the Classroom*. London: Department of Education and Professional Studies, Kings College.

Black, P. and Wiliam, D. (1998). *Inside the Black Box: Raising Standards through Classroom Assessment*. London: Department of Education and Professional Studies, Kings College.

Bourdieu, P. (1990). *The Logic of Practice*, trans. Nice, R. Cambridge: Polity Press. (Original work published in 1980.)

Clay, M.M. (1979). *Reading: The Patterning of Complex Behaviour*. London: Heinemann Educational Books.

DEET:Vic (1997). *Teaching Readers in the Classroom Early Years Literacy Program Stage 1*. S. Melbourne, Victoria: Addison Wesley Longman.

DEET:Vic (1998). *Teaching Writers in the Classroom Early Years Literacy Program Stage 2*. S. Melbourne, Victoria: Addison Wesley Longman.

DEET:Vic (1999). *Teaching Speakers and Listeners in the Classroom Early Years Literacy Program Stage 3*. S. Melbourne, Victoria: Addison Wesley Longman.

Department For Education and Employment (1998). *The National Literacy Strategy*. London: Department for Education and Employment.

Dweck, C. (1989). 'Motivation.' In: Lesgold, A. and Glaser, R. (Eds) *Foundations for a Psychology of Education*. Hillsdale, NJ: Erlbaum.

Earl, L., Watson, N., Levin, B., Leithwood, K., Fullan, M. and Torrance, N. (2003). *Watching and Learning 3: Final Report of the External Evaluation of England's National Literacy and Numeracy Strategies*. (Ontario Institute for Studies in Education, University of Toronto) January 2003.

Garner, R. (1987). *Metacognition and Reading Comprehension*. New Jersey: Ablex Publishing Corporation.

Gipps, C.V. (1994). *Beyond Testing: Towards a Theory of Educational Assessment.* London: The Falmer Press.

Goodman, K. (1967). 'A linguistic study of cues and miscues in English', *Elementary English*, **32**, 639–43.

Hall, K. and Myers, J. (1998). '"That's just the way I am": metacognition, personal intelligence and reading', *Reading*, **32**, 2, 8–13.

Luke, C. (2003). 'Pedagogy, connectivity, multimodality and interdisciplinarity', *Reading Research Quarterly*, **38**, 3, 397–403.

Marshall, B. (2004). Paper given at UKLA Research Day, University of Manchester, July 2004.

Moss, G. (2000). 'Raising boys' attainment in reading: some principles for intervention', *Reading*, **34**, 3, 101–6.

Nisbet, J. (1993). 'Introduction.' In: *Curriculum Reform: Assessment in Question.* Paris: OECD.

O'Sullivan, J. and Joy, R. (1994). 'If at first you don't succeed: Children's metacognition about reading problems', *Contemporary Educational Psychology*, **19**, 118–27.

Quicke, J. and Winter, C. (1994). 'Teaching the language of learning: towards a metacognitive approach to pupil empowerment', *British Educational Research Journal*, **20**, 4, 429–45.

Richmond, J. (1990). 'What do we mean by knowledge about language?' In: Carter, R. (Ed) *Knowledge about Language and the Curriculum.* London: Hodder and Stoughton.

Sadler, R. (1989) 'Formative assessment and the design of instructional systems', *Instructional Science*, **18**, 119–44.

Schonell, F.J.Y. and Schonell, F.E. (1950). *A Graded Word Reading Test.* Edinburgh: Oliver and Boyd.

Slavin, R.E. (1996). *Education for All.* Lisse: Swets and Zeitlinger.

Street, B. (1984). *Literacy in Theory and Practice.* Cambridge: Cambridge University Press.

Torrance, H. and Pryor, J. (1998). *Investigating Formative Assessment: Teaching and Learning in the Classroom.* Buckingham: Open University Press.

Williams, M. (2000). 'The part which metacognition can play in raising standards in English at key stage 2', *Reading*, **34**, 1, 3–8.

[Part 2]

Historical insights as drivers of theory

7 The assessment of reading comprehension: key historical influences in the USA

P. David Pearson and Diane Nicole Hamm

The purpose of this chapter is to build a rich and detailed historical account of reading comprehension, both as a theoretical phenomenon and an operational construct that lives and breathes in classrooms throughout the USA. We will review both basic research, which deals with reading comprehension largely in its theoretical aspect and applied research, which is much more concerned about how comprehension gets operationalised in classrooms, reading materials and tests.

With a renewed professional interest in reading comprehension (e.g. Rand Study Group, 2002), it is an optimal time to undertake a new initiative in the area of reading comprehension assessment. To do so, it needs our rapt and collective attention at this particular point in history. First, reading comprehension, both its instruction and its assessment, is arguably the most important outcome of reform movements designed to improve reading curriculum and instruction. Second, given the national thirst for accountability, we must have better (i.e. conceptually and psychometrically more trust-worthy) tools to drive the engines of accountability at the national, state and local level. Third, and even more important, we need better assessments so that we can respond to the pleas of teachers desperate for useful tools to assist them in meeting individual needs. It is doubly appropriate that the assessment of reading comprehension receive as much attention as the construct itself. In the final analysis, a construct is judged as much by how it is operationalised as by how it is conceptualised.

The process of text comprehension has always provoked exasperated but nonetheless enthusiastic inquiry within the research community. Comprehension, or 'understanding', by its very nature, is a phenomenon that can only be assessed, examined, or observed indirectly (Pearson and Johnson, 1978; Johnston, 1984a). We talk about the 'click' of comprehension that propels a reader through a text, yet we never see it directly. We can only rely on indirect symptoms and artifacts of its occurrence. People tell us that they understood, or were puzzled by, or enjoyed, or were upset by a text. Or, more commonly, we quiz them on 'the text' in some way – requiring them to recall its gist or its major details, asking specific questions about its content and purpose, or insisting on an interpretation and critique of its message. All of these tasks, however challenging or engaging they might be, are little more than the residue of the comprehension process itself. Like it or not, it is precisely this residue that scholars of comprehension and comprehension assessment must work with in order to improve our understanding of the construct. We see little more of comprehension than Plato saw of the shadows in the cave of reality.

Models of reading comprehension and how to assess it have evolved throughout the century (see Johnston, 1984b). Many techniques of assessment have risen to prominence and then fallen out of use, some to be reincarnated decades later, usually with new twists. Our aim is to provide a thorough account of what we know about assessing reading comprehension. Where possible and appropriate, we will take detours into research and theory about the comprehension process, on the grounds that conceptions of the process, because they have influenced how it is assessed, will inform our understanding. We hope to illuminate the patterns, cycles and trends in comprehension assessment. Through these efforts, we hope to provide our readers with a means to evaluate the current state of reading assessment, which we believe has reached a critical juncture, one that can be crossed only by shaping a research agenda that will improve our capacity to create valid, fair and informative assessments of this important phenomenon.

Historical foundations of reading comprehension assessment

Before the beginning

Although reading comprehension assessment as a formal, identifiable activity is a 20th century phenomenon, it has been a part of classrooms as long as there have been schools, required texts, students who are required to read them and teachers wanting or needing to know whether students understood them. In every century and every decade, every assignment given by a teacher, every book report or chapter summary and every conversation about a book, story, article, or chapter has provided an opportunity for assessment. It was not until well into the 20th century that we began to seize those opportunities. There are two plausible explanations for the relatively late arrival of comprehension as an indicator of reading achievement. First, the default indicator of reading prowess in the 17th to 19th centuries was definitely oral capacity, indexed either by accuracy or by expressive fluency, in the tradition of declamation and oratory (see Smith, 1966 or Matthews, 1966 for accounts of this emphasis). Second, within ecclesiastical circles, comprehension, at least in the sense of personal understanding, was not truly valued; if it mattered, it mattered largely as a stepping stone to the more valued commodity of text memorisation (see Olson, 1994, for an account of the various religious traditions in text interpretation).

The beginning

It is well worth our effort to examine early trends in reading assessment, for they suggest that nearly all of the tools we use to measure reading comprehension today made an appearance in some way shape or form before World War II. Granted, today's formats and approaches may look more sophisticated and complex, but, as our review will demonstrate, those formats were there, at least in prototypic form, long ago.

The first systematic attempts to index reading ability by measuring comprehension date back to the period just prior to World War I. Binet, as early as 1895 (cited in Johnston, 1984a), used comprehension test items, ironically, to measure intelligence rather than reading achievement. In 1916, Kelly brought us the first published comprehension assessment, the *Kansas Silent Reading Test* (see Kelly, 1916). Thorndike, in his classic 1917 piece, 'Reading as reasoning', offered us our first professional glimpse 'inside the head' as he tried to characterise what must have been going on in the minds of students to produce the sorts of answers they come up with when answering questions about text (Thorndike, 1917). As we indicated earlier, the quest to get as close as possible to the 'phenomenological act of comprehension' as it occurs has always driven researchers to discover new and more direct indices of reading comprehension.

The scientific movement and the changing demographic patterns of schooling in America were both forces that shaped the way reading was conceptualised and assessed in the first third of the 20th century. Schools had to accommodate to rapid increases in enrolment, due to waves of immigration, a rapidly industrialising society, the prohibition of child labour and mandatory school attendance laws. The spike in school enrolment, coupled with a population of students with dubious literacy skills, dramatically increased the need for a cheap, efficient screening device to determine students' levels of literacy. During this same period, psychology struggled to gain the status of a 'science' by employing the methods that governed physical sciences and research. In America, the behaviorist schools of thought, with their focus on measurable outcomes, strongly influenced the field of psychology (Johnston, 1984a; Resnick, 1982; Pearson, 2000); quantification and objectivity were the two hallmarks to which educational 'science' aspired. When psychologists with their newfound scientific lenses were put to work creating cheap and efficient tests for beleaguered schools, the course of reading assessment was set. Group administered, multiple-choice, standardised tests would be the inevitable result.

The other strong influence in moving toward comprehension as a measure of reading accomplishment was the curricular shift from oral to silent reading as the dominant mode of reading activity in our classrooms. Although the first published reading assessment, circa 1914, was an oral reading assessment created by William S. Gray (who eventually became a pre-eminent scholar in the reading field and the senior author of the country's most widely used reading series), most reading assessments developed in the first third of this century focused on the relatively new construct of silent reading (see Gray, 1917; Pearson, 2000; Johnston, 1984a). Unlike oral reading, which had to be tested individually and required that teachers judge the quality of responses, silent reading comprehension (and rate) could be tested in group settings and scored without recourse to professional judgement; only stop watches and multiple-choice questions were needed. In modern parlance, we would say that they moved from a 'high inference' assessment tool (oral reading and retelling) to a 'low inference' tool (multiple-choice tests or timed readings). It fit the demands for efficiency and scientific objectivity, themes that were part of the emerging scientism of the period. The practice proved remarkably persistent for at least another 40 or 50 years. Significant developments in reading comprehension would occur in the second third of the 20th century, but assessment would remain a *psychometric* rather than a *cognitive* activity until the cognitive revolution of the early 1970s.

It is important to note that comprehension instruction and the curricular materials teachers employed were driven by the same infrastructure of tasks used to create test items – finding main ideas, noting important details, determining sequence of events, cause-effect relations, comparing and contrasting and drawing conclusions.[1] If these new assessments had not found a comfortable match in school curricular schemes, one wonders whether they would have survived and prospered to the degree that they did.

Intelligence and comprehension

Interestingly, it was difficult to tell the difference, in these early years, between reading comprehension assessments and intelligence tests. Freeman (1926) noted that Binet (1895, in Johnston, 1984a) had used reading comprehension items as a part of his IQ battery. Consider, also, this item from an early (but undated) edition of a Thurstone intelligence test:

> *Every one of us, whatever our speculative opinion, knows better than he practices and recognizes a better law than he obeys.* (Froude). Check two of the following statements with the same meaning as the quotation above.

- To know right is to do the right.

- Our speculative opinions determine our actions.

- Our deeds often fall short of the actions we approve.

- Our ideas are in advance of our every day behavior.

(Johnston, 1984a)[2]

Minor anomalies and omens of the future

While behaviorism was the dominant paradigm underlying curricular and assessment work during this period, remnants of a cognitively more complex approach of the sort that Huey described near the turn of the century (Huey, 1908) made minor appearances on the assessment scene. Free recall was used by a few researchers as an index of comprehension. Starch (1915), for example, created a ratio (the number of relevant words a student remembered in a passage in comparison to the proportion of total words remembered) as an index of comprehension. Courtis (1914) developed a similar, but simpler index (ratio of idea units reproduced or interpreted to the number possible). These indices, especially the relevance index, foreshadow work in the 1970s and 1980s on 'importance' (as indexed by the relevance of propositions to a text's ideational structure (e.g. Rumelhart, 1977). Even at this early stage, scholars recognized that recall is not the same process as making or uncovering meaning (Kelly, 1916), but recall continued to be used in research and later in practice, as a direct index of comprehension. This use of recall would be revived in the 1970s as a retelling procedure, which would give us a window on whether students were remembering important ideas in stories (Stein and Glenn, 1977) or in the propositional data base of expository texts (Kintsch and van Dijk, 1978; Turner and Greene, 1977).

Consistent with the efficiency criterion in the new scientific education, speed was often used as an important factor in assessing comprehension. Kelly, the author of the Kansas Silent Reading Test (1916) required students to complete as many of a set of 16 diverse tasks as they could in the 5 minutes allotted. The tasks included some 'fill in the blanks', some verbal logic problems and some procedural tasks (following directions). Monroe (1918) also used a speeded task – asking students to underline the words that answered specific questions.

We can even find foreshadowing of the error detection paradigms that were to be so widely used by psychologists investigating metacognitive processes in the 1970s through the 1990s (Markman, 1977; Winograd and Johnston, 1980). For example, Chapman (1924) asked students to detect words that were erroneous or out of place in the second half of each paragraph (presumably they did so by using, as the criterion for rejection, the set or schema for paragraph meaning that became established as they read the first half). In 1936, Eurich required students to detect 'irrelevant clauses' rather than words.

Thorndike (1917) was probably the first educational psychologist to try to launch inquiry into both the complex thought processes associated with comprehension and assessment methods. He referred to reading 'as reasoning', suggesting there are many factors that comprise it: 'elements in a sentence, their organization … proper relations, selection of certain connotations and the rejection of others and the cooperation of many forces'. He proposed ideas about what should occur during 'correct reading', claiming that a great many misreadings of questions and passages are produced because of under- or over-potency of individual words, thus violating his 'correct weighting' principle:

> *Understanding a paragraph is like solving a problem in mathematics. It consists in selecting the right elements in the situation and putting them together in the right relations and also with the right amount of weight or influence or force of each*

(Thorndike, 1917)

Of course, he assumed that there are such things as 'correct' readings. He argued further that in the act of reading, the mind must organise and analyse ideas from the text. 'The vice of the poor reader is to say the words to himself without actively making judgements concerning what they reveal' (Thorndike, 1917). Clearly for Thorndike, reading was an active and complex cognitive process. Although this perspective did not become dominant in this early period, it certainly anticipated the highly active view of the reader that would become prominent during the cognitive revolution of the 1970s.[3]

Paralleling an active line of inquiry in oral reading error analysis (see Allington, 1984, pp.829–64) during this period, some researchers followed Thorndike's lead and tried to develop taxonomies of the kinds of errors readers make either during decoding or understanding. Touton and Berry (1931) classified errors into six categories based on research on college students:

1. failure to understand the question

2. failure to isolate elements of 'an involved statement' read in context

3. failure to associate related elements in a context

4. failure to grasp and retain ideas essential to understanding concepts

5. failure to see setting of the context as a whole

6. other irrelevant answers.

Even though Goodman is rightfully credited with helping us understand that oral reading errors, or 'miscues' to use his term, can reveal much about the comprehension processes a student engages in; there were inklings of this perspective emerging in the 1930s. Gates (1937), for example, was interested in how readers' fluency may be an indicator of one's ability and understanding. He looked at readers' 'error of hesitation', that is, whether a reader stumbled over a word or phrase. Durrell (1937) and later Betts (1946) sought to use these error patterns as indicators of the level of reading material students could handle, both from a word recognition and comprehension perspective. These early scholars determined that students who misread many words (they found that 2 per cent seems to be our outside limit – although modern scholars often go up to 5 per cent) will have difficulty comprehending a passage. These harbingers notwithstanding, it would be another 30 years before the Goodmans' (Goodman, 1968, 1969; Goodman and Burke, 1970) miscue analysis work prompted us to take oral reading miscues seriously as a lens that would allow us to look into the windows of the mind at the comprehension process.

Psychometrics gathers momentum

Two significant events in the history of assessment occurred during the 1930s and 1940s; both would have dramatic effects on reading comprehension assessment. First, in 1935, IBM introduced the IBM 805 scanner, which had the potential to reduce the cost of scoring dramatically (compared to hand scoring of multiple-choice, or 'even worse', short answer and essay tests) by a factor of 10 (Johnston, 1984a). It is not insignificant that the Scholastic Aptitude Test, which, in the 1920s and early 1930s, had been mostly an essay test, was transformed into a machine-scorable multiple-choice test shortly thereafter (Resnick, 1982). This development paved the way for a new generation of multiple-choice assessments for all fields in which testing is used; reading comprehension assessment proved no exception.

Determining the infrastructure of reading comprehension

The second important event was the publication, in 1944, of Frederick Davis's landmark doctoral dissertation in which he used a brand new statistical tool, factor analysis, to determine whether a set of conceptually distinct subtests of reading comprehension (entities like finding main ideas, selecting details, determining word meanings, drawing conclusions, determining cause-effect relations, distinguishing fact from opinion and the like) were also psychometrically distinct. Factor analysis is a technique, still highly popular among traditional psychometricians, in which the covariation among 'units' (usually items or subtests) is examined to discover which units tend to cluster with (i.e. covary with) which other units. Armed with this new tool, researchers were (at least theoretically) ready to answer a question that had vexed both test makers and curriculum designers for the two or three decades in which reading tests and reading curriculum had become part of the American educational landscape: is comprehension a unitary or a multivariate construct? That is, are there distinct subcomponents, subprocesses, or 'skills' that ought to be measured and perhaps taught separately? Or, alternatively, is reading better construed as a unitary process that ought to be considered holistically?

In his groundbreaking 1944 study, Davis reviewed the literature describing reading comprehension as a construct and found several hundred skills mentioned (Davis, 1944). He sorted them into nine categories that he felt constituted conceptually distinct groups; from these he devised nine testable skills (based also in part on correlation data).

1. word meanings

2. word meanings in context

3. follow passage organisation

4. main thought

5. answer specific text-based questions

6. text-based questions with paraphrase

7. draw inferences about content

8. literary devices

9. author's purpose.

Davis employed the most sophisticated factor analytic tools available (Kelly, 1935) in his search for psychometric uniqueness to match the conceptual uniqueness of his categories. Acknowledging the unreliability of some of the subtests (due among other factors to the small standard deviations and the fact each passage had items from several cognitive categories attached to it), he was able to conclude that reading comprehension consisted of two major factors, word knowledge and 'reasoning about reading', that were sufficiently powerful and reliable to guide us in the construction of tests and reading curriculum. He speculated that another three factors (comprehension of explicitly stated ideas, understanding passage organisation and detecting literary devices) had the potential, with better item development, to reveal themselves as independent factors.

Between 1944 and the early 1970s, several scholars attempted to either replicate or refute Davis' findings. Harris (1948) found only one factor among the seven he tested. Derrik (1953) found three and they were consistent across different levels of passage length. Hunt (1957) used differential item analysis and correction formulae to adjust his correlations, finding vocabulary (i.e. word knowledge) as the single most important factor.

The cloze procedure

In the 1950s, Wilson Taylor (1953) developed the cloze procedure as an alternative to the conventional standardised test. Taylor began with the assumption that even the process of writing multiple-choice items was subjective. Instead of introducing subjectivity by requiring test developers to determine what content and features of a passage should be assessed, Taylor developed the cloze technique, which replaces human judgement with a mechanical approach to item development. A test designer simply deletes every nth word (usually every 5th word) in a passage; the task of the examinee is to fill in each cloze blank. The more blanks filled in, the higher the comprehension score. There was a buzz of excitement about the cloze procedure during the 1960s and 70s (see Rankin, 1965, pp.133–50; also see Bormuth, 1966 for the most elaborate application of cloze). Cloze was touted as the scientific alternative to multiple-choice tests of reading comprehension. It was widely used as the comprehension criterion in studies of readability in the 1960s (see Bormuth, 1966). It became the cornerstone of reading assessment for speakers of English as a Second Language (ESL) (see Bachman, 1982), where it is still widely used (Bachman, 2000).

Cloze has experienced a great deal of adaptation over the years. For example, in the classic cloze procedure, students are asked to write in their responses when every 5th word is deleted. And only exact replacement is scored as correct; synonyms will not do. However, researchers and test developers have created modified cloze using a whole host of variations:

- Allow synonyms to serve as correct answers.

- Delete only every 5th content word (leaving function words intact).

- Use an alternative to every 5th word deletion.

- Delete words at the end of sentences and provide a set of choices from which examinees are to pick the best answer (this tack is employed in several standardised tests, including the Stanford Diagnostic Reading Test and the Degrees of Reading Power).

The unsettled question about cloze tests is whether they are measures of individual differences in comprehension or measures of the *linguistic predictability* of the passages to which they are applied. They have been widely criticised for this ambiguity. But perhaps the most damaging evidence in their role as indices of reading comprehension is that they are not sensitive to 'intersentential' comprehension, i.e. understanding that reaches across sentences in a passage. In a classic study, Shanahan *et al.* (1982) created several passage variations and assessed cloze fill in rates. In one condition, sentence order was scrambled by randomly ordering the sentences. In another condition, sentences from different passages were intermingled and in a third condition, isolated sentences from different passages were used. There were no differences in cloze fill in rate across any of these conditions, indicating that an individual's ability to fill in cloze blanks does *not* depend upon passage context; in short, when people fill in cloze blanks, they do not think across sentence boundaries. In the period of the cognitive revolution of the 1980s, in which comprehension was viewed as an integrative process, a measure that did not require text integration did not fare well.

These findings notwithstanding, modified, multiple-choice versions of cloze are still alive and well in standardised tests (i.e. the Degrees of Reading Power and the Stanford Diagnostic Reading Test referred to earlier) and in ESL assessment for adults and college students (Bachman, 2000).

Passage dependency

Beginning in the late 1960s a new construct arose in reading assessment, one that, at the time, had the impact of a 'the emperor has no clothes' epiphany. Several scholars became concerned about the fact that many of the questions on standardised tests of reading comprehension could be answered correctly without reading the passage (mainly because the information assessed was likely to exist in examinees' prior knowledge, as well as in the text). This problem is particularly exacerbated in passages about everyday or common academic topics (in comparison, for example, to fictional narratives). A number of researchers (e.g. Tuinman, 1974, 1978, pp.165–73) conducted passage dependency studies in which some subjects took the test without the passage present. The difference between the p-value of an item in the two conditions (with and without text) is an index of an item's passage dependency. The logic of this construct is simple and compelling: a reader should have to read a passage in order to answer questions about it. The interest in passage dependency, like the interest in cloze, waned considerably during the cognitive revolution. In the new paradigm, prior knowledge would be embraced as one of the cornerstones of comprehension and scholars would attempt to take prior knowledge into account rather than trying to eliminate or encapsulate its impact on comprehension (see Johnston, 1984b, for an account of these attempts during the early 1980s).

The revolutions begin

Somewhere during this period of active psychometric work on reading assessment (between 1955 and 1975 – the exact point of departure is hard to fix) the field of reading experienced a paradigm shift. Reading became an ecumenical scholarly commodity; it was embraced by scholars from many different fields of inquiry (see Pearson and Stephens, 1993, for a complete account of this phenomenon). In terms of reading comprehension assessment, three movements are particularly important: cognitive psychology, sociolinguistics (and more general sociocultural perspectives) and literary theory (in the form of reader response theory). Cognitive psychology spawned the first of two major shifts in comprehension assessment; the second was prompted by the joint influence of sociolinguistics and literary theory.

Cognitive psychology

In rejecting behaviorism, cognitive psychology allowed psychologists to extend constructs such as human purpose, intention and motivation to a greater range of psychological phenomena, including perception, attention, comprehension, learning, memory and executive control or 'meta-cognition' of all cognitive process. All of these would have important consequences in reading pedagogy and, to a lesser extent, reading assessment.

The most notable change within psychology was that it became fashionable for psychologists, for the first time since the early part of the century, to study complex phenomena such as language and reading.[4] And in the decade of the 1970s works by psychologists flooded the literature on basic processes in reading. One group focused on text comprehension, trying to explain how readers come to understand the underlying structure of texts. We were offered story grammars – structural accounts of the nature of narratives, complete with predictions about how those structures impede and enhance story understanding and memory (Rumelhart, 1977; Mandler and Johnson, 1977; Stein and Glenn, 1977). Others chose to focus on the expository tradition in text (e.g. Kintsch, 1974; Meyer, 1975). Like their colleagues interested in story comprehension, they believed that structural accounts of the nature of expository (informational) texts would provide valid and useful models for human text comprehension. And in a sense, both of these efforts worked. Story grammars did provide explanations for story comprehension. Analyses of the structural relations among ideas in an informational piece also provided explanations for expository text comprehension. But neither text-analysis tradition really tackled the relationship between the knowledge of the world that readers bring to text and comprehension of those texts. In other words, by focusing on structural rather than the ideational, or content, characteristics of texts, they failed to get to the heart of comprehension. That task, as it turned out, fell to one of the most popular and influential movements of the 70s, schema theory.

Schema theory (see Anderson and Pearson, 1984, pp.255–90; Rumelhart, 1981, pp.3–26; Rumelhart and Ortony, 1977) is a theory about the structure of human knowledge as it is represented in memory. In our memory, schemata are like little containers into which we deposit the particular traces of particular experiences as well as the 'ideas' that derive from those experiences. So, if we see a chair, we store that visual experience in our 'chair schema'. If we go to a restaurant, we store that experience in our 'restaurant schema', if we attend a party, our 'party schema' and so on.

Schema theory also provided a credible account of reading comprehension, which probably, more than any of its other features, accounted for its popularity within the reading field in the 1970s and 80s.[5] Schema theory struck a sympathetic note with researchers as well as practitioners. It provided a rich and detailed theoretical account of the everyday intuition that we understand and learn what is new in terms of what we already know. It also accounted for the everyday phenomenon of disagreements in interpreting stories, movies and news events – we disagree with one another because we approach the phenomenon with very different background experiences and knowledge.

With respect to reading comprehension, schema theory encouraged educators to examine texts from the perspective of the knowledge and cultural backgrounds of students in order to evaluate the likely connections that they would be able to make between ideas inscribed[6] in the text and the schema that they would bring to the reading task. Schema theory also promoted a constructivist view of comprehension; all readers, at every moment in the reading process, construct the most coherent model of meaning for the texts they read.[7] Perhaps the most important legacy of this constructivist perspective was that it introduced ambiguity about the question of where meaning resides. Does it reside in the text? In the author's mind as she sets pen to paper? In the mind of each reader as she builds a model of meaning unique to her experience and reading? In the interaction between reader and text? Schema theory raised, but did not settle these questions.

The impact of cognitive science on assessment

The impact of this new work in comprehension on curriculum and classroom teaching was immediate. We saw huge changes in basal readers, which, even until the late 1980s, remained the core tool of classroom practice. These included (a) more attention to the role of prior knowledge introducing new texts, explicit teaching of comprehension strategies, (b) attention to text structure (in the form of story maps and visual displays to capture the organisational structure of text) and (c) the introduction of metacognitive monitoring (reflecting on what one has read, said, or written to see if it makes sense) (see Pearson, 2000).

The impact on assessment, in particular, the unsettled question of where meaning resides, was fairly transparent: how, with even a modicum of respect for fairness, can we use tests with single correct answers if we know that answers are influenced by experience and background knowledge? It was not long before educators began to ask questions about whether the long tradition of standardised, multiple-choice assessments could or should continue to be used as measures of program quality or teacher effectiveness.

By the late 1980s, constructivist approaches to reading assessment began to emerge. These were new efforts and new perspectives and they sought new formats and new approaches to question generation for assessments. They privileged conceptual over psychometric criteria in building new reading assessments. They emphasised the need for assessments to reflect resources such as prior knowledge, environmental clues, the text itself and the key players involved in the reading process. They emphasised metacogntion as a reflective face of comprehension. And they championed the position that only a fresh start in assessments would give us tests to match our models of instruction.

Major changes

Changes included longer text passages, more challenging questions, different question formats (such as the more than one right answer format and open-ended questions). Reading scholars acknowledged that while all multiple-choice items include answers that are plausible under certain conditions, they did not necessarily invite reflection or interactive learning. Assessment efforts in Illinois and Michigan (see Valencia *et al.*, 1989) led the charge in trying to incorporate these new elements. In the spirit of authenticity, they included longer and more naturally occurring or 'authentic' text selections in tests. And both included test items that measured prior knowledge rather than trying to neutralise its effects (i.e. the passage dependency phenomenon). They also included items that were designed to measure students' use of reading strategies and their dispositions toward reading.

A systematic research program

A fair amount of research on these new assessment practices was carried out in the 1980s, much of it conducted at the Center for the Study of Reading under the leadership of Valencia and Pearson (Valencia *et al.*, 1986; Valencia and Pearson, 1987; Pearson *et al.*, 1990). For example, several candidate measures of prior knowledge were compared to a common criterion, an individual interview, to determine which exhibited the greatest concurrent validity (Pearson *et al.*, 1990). This work was a part of a new way of dealing with the prior knowledge problem in reading comprehension assessment. As we mentioned before, the traditional approach to dealing with prior knowledge in standardised tests was to neutralise it. Test writers would provide lots of short passages covering a wide variety of topics, the hope being that the variety would prevent any given type of individual from being consistently advantaged because of prior experiences.[8] The solution advocated in the 1960s was to use passage dependency analyses as a means of culling out items that could be answered without reading the text. The solution in these new assessments was to embrace prior knowledge as a part of the process of making meaning and then to assess it independently of comprehension so that its impact could be separately indexed.

Similar criterion validity studies were carried out for measures of comprehension monitoring, dispositions for reading and comprehension. While this work addressed a broad range of psychometric and conceptual issues, item format and test infrastructure is of greatest interest to the problems still lingering in the field. Central questions still plaguing us are which formats have the greatest validity as indices of comprehension and how do the various items in a comprehension assessment cluster to form independent factors.

Classroom assessment

The most significant advances in classroom comprehension assessment tools during this period also came from cognitive science. First was the spread of retellings as a tool for assessing comprehension. Driven by the 1970s advances in our knowledge about the structure of narrative and expository text (see Meyer and Rice, 1984), many scholars (see Irwin and Mitchell, 1983; Morrow, 1988, pp.128–49) developed systems for evaluating the depth and breadth of students' text understandings, based upon their attempts to retell or recall what they had read. Like the formal efforts of this era, there was a conscious attempt to take into account reader, text and context factors in characterising students' retellings.

Second was the use the think-aloud protocol as a measure of comprehension. Think-alouds had become respectable research tools by virtue of the important work on self-reports of cognitive processes popularised by Ericsson and Simon (1984). In attempting to characterise the nature of expertise in complex activities, such as chess, Ericsson and Simon learned that the most effective way inside the heads of expertise was to engage the players in thinking aloud about the what, why and how of their thing and actions during the activity.

This led to the wider use of think-alouds. First it became a research tool to get at the process, not just the product of student thinking (e.g. Olshavsky, 1977; Hartman, 1995). Then, it became an instructional practice (Baumann *et al.*, 1993) and finally, it was used as an assessment practice (Farr and Greene, 1992; California Learning Assessment System, 1994). With the ostensible purpose of assessing metacognitive processes during reading, Farr and Greene engaged students in write-along tasks (a kind of mandatory set of marginal notes prompted by a red dot at key points in the text). Students were encouraged, as they are in think-alouds, to say (in this case make a few notes about) what they thought at a given point. A similar practice was a standard part of the now defunct California Learning Assessment System: marginal notes were allowed, even encouraged, in the initial reading of the texts and those notes were fair game for review when the tasks were scored. Unfortunately, with the exception of a very thorough account of the research and theoretical background on verbal protocols by Pressley and Afflerbach (1995), very little careful work of either a conceptual or psychometric nature on the use of think-alouds as a viable assessment tool has emerged, although there was one effort to evaluate different approaches to metacognitive assessment in the special studies of NAEP in 1994.

Sociocultural and literary perspectives

We are not sure whether what happened next constitutes a second major shift or is better thought of as an extension of the first shift. It came so fast on the heels of the cognitive revolution that it is hard to pinpoint its precise beginning point. But by the late

1980s and early 1990s, a new contextual force was at work in shaping our views of comprehension assessment.

Sociolinguistics

In fact, harbingers of this socio-cultural revolution, emanating from sociolinguistic perspectives (see Bloom and Greene, 1984, pp.394–421) and the rediscovery of Vygotsky (see Vygotsky, 1978; Wertsch, 1985) were around in the early to mid-1980s, even as the cognitive revolution was exercising its muscle on assessment practices. For example, in cognitively motivated teaching approaches such as reciprocal teaching, students took on more responsibility for their own learning by teaching each other. In process writing, revision and conversation around revision delved more deeply into the social nature of reading, writing and understanding. Teachers used such practices to engage students to reflect on their work as well as interact with others around it. The concept of 'dynamic assessment' also emerged in this period. Dynamic assessment (Feuerstein *et al.*, 1979) allows the teacher to use student responses to a given task as a basis for determining what sort of task, accompanied by what level of support and scaffolding from the teacher, should come next. Here we see both cognitive and socio-cultural influences in assessment.

These early developments notwithstanding, the next round of assessment reforms carried more direct signs of the influence of these new social perspectives of learning, including group activities for the construction of meaning and peer response for activities requiring writing in response to reading.

Literary theory

The other influential trend was a renaissance in literary theory in the elementary classroom. One cannot understand the changes in pedagogy and assessment that occurred in the late 1980s and early 1990s without understanding the impact of literary theory, particularly reader response theory. In our secondary schools, the various traditions of literary criticism have always had a voice in the curriculum, especially in guiding discussions of classic literary works. Until the middle 1980s, the 'New Criticism' (Richards, 1929) that began its ascendancy in the depression era dominated the interpretation of text for several decades. It had sent teachers and students on a search for the one 'true' meaning in each text they encountered.[9] With the emergence (some would argue the re-emergence) of reader response theories, all of which gave as much authority to the reader as to either the text or the author, theoretical perspectives, along with classroom practices, changed dramatically. The basals that had been so skill-oriented in the 1970s and so comprehension oriented in the 1980s, became decidedly literature-based in the late 1980s and early 1990s. Comprehension gave way to readers' response to literature. Reader response emphasises affect and feeling that can either augment or replace cognitive responses to the content. To use the terminology of the most influential figure in the period, Louise Rosenblatt (1978), the field moved from efferent to aesthetic response to literature. And a 'transactive model' replaced the 'interactive model' of reading championed by the cognitive views of the 1980s. According to Rosenblatt, meaning is created in the transaction between reader and text. This meaning, which she refers to as the 'poem', is a new entity that resides above the reader–text interaction. Meaning is therefore neither subject nor object nor the interaction of the two. Instead it is transaction, something new and different from any of its inputs and influences.[10]

Illustrating the impact on reading assessment

Nowhere was the influence of these two new perspectives more prominent than in the development of the California Language Arts Framework (California State Department of Education, 1987) and in the assessment systems that grew out of the framework. There was a direct attempt to infuse social, cultural and literary perspectives into comprehension assessment processes more transparent than in the work of the California Learning Assessment System (CLAS, 1994). CLAS, which died an unhappy death via legislative mandate in the mid 1990s, nonetheless paved the way for more open assessments by emphasising response to literature formats and the social aspects of learning. Response to literature questions articulated a more open and reflective stance toward reading rather than a skills-based approach:

- If you were explaining what this essay is about to a person who had not read it, what would you say?

- What do you think is important or significant about it?

- What questions do you have about it?

- This is your chance to write any other observations, questions, appreciations and criticisms of the story. (CLAS, 6–9)

Response to literature formats demanded students to be able to summarise, explain, justify, interpret and provide evidence in their answers. In other words, assessment of reading comprehension reached a new stage, one much more compatible with what society might expect of students in the real world.

Critiques of the new assessments

As with other novel approaches in comprehension assessment, these new assessments came under fire as teachers and test developers struggled with issues of validity (particularly for individual scores), external accountability, reliability and generalisability (Linn, 1999; Pearson et al., 1998). Given what we know about the high-stakes functions for which assessments are used to make decisions about individuals (e.g. decisions about entry into or exit from special programs or 'certifying' or licensure decisions), these criticisms should not be surprising.

The social nature of the assessments

Performance assessments, probably because of their strong connection to everyday classroom activity and real world workplace contexts, tended to encourage teachers to have students work in groups. This led to an essential dilemma: what are we to do when we know that the performance of an individual student is influenced by the work, comments and assistance of peers and/or teachers? The essence of this dilemma was captured well in an essay by Gearhart *et al.* (1993) entitled, 'Whose work is it?' This 'contamination' of individual student scores has prompted great concern on the part of professionals who need to make decisions about individuals. The social components of the reading process can be grounded in theories that may even deny the existence, or at least the significance, of the 'individual'. This makes assessment doubly difficult.

Task generalisability

Task generalisability, the degree to which performance on one task predicts performance on a second, is a major concern with these performance tasks. The data gathered from the first scoring of New Standards tasks (Linn *et al.*,1995) indicate that indices of generalisability for both math and reading tasks were quite low. That essentially means that performance on any one task is not a good predictor of scores on other tasks. Shavelson and his colleagues encountered the same lack of generalisability with science tasks (Shavelson *et al.*, 1992), as have other scholars (e.g. Linn, 1993) even on highly respected enterprises such as the advanced placement tests sponsored by the College Board. The findings in the College Board analysis are noteworthy for the incredible variability in generalisability found as a function of subject matter. For example, in order to achieve a generalisability coefficient of .90, estimates of testing time range from a low of 1.25 hours for Physics to over 13 hours for European History. These findings suggest that we need to measure students' performance on a large number of tasks before we can feel confident in having a stable estimate of their accomplishment in a complex area such as reading, writing, or subject matter knowledge. Findings such as these probably explain why standardised test developers have included many short passages on a wide array of topics in their comprehension assessments. They also point to a bleak future for performance assessment in reading; one wonders whether we can afford the time to administer and score the number of tasks required to achieve a stable estimate of individuals' achievement.

The legacy

If one examines trends in the assessment marketplace and in state initiatives, one can make predictions based on usually a reliable indicator of the latest trends in assessment. Now the revolution begun in the 1980s is over, or at least inching along in a very quiet cycle. Granted, successful implementations of authentic wide-scale assessment have been maintained in states like Maryland (Kapinus *et al.*, 1994, pp.255–76), Kentucky and Oregon (see Pearson *et al.*, 2002). However, other states (e.g. California, Wisconsin,

Arizona and Indiana) have rejected performance assessment and returned to off-the-shelf, multiple-choice, standardised reading assessments. Pearson *et al.* (2002), found a definite trend among states in which performance assessment is still alive to include it in a mixed model, not unlike NAEP, in which substantive, extended response items sit along side more conventional multiple-choice items. Both these item formats accompany relatively lengthy passages. Even the more modest reforms in Illinois (the multiple-correct answer approach) were dropped in 1998 (interestingly, in favour of a NAEP-like mixed model approach). And it is the NAEP model that, in our view, is most likely to prevail. It is within the NAEP mixed model that the legacy of the reforms of the early 1990s are likely to survive, albeit in a highly protracted form (see chapter 18 for an account of the NAEP approach to reading assessment).

Concluding statement

Reading comprehension assessment has been a significant landmark in the educational landscape for just over 80 years. Its history is a remarkable story, one characterised by cycles of great hope and expectation alternating with periods of disappointment and frustration. A disappointment general to scholars throughout its history has been our persistent inability to see comprehension as it happens, what we have referred to as the phenomenological 'click' of comprehension. Instead, they have had to content themselves with 'artifacts' and residual traces of the comprehension process – indirect indices of its occurrence. Each of these indirect indices carries with it a cost, one that can be measured by the inferential distance between the evidence and the phenomenon itself. Many of the advances in comprehension assessment have, at least in a virtual sense, narrowed the distance between evidence and the process, providing us with greater confidence in our measures.

Other hopes and disappointments have been particular to specific periods. Two examples stand out: (a) the great expectations built up around performance assessments in the early 1990s, followed by the disappointment at their failure to stand psychometric tests of generalisability and reliability and (b) the short-lived exhilaration so prominent in the late 1980s which held a promise that we might find assessments that would match the models of instruction built on the principles governing allegedly challenging constructivist curriculum. While the disappointments and frustrations are real, there has also been genuine progress. That progress is probably best represented by NAEP and some of our other mixed model, wide-scale assessments.

And, of course, there is still much more to learn about how to measure a phenomenon that is as elusive as it is important. It is our modest hope that this manuscript will serve as a catalyst for both lively conversation and concentrated work to improve our capacity to assess what is assuredly most important about reading – our ability to marshal all of our resources to make sense of the texts we encounter.

References

Allington, R.L. (1984). 'Oral reading.' In: Pearson, P.D., Barr, R., Kamil, M. and Mosenthal, P. (Eds) *Handbook of Reading Research*. New York: Longman.

Anderson, R.C. and Pearson, P.D. (1984). 'A schema-theoretic view of basic processes in reading comprehension.' In: Pearson, P.D., Barr, R., Kamil, M. and Mosenthal, P. (Eds), *Handbook of Reading Research*. New York: Longman.

Bachman, L.F. (1982). 'The trait structure of cloze test scores', *TESOL Quarterly*, **16**, 1, 61–70.

Bachman, L.F. (2000). 'Modern language testing at the turn of the century: assuring that what we count counts', *Language Testing*, **17**, 1, 1–42.

Baumann, J., Jones L. and Seifert-Kessell, N. (1993). 'Using think alouds to enhance children's comprehension monitoring abilities', *The Reading Teacher*, **47**, 184–93.

Betts, E. (1946). *Foundations of Reading Instruction*. New York: American Book.

Binet, A. (1895). Cited in Johnston, P.H. (1984a) 'Assessment in reading.' In: Pearson, P.D., Barr, R., Kamil, M. and Mosenthal, P. (Eds) *Handbook of Reading Research*. New York: Longman, 147–82.

Bloom, D. and Greene, J. (1984). 'Directions in the sociolinguistic study of reading.' In: Pearson P.D., Barr, R., Kamil, M. and Mosenthal, P. (Eds) *Handbook of Reading Research*. New York: Longman.

Bormuth, J.R. (1966). 'Reading: a new approach', *Reading Research Quarterly*, **1**, 79–132.

California Learning Assessment System. (1994). *Elementary Performance Assessments: Integrated English-Language Arts Illustrative Material*. Sacramento, CA: California Department of Education.

California State Department of Education. (1987). *English Language Arts Framework*. Sacramento, CA: California Department of Education.

Chapman, J.C. (1924). *Chapman Unspeeded Reading-Comprehension Test*. Minneapolis: Educational Test Bureau.

Courtis, S.A. (1914). 'Standard tests in English', *Elementary School Teacher*, **14**, 374–92.

Davis, F.B. (1944). 'Fundamental factors of comprehension of reading', *Psychometrika*, **9**, 185–97.

Davis, F.B. (1968). 'Research in comprehension in reading', *Reading Research Quarterly*, **3**, 499–545.

Derrik, C. (1953). 'Three aspects of reading comprehension as measured by tests of different lengths', *Research Bulletin* 53–8. Princeton, NJ: ETS.

Dewey, J. (1938). *Experience and Education*. New York: Collier Books.

Durrell, D.D. (1937). *Durrell Analysis of Reading Difficulty*. New York: Harcourt, Brace and World.

Ericsson, K.A. and Simon, H.A. (1984). *Protocol Analysis: Verbal Reports as Data*. Cambridge, MA: MIT Press.

Farr, R. and Greene, B. G. (1992). 'Using verbal and written think-alongs to assess metacognition in reading.' Paper presented at the 15th annual conference of the Eastern Education Research Association Hilton Head, SC.

Feuerstein, R.R., Rand, Y. and Hoffman, M.B. (1979). *The Dynamic Assessment of Retarded Performance*. Baltimore, MD: University Park Press.

Freeman, F.N. (1926). *Mental Tests: Their History, Principles and Applications*. Chicago: Houghton Mifflin.

Gates, A.I. (1937). 'The measurement and evaluation of achievement in reading.' In: *The Teaching of Reading: A Second Report (Forty-Sixth Yearbook of the National Society for Studies in Education, Part 1)*. Bloomington, IL: Public School Publishing.

Gearhart, M., Herman, J., Baker, E. and Whittaker, A.K. (1993). *Whose Work is It? A Question for the Validity of Large-Scale Portfolio Assessment*. CSE Technical report 363. Los Angeles: University of California, National Center for Research on Evaluation, Standards and Student Testing.

Goodman, K.S. (1968). *The Psycholinguistic Nature of the Reading Process*. Detroit: Wayne State University Press.

Goodman, K.S. (1969). 'Analysis of oral reading miscues: applied psycholinguistics', *Reading Research Quarterly*, **5**, 1.

Goodman, Y.M. and Burke, C.L. (1970). *Reading Miscue Inventory Manual Procedure for Diagnosis and Evaluation*. New York: Macmillan.

Gray, W.S. (1917). *Studies of Elementary School Reading through Standardized Tests (Supplemental Educational Monographs No. 1)*. Chicago: University of Chicago Press.

Harris, C.W. (1948). 'Measurement of comprehension in literature', *The School Review*, **56**, 280–89 and 332–42.

Huey, E. (1908). *The Psychology and Pedagogy of Reading*. Cambridge, MA: MIT Press.

Hunt, L.C. (1957). 'Can we measure specific factors associated with reading comprehension?', *Journal of Educational Research*, **51**, 161–71.

Irwin, P.A. and Mitchell, J.N. (1983). 'A procedure for assessing the richness of retellings', *Journal of Reading*, **26**, 391–96.

Johnston, P. H. (1984a). 'Assessment in reading.' In: Pearson, P.D., Barr, R., Kamil, M. and Mosenthal, P. (Eds) *Handbook of Reading Research*. New York: Longman.

Johnston, P.H. (1984b). *Reading Comprehension Assessment: A Cognitive Basis*. Newark, DE: International Reading Association.

Kapinus, B., Collier, G.V. and Kruglanski, H. (1994). 'The Maryland school performance assessment program: a new wave of assessment.' In: Valencia, S., Hiebert, E. and P. Afflerbach (Eds) *Authentic Reading Assessment: Practices and Possibilities*. Newark, DE: International Reading Association.

Kelly, E.J. (1916). 'The Kansas silent reading tests', *Journal of Educational Psychology*, **7**, 63–80.

Kelly, T.L. (1935). *Essential Traits of Mental Life*. Cambridge, MA: Harvard University Press.

Kintsch, W. (1974). The Representation of Meaning in Memory. Hillsdale, NJ: Erlbaum.

Kintsch, W. and van Dijk, T.A. (1978). 'Toward a model of text comprehension and production', *Psychological Review*, **85**, 366–94.

Linn, R. (1993). 'Educational assessment: expanded expectations and challenges', *Educational Evaluation and Policy Analysis*, **15**, 1–16.

Linn, R. (1999). 'Assessments and accountability', *Educational Researcher*, **29**, 2, 4–16.

Linn, R., DeStefano, L., Burton, E. and Hanson, M. (1995). 'Generalizability of New Standards Project 1993 pilot study tasks in mathematics', *Applied Measurement in Education*, **9**, 2, 33–45.

Mandler, J.M. and Johnson, N.S. (1977). 'Remembrance of things parsed: story structure and recall', *Cognitive Psychology*, **9**, 111–51.

Markman, E.M. (1977). 'Realizing that you don't understand: a preliminary investigation', *Child Development*, **48**, 986–92.

Matthews, M. (1966). *Teaching to Read*. Chicago: University of Chicago Press.

McNamara, T.P., Miller, D.L. and Bransford, J.D. (1991). 'Mental models and reading comprehension.' In: Pearson, P.D., Barr, R., Kamil, M. and Mosenthal, P. (Eds) *Handbook of Reading Research, Vol. 2*. New York: Longman.

Meyer, B.J.F. (1975). *The Organization of Prose and its Effects on Memory*. Amsterdam: North Holland Publishing.

Meyer, B.J.F. and Rice, E. (1984). 'The structure of text.' In: Pearson, P.D., Barr, R., Kamil, M. and Mosenthal, P. (Eds) *The Handbook of Reading Research*. New York: Longman.

Monroe, W.S. (1918). *Monroe's Standardized Silent Reading Tests*. Bloomington, IL: Public School Publishing.

Morrow, L.M. (1988). 'Retelling stories as a diagnostic tool.' In: Glazer, S.M., Searfoss, L.W. and Gentile, L.M. (Eds) *Reexamining Reading Diagnosis: New Trends and Procedures*. Newark, DE: International Reading Association.

Olshavsky, J.E. (1977).'Reading as problem solving: an investigation of strategies', *Reading Research Quarterly*, **12**, 4, 654–74.

Olson, D.R. (1994). *The World on Paper: The Conceptual and Cognitive Implications of Writing and Reading*. Cambridge: Cambridge University Press.

Pearson, P.D. (2000). 'Reading in the 20th century.' In: Good, T. (Ed) *American Education: Yesterday, Today and Tomorrow. Yearbook of the National Society for the Study of Education*. Chicago: University of Chicago Press.

Pearson, P.D., Calfee, R., Walker-Webb, T. and Fleischer, S. (2002). *The Role of Performance Assessment in Large Scale Accountability Systems: Lessons Learned from the Inside*. Washington, DC: Council of Chief State School Officers.

Pearson, P.D., Greer, E.A., Commeyras, M., Stallman, A., Valencia, S.W., Krug, S.E., Shanahan, T. and Reeve, R. (1990). *The Validation of Large Scale Reading Assessment: Building Tests for the Twenty-First Century*. Urbana, IL: Center for the Study of Reading: Reading Research and Education Center research report, under grant number G 0087–C1001–90 with the Office of Educational Research and Improvement.

Pearson, P.D. and Johnson, D.D. (1978). *Teaching Reading Comprehension*. New York: Holt, Rinehart and Winston.

Pearson, P.D., DeStefano, L. and Garcia G.E. (1998). 'Ten dilemmas of performance assessment.' In: Harrision, C. and Salinger, T. (Eds) *Assessing Reading 1, Theory and Practice*. London: Routledge.

Pearson, P.D. and Stephens, D. (1993). 'Learning about literacy: a 30-year journey.' In: Gordon, C.J., Labercane, G.D. and McEachern, W.R. (Eds) *Elementary Reading: Process and Practice*. Boston: Ginn Press.

Pressley, M., and Afflerbach, P. (1995).*Verbal Protocols of Reading: The Nature of Constructively Responsive Reading*. Hillsdale, NJ: Erlbaum.

RAND Reading Study Group. (2002). *Reading for understanding: Toward an R&D program in reading comprehension*. Santa Monica, CA: RAND Corporation.

Rankin, E.F. (1965). 'The cloze procedure: a survey of research.' In: Thurston, E. and Hafner, L. (Eds) *Fourteenth Yearbook of the National Reading Conference*. Clemson, SC: National Reading Conference.

Resnick, D.P. (1982). 'History of educational testing.' In: Wigdor, A.K. and Garner, W.R. (Eds) *Ability Testing: Uses, Consequences and Controversies (Part 2)*. Washington, DC: National Academy Press.

Richards, I.A. (1929). *Practical Criticism*. New York: Harcourt, Brace.

Rosenblatt, L.M. (1978). *The Reader, the Text, the Poem: The Transactional Theory of the Literary Work*. Carbondale, IL: Southern Illinois University Press.

Rumelhart, D.E. (1977). 'Understanding and summarizing brief stories.' In: LaBerge, D. and Samuels, J. (Eds) *Basic Processes in Reading Perception and Comprehension*. Hillsdale, NJ: Erlbaum.

Rumelhart, D.E. (1981). 'Schemata: the building blocks of cognition.' In: Guthrie, J.T. (Ed) *Comprehension in Teaching*. Newark, DE: International Reading Association.

Rumelhart, D.E. and Ortony, A. (1977). 'The representation of knowledge in memory.' In: Anderson, R.C., Spiro, R.J. and Montague. W.E. (Eds) *Schooling and the Acquisition of Knowledge*. Hillsdale, NJ: Erlbaum.

Shanahan, T., Kamil, M.L. and Tobin, A.W. (1982). 'Cloze as a measure of intersentential comprehension', *Reading Research Quarterly*, **17**, 2, 229–55.

Shavelson, R.J., Baxter, G.P. and Pine, J. (1992). 'Performance assessments: political rhetoric and measurement reality', *Educational Researcher*, **21**, 4, 22–7.

Smith, N.B. (1966). *American Reading Instruction*. Newark, DE: International Reading Association.

Spiro, R. and Jehng, J. (1990). 'Cognitive flexibility and hypertext: theory and technology for the linear and nonlinear multidimensional traversal of complex subject matter.' In: Nix, D. and Spiro, R. (Eds) *Cognition, Education and Multimedia: Exploring Ideas in High Technology*. Hillsdale, NJ: Erlbaum.

Starch, D. (1915). 'The measurement of efficiency in reading', *Journal of Educational Psychology*, **6**, 1–24.

Stein, N.L. and Glenn, C.G. (1977). 'An analysis of story comprehension in elementary school children.' In: Freedle, R.O. (Ed) *Discourse Processing: Multidisciplinary Perspective*. Norwood, NJ: Ablex.

Taylor, W. (1953). 'Cloze procedure: a new tool for measuring readability', *Journalism Quarterly*, **9**, 206–223.

Thorndike, E.L. (1917). 'Reading as reasoning: a study of mistakes in paragraph reading', *Journal of Educational Psychology*, **8**, 323–32.

Touton, F.C. and Berry, B.T. (1931). 'Reading comprehension at the junior college level', *California Quarterly of Secondary Education*, **6**, 245–51.

Tuinman, J.J. (1974). 'Determining the passage-dependency of comprehension questions in 5 major tests', *Reading Research Quarterly*, **9**, 2, 207–23.

Tuinman, J.J. (1978). 'Criterion referenced measurement in a norm referenced context.' In: Samuels, J. (Ed) *What Research has to Say about Reading Instruction*. Newark, DE: International Reading Association.

Turner, A. and Greene, E. (1977). *The Construction of a Propositional Text Base (Technical Report No. 63)*. Boulder: University of Colorado Press.

Valencia, S. and Pearson, P.D. (1987). *New Models for Reading Assessment* (Read Ed. Report No. 71). Urbana: University of Illinois, Center for the Study of Reading.

Valencia, S., Pearson, P.D., Peters, C.W. and Wixson K.K. (1989). 'Theory and practice in statewide reading assessment: closing the gap', *Educational Leadership*, **47**, 7, 57–63.

Valencia, S.V., Pearson, P.D., Reeve, R., Shanahan, T., Croll, V., Foertsch, D., Foertsch, M. and Seda, I. (1986). *Illinois Assessment of Educational Progress: Reading (for grades 3, 6, 8, 10)*. Springfield, IL: Illinois State Board of Education.

Vygotsky, L. (1978). *Mind in Society: The Development of Higher Psychological Processes*. Cambridge, MA: Harvard University Press.

Wertsch, J.V. (1985). *Vygotsky and the Social Formation of Mind*. Cambridge, MA: Harvard University Press.

Winograd, P. and Johnston, P. (1980). *Comprehension Monitoring and the Error Detection Paradigm (Tech. Rep. No. 153)*. Urbana: University of Illinois, Center for the Study of Reading (ED 181 425).

Further reading

Bloom, B.S. (1968). 'Learning for mastery', *Evaluation Comment*, **1**, 2, 1–12.

Bloom, B.S. (1956). 'Taxonomy of educational objectives.' In: *Handbook 1: Cognitive Domain*. New York: McKay.

Board of Education, City of Chicago. (1984). *Chicago Mastery Learning Reading*. Watertown, MA: Mastery Education Corporation.

Bormuth, J.R. (1970). *On the Theory of Achievement Test Items*. Chicago: University of Chicago Press.

Buly, M. and Valencia, S.W. (in press) 'Below the bar: profiles of students who fail state reading assessments', *Educational Evaluation and Policy Analysis*.

Campell, J.R. (1999). Cognitive processes elicited by multiple-choice and constructed-response questions on an assessment of reading comprehension. Unpublished doctoral dissertation, Temple University.

Campell, J.R., Voelkl, K.E., and Donahue, P.L. (1998). *NAEP 1996 Trends in Academic Progress: Achievement of U.S. Students in Science 1969 to 1996, Mathematics, 1973 to 1996, Reading, 1971 to 1996 and Writing, 1984 to 1996. NCES 97–985*. Washington DC: U.S. Department of Education.

Carroll, J. (1963). 'A model of school learning', *Teachers College Record*, **64**, 723–32.

Davis, F. B. (1972). 'Psychometric research on comprehension in reading', *Reading Research Quarterly*, **7**, 4, 628–78.

Destefano, L., Pearson, P.D. and Afflerbach, P. (1997). 'Content validation of the 1994 NAEP in Reading: Assessing the relationship between the 1994 assessment and the reading framework.' In: Linn, R., Glaser, R. and Bohrnstedt G. (Eds) *Assessment in Transition: 1994 Trial State Assessment Report on Reading: Background Studies*. Stanford, CA: The National Academy of Education.

Durrell, D.D. (1955). *Durrell Analysis of Reading Difficulty*. New York: Harcourt, Brace and World.

Eurich, A.C. (1936). *Minnesota Speed of Reading Test for College Students*. Minneapolis: University of Minnesota Press.

Frederiksen, N. (1984). 'The real test bias: influences of testing on teaching and learning', *American Psychologist*, **39**, 193–202.

Gagné, R.M. 1965. *The Conditions of Learning*. New York: Holt, Rinehart and Winston.

Garavalia D. (in press). The impact of item format on depth of cognitive engagement. Unpublished doctoral dissertation, Michigan State University.

Gardner, H. (1985). *The Mind's New Science: A History of the Cognitive Revolution*. New York: Basic Books.

Ginn and Company. (1982). *The Ginn Reading Program*. Lexington, MA: Ginn and Company.

Glaser, R., Linn, R. and Bohrnstedt, G. (1997). *Assessment in Transition: Monitoring the Nation's Educational Progress*. Stanford, CA: National Academy of Education.

Hartman, D.K. (1995). 'Eight readers reading: the intertextual links of proficient readers reading multiple passages', *Reading Research Quarterly*, **30**, 3.

Illinois Goal Assessment Program. (1991). *The Illinois Reading Assessment: Classroom Connections*. Springfield, IL: Illinois State Board of Education.

Johnson, D.D. and Pearson, P.D. (1975). 'Skills management systems: a critique', *The Reading Teacher*, **28**, 757–64.

Jones L.V. (1996). 'A history of the National Assessment of Educational Progress and some questions about its future', *Educational Researcher*, **25**, 7, 1–8.

Klare, G.R. (1984). 'Readability.' In: Pearson, P.D., Barr, R., Kamil, M. and Mosenthal, P. (Eds) *Handbook of Reading Research*. New York: Longman.

Langer, J. (1995). *Envisioning Literature: Literary Understanding and Literature Instruction*. New York: Teachers College Press.

NAEP Reading Consensus Project. (1992). *Reading Framework for the 1992 National Assessment of Educational Progress*. Washington, DC: US Printing Office.

National Voluntary Reading Test. (1995). *National Voluntary Reading Test*. Washington, DC: US Printing Office.

Naylor, M. (1972). Reading skill variability within and among fourth-grade, fifth-grade and sixth-grade students attaining the same reading achievement score. Unpublished doctoral dissertation. Minneapolis: University of Minnesota.

Otto, W. (1977). 'The Wisconsin design: a reading program for individually guided elementary education.' In: Klausmeier, R.A., Rossmiller, R.A. and Saily, M. (Eds) *Individually Guided Elementary Education: Concepts and Practices*. New York: Academic Press.

Otto, W.R. and Chester, R.D. (1976). *Objective-Based Reading*. Reading, MA: Addison-Wesley.

Paris, S.G. and Winograd, P. (1989). 'How metacognition can promote academic learning and instruction.' In: Jones, B.F. and Idol, L. (Eds) *Dimensions of Thinking and Cognitive Instruction, Vol. 1*. Hillsdale, NJ: Erlbaum.

Pearson, P.D., Garavaglia, D., Danridge, J., Hamm, D., Lycke, K., Roberts, E. and Walker-Webb, T. (in press). *The Impact of Item Format on the Depth of Students' Cognitive Engagement*. Washington, DC: American Institutes for Research.

Pearson, P.D., Spalding, E. and Meyers, M. (1998) 'Literacy assessment in the New Standards Project.' In: Coles, M. and Jenkins, R. (Eds) *Assessing Reading to Changing Practice in Classrooms*. London: Routledge.

Pellegrino, J., Jones, L. and Mitchell, K. (1999). *Grading the Nation's Report Card: Evaluating NAEP and Transforming the Assessment of Educational Progress*. Washington, DC: National Academy Press.

Ramanuskas, S. (1972). 'The responsiveness of cloze readability measures to linguistic variables operating over segments of text longer than a sequence', *Reading Research Quarterly*, **8**, 1.

Resnick, D.P. and Resnick, L. (1977). 'The nature of literacy: an historical exploration', *Harvard Educational Review*, **47**, 37, 385.

Royer, J.M. (1987). 'The sentence verification technique: a practical procedure for testing comprehension', *Journal of Reading*, **30**, 5, 14–22.

Royer, J.M. and Cunningham, D. J. (1981). 'On the theory and measurement of reading comprehension,' *Contemporary Educational Psychology*, **6**, 3, 187–216.

Royer, J.M. and Hambleton, R.K. (1983). Normative study of 50 reading comprehension passages that use the sentence verification technique. Unpublished study. Amherst: University of Massachusetts.

Royer, J. M., Hastings, N. and Hook, C. (1979). 'A sentence verification technique for measuring reading comprehension tests', *Journal of Reading Behavior*, **11**, 355–63.

Royer, J.M., Kulhavy, R.W., Lee, J.B. and Peterson, S.E. (1984). 'The sentence verification technique as a measure of listening and reading comprehension', *Educational and Psy5chological Research*, **6**, 299–314.

Royer, J.M., Lynch, D.J., Hambleton, R.K. and Bulgarelli, C. (1984). 'Using the sentence verification technique to assess the comprehension of technical text as a function of subject matter expertise', *American Educational Research Journal*, **21**, 839–69.

Salinger, T. and Campbell, J. (1998). 'The national assessment of reading in the USA.' In: Harrison, C. and Salinger, T. (Eds) *Assessing Reading: Theory and Practice*. London: Routledge, 96–109.

Sarroub, L. and Pearson, P.D. (1998). 'Two steps forward, three steps back: the stormy history of reading comprehension assessment', *The Clearing House*, **72**, 2, 97–105.

Schreiner, R.L., Heironymus, A.N. and Forsyth, R. (1969). 'Differential measurement of reading abilities at the elementary school level', *Reading Research Quarterly*, **5**, 1.

Silver, Burdett, and Ginn. (1989). *World of Reading*. Needham, MA: Silver, Burdett, and Ginn.

Spearitt, D. (1972). 'Identification of subskills of reading comprehension by maximum likelihood factor analysis', *Reading Research Quarterly*, **8**, 92–111.

Stenner, A.J. and Burdick, D.S. (1997). *The Objective Measurement of Reading Comprehension*. Durham, NC: MetaMetrics Inc.

Stenner, A.J., Smith, D.R., Horabin, I. and Smith, M. (1987). *Fit of the Lexlie Theory to Item Difficulties on Fourteen Standardized Reading Comprehension Tests*. Durham, NC: MetaMetrics Inc.

Thurstone, L.L. (no date). *Psychological examination (Test 4)*. Stoelting.

Touchstone Applied Science Associates. (1995). *Degrees of Reading Power*. Benbrook, TX: Touchstone Applied Science Associates.

Valencia, S. and Pearson, P.D. (1987). 'Reading assessment: time for a change', *The Reading Teacher*, **40**, 726–33.

White, E.B. (1952). *Charlotte's Web*. New York: Harper and Row.

Yepes-Bayara, M. (1996). 'A cognitive study based on the National Assessment of Educational Progress (NAEP) Science Assessment.' Paper presented at the annual meeting of the National Council on Measurement in Education, New York.

Notes

1   This tradition of isomorphism between the infrastructure of tests and curriculum has been a persistent issue throughout the century. See, for example, Johnson and Pearson (1975) and Resnick (1982). Also see Smith (1966) for an account of the expansion of reading comprehension as a curricular phenomenon.

2   The use of more than one right answer predates the infamous a, b, c (a and b) multiple-choice format as well as the systematic use of the 'more than one right answer' approach used in some state assessments in the 1980s and 1990s (Pearson *et al.*, 1990).

3 It is somewhat ironic that the sort of thinking exhibited in this piece did not become dominant view in the teens and twenties. Unquestionably, Thorndike was the pre-eminent educational psychologist of his time (Thorndike, 1917). Further, his work in the psychology of learning (the law of effect and the law of contiguity) became the basis of the behaviorism that dominated educational psychology and pedagogy during this period and his work in assessment led was highly influential in developing the components of classical measurement theory (reliability and validity). Somehow this more cognitively oriented side of his work was less influential, at least in the period in which it was written.

4 During this period, great homage was paid to intellectual ancestors such as Edmund Burke Huey, who as early as 1908 recognized the cognitive complexity of reading. Voices such as Huey's, unfortunately, were not heard during the period from 1915 to 1965 when behaviorism dominated psychology and education.

5 It is not altogether clear that schema theory is dead, especially in contexts of practice. Its role in psychological theory is undoubtedly diminished due to attacks on its efficacy as a model of memory and cognition. See McNarmara et al. (1991) or Spiro and Jehng (1990, pp.163–205).

6 Smagorinsky (in press) uses the phrase 'inscribed' in the text as a way of indicating that the author of the text has some specific intentions when he or she set pen to paper, thereby avoiding the thorny question of whether meaning exists 'out there' outside of the minds of readers. We use the term here to avoid the very same question.

7 Most coherent model is defined as that model which provides the best account of the 'facts' of the text uncovered at a given point in time by the reader in relation to the schemata instantiated at that same point in time.

8 Note that this approach tends, on average, to favor those students who have high general verbal skills as might be indexed by an intelligence test, for example. These will be the students who will possess at least some knowledge on a wide array of topics (Johnston, 1984a, 1984b).

9 We find it most interesting that the ultimate psychometrician, Frederick Davis (e.g. 1968), was fond of referencing the New Criticism of I.A. Richards (1929) in his essays and investigations about comprehension.

10 Rosenblatt credits the idea of transaction to John Dewey, who discussed it in many texts, including *Experience and Education* (Dewey, 1938).

8 Significant moments in the history of reading assessment in the UK

Chris Whetton

It was the initial hope and aim of the discussion series of seminars which gave rise to this book, that a unified theory of reading assessment would be produced. If successful, this would give a relationship between the psychological approaches to reading and the view of literacy as a process steeped in the understanding of all the information imparted by text. As with many endeavours, this has had to be modified over time into a lesser objective (see Marian Sainsbury's introduction.)

This chapter will take one view, based on a historical survey of some important tests in use in the UK over the last eighty years. This view is that the prevailing definition of reading is a reflection of the needs and values of the education system at the time, which themselves arise from the prevailing attitudes and requirements of society in general.

This viewpoint is best illustrated by a personal anecdote. In 1990, the first National Curriculum assessments for England were under development. The present author was the Director of the NFER project which was creating 'standard assessment tasks' (SATs) for the assessment of seven-year-old pupils. The specification had said that these were to be naturalistic tasks to be used by teachers in the classroom as a part of their usual practice. Many aspects of the curriculum from science through to history were to be assessed, but a particular bone of contention was the assessment of reading. The political background of the time was that claims were being made that standards had fallen during the 1980s, due to teachers' reliance on children's books to teach reading using whole-word and context strategies (summarised as 'real books') as opposed to phonics methods advocated by the criticising educational psychologists and others. (Turner, 1990a and 1990b.) This debate had developed such importance that the issue of how to assess was to be resolved by the responsible minister himself – the Secretary of State for Education. At the time, this was Kenneth Clarke, famous as a 'big picture' strategist with little wish to grapple with detail.

A meeting was arranged to discuss the issue of reading assessment. Representatives of the Schools' Examination and Assessment Council (SEAC) (the government agency then responsible), Her Majesty's Inspectors of Schools (HMI) (involved in steering the process) and the education ministry, then called the Department for Education and Science (DES) gathered in a meeting room and waited. The minister, Mr Clarke, swept in surrounded by an entourage of (about six) political advisers. He listened for a short time to the muddled arguments of the education professionals and then pronounced, with words along the lines of:

It doesn't seem so difficult to me to find if a child can read. You give them a book and ask them to read. If they can read, they read the book, if they can't read they don't read the book. It's perfectly simple. Mind you, I'm not having anything to do with this real books nonsense.

With that Delphic remark he and his entourage departed from the room, moving on to their next decision.

Translated into policy by SEAC, HMI and DfES, this meant that the reading assessment was one in which children read from actual books, with a choice of book; reading individually to the teacher who maintained a running record, including a miscue analysis. The children also answered questions about the meaning of what they had read. The assessment is described more fully in the last section of this chapter.

While there was a wealth of educational and assessment research behind this form of assessment, ultimately it was the person empowered by society who determined the nature of the assessment. This story is unusual in that the individual concerned was such a high-ranking representative of society and the decision so abrupt. However, the contention of this article is that this is always the case, but that the representative(s) concerned varies according to time and circumstances, being in some cases an educational psychologist, in others a curriculum developer and in others an examination officer.

The plan for this chapter has therefore been to select tests which have had an historical importance in Britain and then to use these to illustrate the view of the construct of reading prevailing at the time. This is related as far as possible to the prevailing views of education and society at that time. In determining which reading tests are considered to be those with historical importance, a set of general principles has been followed. First, the tests should have been influential, that is, they should have been widely used in the education system and they should have been referred to in the research literature and in books for teachers and students. They should also have served as models for other tests, so that other authors and publishers produced tests of the same general type. A second principle has been that the tests should have had 'staying power', that is they should have been used over a long period of time. Finally, tests have been selected for their importance in serving the educational priorities of their time.

A preliminary list of tests meeting these principles was proposed to the group attending the third ESRC seminar. This was largely accepted and one or two additions were proposed. This led to the final list of 'important' tests which is:

• Burt Word Reading Test (1921)

• Schonell Reading Tests (1942)

• Reading Test AD (NFER, 1955) A.F. Watts

• Neale Analysis of Reading Ability (1958)

• Gap and Gapadol (1970, 1973)

• Edinburgh Reading tests (1975)

- APU Reading Assessment National Surveys (1979–1988)

- Key Stage 1 National Curriculum Reading Assessment (1990–present).

Burt Word Reading Test

The Burt Word Reading Test was first published in 1921 and consists of a set of 110 words, printed with five on each line. The words are in (broadly) increasing order of difficulty and the child is asked to read them aloud, continuing until they fail to read any word on two consecutive lines. The first line is:

    to   *is*   *up*   *he*   *at*

and the final line is:

    alienate   *phthisis*   *poignancy*   *ingratiating*   *subtlety*

The score is the number of words read aloud correctly which can then be converted to a reading age. The concept of reading is very rudimentary. Provided words are pronounced aloud, success is assumed. The child may be unfamiliar with the word or its meaning but still be regarded as able to read it.

The information in the following section is derived largely from Hernshaw's (1979) biography of Burt.

The initial version of the test was produced by Cyril Burt as one of a battery of Mental and Scholastic tests. They were devised for use in London, where Burt was working as a psychologist for London County Council. The primary reason for his appointment in 1913 was to assist with the examination of pupils in elementary schools nominated for admission to schools for the mentally deficient. Previously this had been the province of medical officers, who were suspected of sending many pupils to special schools incorrectly and it was hoped that such errors could be avoided through the use of psychological testing. Burt was the sole psychologist (and only part-time) but set up a programme in which he spent two days a week testing in schools and a third on test construction. He initially published a report on the *Distribution and Relation of Educational Abilities*, concluding that the educational system was failing to push the brightest to the limits of their potentialities (*plus ça change*) and was also failing to make provision for the backward, defined as children, though not defective, who were unable to do the work of even a class below their age. Burt utilised the tests he adapted (such as Binet's intelligence scale) or devised, to underpin this practical work on educational attainment. In 1921 he published *Mental and Scholastic Tests* which contained sections on the validity of the tests which among other matters described test development, item analysis and other statistical methods. It also contained the series of scholastic tests for reading, spelling, arithmetic, writing, drawing, handwork and composition. Among these was the Word Reading Test. The book was also balanced in its advocacy of testing, stressing that tests should be regarded as 'but the beginning, never the end, of the examination of the child ... to appraise the results demands the tact, the experience, the imaginative insight of the teacher born and trained'.

Always immodest, Burt claimed that many of the technical procedures used in developing the tests were used for the first time. These included item analysis, tetrachoric correlations, factor scores, correlations of person's scores, representative sampling and practical regression equations. Some of these he devised, but others were adapted from the work of others. However, what this did represent was the first application of test development technology, as now understood, to educational assessment in Britain.

In terms of defining the construct of reading, Burt said that he had selected words, sentences and passages from a large preliminary collection taken from reading books used in schools, from children's own talk and compositions and from books and magazines which children read out of school. Teachers then assisted with the selection of the texts, since a variety of methods of teaching reading was in vogue, resulting in different vocabularies in each. The words selected were common to all. The final selection of words was based on an item analysis and correlations of each word with teachers' ratings of children's reading ability.

This account is of interest since it shows that two elements of the process of developing reading tests – the attempt to find material of interest to children and common to all their experiences and the relationship of the test outcomes to teachers' ratings of children – which we sometimes think of as modern concerns have been in place from the start of the systematic testing of reading.

Mental and Scholastic Tests was an influential publication and second, third and fourth editions followed, the final one in 1962. The Word Reading Test was re-standardised by P.E. Vernon in 1938 using a Scottish sample and the Scottish Council for Research in Education (SCRE) undertook a slight revision (some words were moved to new positions) and re-standardisation in 1974. By that time, the utility of the test was being questioned and a 1976 review says of this last exercise that 'it seems a pity in view of the basically archaic conception of reading underlying the tests' (Vincent and Cresswell, 1976).

Nevertheless, this type of reading test provided a model for many other tests and appears even in modern psychological batteries as a means of assessing children's reading ability (e.g. *British Ability Scales*, Elliott *et al.*, 1997).

In terms of its vision of the concept of reading, it can be seen in its context of attempting to provide a rapid measure, usable with individuals, to help identify children who were under-performing in an urban education system which was trying to cope with a large number of pupils from impoverished backgrounds. It brought psychometrics into educational measurement for the first time and became a test with great longevity and influence.

Schonell Reading Tests

Just as the First World Was provided the background to the development of Burt's Mental and Scholastic Tests, the Second World War provided the context for the development of the Schonell Reading Tests. These consist of four tests, shown in Table 8.1.

Table 8.1 Schonell Reading Tests

R1	Graded Word Reading Test (GWRT)	Ages 5–15 years
R2	Simple Prose Reading Test (SPRT)	Ages 6–9 years
R3	Silent Reading Test A	Ages 7–11 years
R4	Silent Reading Test B	Ages 9–13 years

The Graded Word Reading Test follows Burt's model almost exactly. There are 100 words, five to a line, with the lines in pairs. Children read the words aloud to the tester until ten successive mistakes are made. The score is the number of words said aloud correctly. This is converted to a Reading Age.

The Simple Prose Reading Test has four paragraphs of prose which are read aloud to the tester. The time taken is recorded. The passage is then removed and several comprehension questions asked. Reading Ages can be derived for word recognition, comprehension and speed.

In a review of the tests undertaken in 1984, Stibbs refers to them as 'self-validating'. They had become such familiar instruments and were so widely used by teachers that 'to say they had content validity would be almost tautologous'. The norms were so long established they were used as benchmarks against which to standardise other tests.

The Graded Word Reading Test is criticised (by Stibbs) for the concept of reading it espouses. This is inferred, rather than stated by the test authors, but seems to be that the essence of reading is recognising words and that only words pronounced correctly are recognised. Recognition is gained through phonic analysis and synthesis together with guessing. This conception had hardly moved on from that of Burt thirty years before.

There were though the other three tests which did provide other measures – comprehension and speed. The conception of reading has become somewhat broader, though only one passage is used and this has relatively mundane subject matter ('My Dog').

The importance of the Schonell tests lies in their acceptance and use by the teaching profession. The survey of test use for the Bullock Report *A Language for Life* (DES, 1975) found that they were by far the most popular reading tests in schools (thirty years after publication!). The Graded Word Reading Test was the most used test in both primary and secondary schools and the two silent reading tests were second and third most popular in secondary schools and fourth and fifth in primary schools. This popularity reflected the tests' use for a wide range of purposes: screening for remedial attention; streaming and setting; monitoring progress of individuals; informing parents and providing transfer information either prior to the move to secondary school or on entry to the secondary school.

With their different measures, there was some scope for the Schonell Reading Tests to give some diagnostic information. However, this function was left to a separate set of diagnostic tests.

Reading Test AD (NFER, 1955) Author A.F. Watts (also Watts-Vernon, 1938)

Reading Test AD has been included in this list as a representative of a large number of multiple-choice sentence-completion tests. These are important because during the 1950s and on into the 60s and 70s, they came to be the most widely used form of group reading test. As such they defined a view of reading comprehension as operating at a sentence level with understanding largely dependent on vocabulary and on word order and the other structures of English. A larger text or authenticity were not regarded as important as the virtues of reliability and ease of marking.

Reading Test AD is a 35 item multiple-choice sentence-completion test. It is speeded, having a short administration time of 15 minutes. The target age group is 8–10-year-olds. An example item is:

The engine driver and the guard left the train on reaching the (door, hill, farm, station, street)

The test was first published in 1955 and is very similar to a series of other NFER reading tests of the period (Reading Test BD for 7–11-year-olds; Reading Test EH1 for 11–15-year-olds). However, it had formerly been known as Sentence Reading Test 1 and had been used in an enquiry of the standards of reading conducted in Kent in 1954 (Morris, 1959).

The manual of the published test gave no indication of its intended purpose, but its first use and the author give the clue to this. It was designed as a test for use in surveys and monitoring of standards. As such its reliability and ease (cheapness) of marking were important and its validity (again no comments on this in the manual) reflect a behaviourist view of reading, as in the USA at the time (Pearson and Hamm, this volume).

Watts was also an author of the Watts-Vernon test[1] which was used in national surveys of schoolchildren in England and Wales. It was first developed in 1938 and was used in national surveys in 1948, 1952, 1956, 1961, 1964 and 1970–71. Brooks *et al.*, (1995) summarises the results of these surveys as showing that average reading score rose slightly between 1948 and 1952 (the improvement being attributed to recovery of the education system after the war years) followed by a period of little change. The stability, as measured by other tests, in fact continued until around 1987 and 1988, when a decline was perceived. The successor test in use for national surveys, NS6, was also a multiple-choice sentence completion test.

The failure for reading scores to increase, despite periods of increased expenditure on education was one of the reasons for the introduction of a National Curriculum in England and Wales and was still being cited by a government minister in 2003 as a reason for continuing with a programme of National Curriculum Assessment (including reading tests) (Miliband, 2003). It is of interest, but idle to speculate, that one reason for the lack of an increase in scores may have been that the monitoring tests espoused a different view of reading attainment than that current in primary schools. A test used in this way with no accountability for individual schools had little backwash effect on teaching and consequently the efforts of schools may not have been directed to the skills required for sentence completion tests.

Reading Test AD differed from the earlier tests also in the manner of its results. Rather than reading ages (easily interpretable by teachers but statistically suspect), the outcomes were standardised scores, normalised and age-adjusted with a neat mean of 100 and standard deviation of 15. These have very nice statistical properties, useful in averaging and manipulation for survey results, but much less intuitively useful for teachers.

Successors to these sentence completion tests remain in use in the new millennium. Two examples are the Suffolk Reading Test (Hagley, 1987) and The Group Reading Test (Macmillan Test Unit, 1997) which is currently very popular.

An important successor test, which might have stood alone in this listing, except that it offers little really new in terms of its conception of reading is Young's Group Reading Test. This is a test for the transition from infant to junior school (now years 2 and 3; 6–8-year-olds). It was published in 1968, restandardised in the late 1970s, with a second edition in 1980. Its importance lies in that by 1979, 33 local education authorities (LEAs) used this test for monitoring and record-keeping purposes (about a third of the LEAs at that time). As such and as a rapidly administered (13 minutes) multiple-choice sentence completion test it is clearly in the Watts-Vernon, NS6, Reading Test AD mould. The innovation was the first section where pictures are given and the child must circle the word matching the picture. Here the construct of reading therefore incorporates not only recognising the written word but identifying the object in the picture which must be matched. The manual gives no evidence of construct or content validity but does offer evidence of concurrent and predictive validity with impressive correlations to a range of other reading tests.

Neale Analysis of Reading Ability

The Neale Analysis of Reading Ability is an individual test of reading in which the child must read aloud a complete narrative passage. This process provides measures of their rate of reading, accuracy and comprehension. There are three parallel forms, each with six passages. The passages are ordered in terms of difficulty as indicated by length, vocabulary and sentence structure. There are criteria for which passage to begin the test with and for stopping the test, providing a measure of tailored testing. For each passage, the time taken to read it is measured and recorded; scores from the passages being combined to give an overall measure of rate of reading. As the child reads, the tester records errors on a record sheet and codes these into six types of error in oral reading (mispronunciations, substitutions, refusals, additions, omissions, reversals). Finally, a set of comprehensive questions are asked and the number correct provides a raw score for comprehension.

All three measures can be converted, using tables, to give reading ages for accuracy, rate and comprehension.

The first edition of the Neale Analysis was published in 1958 and arose from Marie Neale's PhD thesis undertaken at Birmingham University in the early 1950s. (When the present author met Neale during the 1990s as part of discussions about the second edition, she spoke of the work she did alone for the standardisation, cycling along snowy country lanes to village schools to test their pupils.)

The manual gives a clear purpose for the test as to 'provide a sympathetic and stimulating situation in which (the child's) difficulties, weaknesses, types of error, persistence and attitudes could be assessed'. The miscue analysis in the accuracy assessment, the provision of three measures and the inclusion in the package of a further set of optional supplementary diagnostic tests all point clearly to its conception as a diagnostic instrument, intended to be of use to classroom teachers in a clinical informative sense. Again, the test is reflecting its times with its post-war concerns to raise levels of literacy following a long period of disruption of the educational process. The means of doing this is through improving the knowledge that teachers had about the profile of skills of their pupils, helping them to decide on the next steps.

With this diagnostic intent, the conception of reading has become broader than in any of the previous tests described. The intention is that the reading experience should be authentic. Children read whole passages from a reader which is designed to appear as a children's book with illustrations, large print and white space on the page. The manner of testing, too, is authentically like classroom practice of the child reading to an adult. The provision of parallel forms allows teachers to conduct investigations, even to use the material for teaching after the test and yet still re-assess the child in the future in the same way and with the same construct of reading.

For these reasons, the Neale Analysis remained popular with teachers through to the 1980s. By then, Marie Neale had emigrated to Australia where she produced a second edition (Neale, 1988). This was re-imported, revised and restandardised for British use (Neale *et al.*, 1989).

Gap Reading Comprehension Test and Gapadol Reading Comprehension Test

In the 1960s and 1970s, a new form of assessment of reading comprehension began to appear. This was the cloze procedure credited as the invention of W.L. Taylor.[2] The procedure had originally been developed by Taylor (1953) as a means of estimating the readability of children's books. Words are removed from a passage in a systematic manner (say every 5th word) and the readability of the text was defined as the ease of supplying the missing words. This soon became extended into a method of assessing the persons supplying the words rather than the readability of the passage. As Pearson (this volume) describes, the classic cloze procedure has evolved in many directions in terms of the manner of selecting the deleted words and the level of assistance in providing the missing word. This can extend from no clues, through providing the first letter, to giving several multiple-choice alternatives.

In the UK, the first influential tests to use cloze for native speakers were the Gap and Gapadol tests. (The qualification of 'native speakers' is required since cloze was and remains, much more important in tests of English as an additional/foreign/second language.) In fact, the two tests were Australian in origin, devised by John McLeod. Each was adapted for British use by a second author.

The Gap Reading Comprehension Test consists of a series of short passages of increasing difficulty. It has two forms: B with seven passages and R with eight. The tests use a modified cloze procedure, having 44 gaps at irregular intervals. The child has to write in the missing words. For scoring, there is one acceptable word for each gap. This was determined during development as the response of 'expert readers' (university undergraduates). Incorrect spelling is permitted but the word must be grammatically correct. The test is aimed at primary school pupils, aged 8–12 years. British norms were obtained from Scotland, Wales and England.

The Gapadol Reading Comprehension Test is very similar to the Gap test, but it covers a wider age range: from 7 to 17. There is no UK standardisation data. For this test there are again two forms, but each with eight passages, including practice. The cloze gaps are at irregular intervals with 83 in one form and 81 in the other. The student writes a word into each gap and if this matches that of the 'first class readers' a mark is scored. Details are given in McLeod and Anderson (1970).

These two tests do not appear ever to have obtained a wide set of users. Their importance lies in their introduction of a new technique (to teachers as well as testers) that appeared to be a truer measure of reading comprehension than methods requiring a mediating vehicle like an open-ended or multiple-choice question on the text. Certainly, this is the claim made in the manual of the Gap test: 'the only stimulus to which the child must respond is the reading passage itself; there are no extraneous questions to constitute an intervening variable'. This is a more valid test of reading comprehension than completing questions based on a written passage.

The popularity of cloze techniques as assessments for second language learners arises from the fact that the technique gives information on the extent to which grammatical processes are understood. Taylor (1953) himself used the notion of 'grammatical expectation' to justify the validity of cloze. Some combinations of words are more likely than others: 'Merry Christmas' is more likely than 'Merry Birthday'. It is not easy to explain why (as anyone who tries to explain English to non-native speakers knows) but custom, history and cliché contribute to certain combinations being more probable. A second factor is redundancy. Taylor cites 'A man is coming this way now' as having a great deal of redundancy. The singular 'man' is signalled three times ('a', 'man' and 'is'), the present tense twice ('is' and 'now'), direction twice ('coming' and 'this way'). He attributes probability differences in grammatical expectation to this redundancy.

For many purposes, cloze tests have drawbacks. Classic cloze tests are tedious to mark and despite demonstrations of reliability, there is the constant carping that other words are possible in the gaps than those produced by the expert/first class readers.

Perhaps for these reasons, there are few (if any) pure classic cloze tests in use now. However, variants of the cloze technique occur in many tests of reading comprehension, for example key stage 2 National Curriculum tests in England which frequently incorporate a cloze retelling of a passage or text.

Edinburgh Reading Tests

The construction of these tests was undertaken in the belief that instruments of this kind, designed for use by teachers and requiring no special psychological expertise in administration or in interpretation of results, were needed urgently to assist in the teaching of reading.

In the light of the results she [the teacher] *can adapt her methods and choose her teaching material to remedy a weakness or satisfy a strength.*

These quotations from the early manuals of the Edinburgh Reading Tests sets out the purpose of the tests and their attempt at a unique selling point. If earlier published tests had aspired to be diagnostic, it was through looking at reading rate, accuracy and understanding separately. In contrast, the Edinburgh Reading Tests attempted to have many sub-tests and hence to give detailed diagnostic information on the processes of reading. Through this means, it was 'hoped in particular that the tests will help the primary school teacher to ensure that all her pupils, within reason, pass to the secondary school with no outstanding reading disability'.

This was (and is) an extremely laudable aim. It reflects the commissioning of the tests in the early 1970s by the Scottish Education Department and the Educational Institute of Scotland (a professional association of teachers).

The Edinburgh Reading Tests have four 'stages' each for a different age group and each with a different set of sub-tests, as shown in Table 8.2.

Table 8.2 The Edinburgh Reading Tests

Stage	Ages	Content
1	7.0–9.0	Vocabulary, Syntax, Sequences and Comprehension
2	8.6–10.6	Vocabulary, Comprehension of Sequences, Retention of Significant Details, Use of Context, Reading Rate and Comprehension of Essential Ideas
3	10.0–12.6	Reading for Facts, Comprehension of Sequences, Retention of Main Ideas, Comprehension of Points of View and Vocabulary
4	12.0–16.0	Skimming, Vocabulary, Reading for Facts, Points of View and Comprehension

Each sub-test in each stage contains two or three different types of item and these also develop across the stages. For some scales, this has a type of logic. In vocabulary for example, there is:

- recognition of pictures (Stage 1)

- sentence completion (Stages 1, 2 and 3)

- selection of a word to give the meaning of a phrase (Stage 2)

- selection of a word or phrase to fit a precis (Stage 3)

- synonyms (Stages 3 and 4).

However, most sub-tests do not have such a systematic development across the stages.

The summation of the various sub-tests leads to overall test scores which give rise to 'deviation quotients' (standardised scores or reading ages) giving an overall measure of ability in reading. However, in line with the stated purposes of the tests, users can compile a subtest profile and plot this on a chart. Teachers are then able to identify those pupils' results which are 'sufficiently exceptional to demand special attention'. This can be done for individuals or whole classes.

Through its wide range of sub-tests and its approach to profiling reading, the Edinburgh Tests attempted to provide rich information on the skills of each pupil and to relate this to helpful diagnostic information, leading to improvements in children learning to read.

The approach was essentially an atomised and psychometric one, which had the intention of providing differentiated information. However, this was not achieved in a statistical sense. The subtests tend to be highly correlated and therefore not to provide distinctive or useful diagnostic information. This leads even the authors to conclude that 'children in general do equally well or poorly on all the sub-tests and the various reading tasks involve the same competencies to a high degree' (e.g. Stage 3 manual (Moray House College of Education (1981, p.28)).

The importance of the Edinburgh Reading Tests lies in their attempt to identify the underlying processes of reading and to separate them out in a helpful diagnostic way. This work seems to have been guided initially by agreements on the theoretical structure by the steering committee. However, it was not ratified and supported by the psychometric examinations of structure, leading the authors back to a view of reading as a unified process.

The large role of a government department and a teachers' association in commissioning the tests and then steering their development illustrates the growing role of society's representatives in determining the nature of reading as a construct. However, the failure to identify psychometrically rigorous and useful sub-tests making up reading, may also have been influential in causing later individuals and groups to regard reading as a unified construct and define their tests accordingly.

APU Reading Assessment National Surveys

In the mid 1970s a trend began in England (or perhaps the UK as a whole) to recognise the importance of education in promoting the economic well-being of the country. A debate on the need for improvements in education was begun by the Prime Minister, James Callaghan, with an important speech at Ruskin College in 1976.

One strand in this concern was the establishment of a commission of enquiry into the teaching of English. The Bullock committee published their report, *A Language for Life* in 1975. This included a review of evidence from earlier national surveys or reading and the conclusion that there was a need for a new type of test which would indicate the extent to which pupils had developed a proficiency in reading, sufficient to serve their personal and social needs. They proposed that new instruments should be developed which would 'embrace teaching objectives for the entire ability range'. Tests should also draw on a variety of sources to ensure an extensive coverage, rather than focusing narrowly on a single text.

In this they were echoing the worldwide shift in thinking about the nature of literacy. La Fontaine (2004) describes this as the move from comprehension to literacy. In the context of international comparative studies, definitions of reading broadened so that the concept became one of a process which regards comprehension as the outcome of an interaction between the text and the reader's previous knowledge, a process of construction. However, outside this, the pragmatic requirements of society are also relevant. This change reflected the influence of the 'response to literature' movement and the new focus on literacy as relating to a wide range of text types. This type of definition became the currency of international survey of reading and alongside this, the same movement in definition seems to have taken place within the UK.

One of the recommendations of the Bullock report was to advocate a proper programme of monitoring of standards of literacy. The government responded by establishing monitoring in English, mathematics, science and, briefly, foreign languages. The surveys were to be undertaken by an Assessment of Performance Unit (APU). For English the content of the survey was determined by a 'Language Steering Group' which comprised teachers, members of Her Majesty's Inspectorate of Schools (HMIS), LEA advisers and academics (two professors of linguistics). This group addressed theoretical and practical issues, including questions such as the following.

- How would the tests represent the range of reading activities that children might be engaged in?

- What account, if any, should be taken of the many inconclusive attempts to differentiate the so called 'sub-skills' in reading? (This phrasing gives a clue to what would be decided in relation to this issue! It is probably a reference to the Edinburgh Reading Tests.)

- To what extent is it appropriate in tests of reading to require pupils to provide extended written answers?

The resolution of these issues was to reject reading 'sub-skills' and any attempt to isolate factors underlying reading. Comprehension was said to be as complex as thinking itself and therefore no model of the reading process was possible. The previous use of sentence completion tests was rejected in favour of tests which had coherence in content and structure. Three categories of material were used in the surveys: works of reference, works of literature, and everyday reading materials which pupils would encounter for practical purposes in everyday life (comics, newspapers, forms, notices, brochures, instructions etc.). The reading stimulus material consisted of booklets which were intended to be naturalistic, with coherent organisation in terms of content and structure, including contents pages, indexes, chapters etc. The works of literature used were complete, rather than extracts, and covered a range of genres such as short stories and poems.

Attempts were made to include different types of response to the questions asked about the stimulus material. Most questions required a written response, but pupils also had to complete forms, fill in tables, label diagrams, make notes, prepare summaries and design posters. The stated guiding principle was that the tasks should be similar to those an experienced teacher would be likely to ask, taking into account the subject matter, form and function of the reading material.

This expansive approach to the assessment of reading (and the definition of reading) was possible because of the purpose of the exercise as a national survey with many tests each being used with a defined randomly selected group of pupils. Five surveys of reading were undertaken each year from 1979 to 1983, with all involving both 11- and 15-year-olds, chosen as the end points of primary and secondary schooling. A full account of the APU Language Monitoring Programme can be found in Gorman *et al.* (1988). In addition to reading, writing and speaking and listening were also surveyed.

In terms of a definition of reading to be assessed, the APU tests were important in a number of ways. They gave an even greater emphasis to the use of actual or realistic material, reflecting the notion of an actual purposeful activity, rather than an abstraction or simulation as in most of the earlier tests. The range of genres was also important, moving away from a constant reliance on story and narrative. Finally, the range of questioning was broadened and the styles of responding became more varied. To some extent, this represented the introduction of a more literary approach in which pupils were expected to understand the roles and meanings of test types and also provide a personal response.

The 'official' nature of the material, as a government-sponsored project led to a process for defining the construct of reading which was based on consensus among a variety of representatives. This contrasts with the earlier national surveys where the test used was devised by a single researcher. This democratisation and centralisation of the process illustrates the view taken here that the constructs of reading assessed over the years have reflected the needs of both the educative endeavour and wide society, reflecting their concerns at a given time and the prevailing views of the functions of the assessment.

In historical terms, the APU monitoring programme was not long-lived. It functioned from 1979 to about 1989, unlike its US cousin NAEP, which has continued to the present.

The government's decision to cease national monitoring through a low-stakes survey-based approach signalled the end of a tolerant monitoring approach to educational outcomes and the beginning of an evolution to a process which became a high-stakes accountability system based on population testing.

Any evaluation of the success of APU can be contentious. However, its demise points to a failure (in the view of government) to provide useful information on the education system. Nor did it provide the pressure desired of an accountability system in promulgating change. What it was successful in (and this was done too in science and mathematics) was developing new forms of educational assessment and gaining acceptance of these.

When National Curriculum testing of English for 11-year-olds was introduced, the style of reading tests specified and developed followed closely the models pioneered by the APU assessment. The tests (see chapter 14 for a current description) are necessarily narrower than in the full survey which included many booklets of stimulus material. However, each year the National Curriculum tests feature a booklet containing three or four types of texts, linked thematically. The questions have a range of styles from multiple-choice to those requiring extended text answers, via matching the completion of tables and single sentences. It is in this influence on the high-stakes assessment which replaced it that the influence of the APU on reading assessment survives.

Key Stage 1 National Curriculum Reading Assessment (1990–present)

In 1989, the structure and responsibility for education in England and Wales received its biggest change for forty years. A National Curriculum was introduced, passing responsibility for what was taught from local control by teachers, schools and LEAs to central government. This was intended to radically alter the nature of compulsory education in the UK. The genesis of the reform was concerns over many aspects of the process of schooling and its outcomes. There was a growing view that despite increases in resources, standards of attainment had not improved since the Second World War. Indeed, national surveys seemed to support such a view (Brooks *et al.*, 1995). This poor achievement was in contrast to students in other countries and low ability students were thought to be most at risk, giving rise to very wide ranges of attainment. Prior to that time, teachers, schools and local education authorities had determined the curriculum in each locality, leading to large variations in standards. During the 1970s, some pedagogic practices received high levels of publicity and condemnation. In other spheres of government, the ideology of the time had been based on the introduction of market forces in order to raise standards and this philosophy was now to be applied to education.

The National Curriculum approach to English was set out in the Cox proposals (DES and WO, 1989) and continues to underlie the curriculum, even after several revisions.

There is a vision of children developing as independent readers, writers, speakers and listeners. The point and purpose of language use is regarded as inseparable from the acquisition of skills. Real audiences, genuine purposes and stimulating texts are requirements both for production of work in the classroom and for assessment.

Without acknowledgement, it is clear that these notions had drawn on the Bullock (1975) view of language and more deeply embedded, the change from a psychological view of reading to a literary one. Sainsbury (1996) sets out the tensions involved in the development of a reading test for 7-year-olds to meet this new type of requirement.

The assessment has different tasks for children operating at different National Curriculum levels. Hence, there is immediately a tailoring of the demand according to the teacher's assessment. For level 1 (the lowest level), the reading activity takes the form of a discussion of a book chosen by the child from a short list. This is really an assessment of emergent reading since it addresses the child's interest in books, concept of print and recognition of letters and words. With revisions to the National Curriculum, from 1996, more evidence of the child's ability to read text with support was required.

The level 2 task had some of the same features as that for level 1. At level 2, there is not yet an expectation that a child can read silently and independently. This makes a reading aloud assessment the natural approach and gives opportunities for a miscue analysis. A list of books was provided to schools and the teacher had to select a book to use in assessing each child, matching their interests so that a best performance could be produced. The teacher had to read through the beginning of the book, with the child, until a specific set passage was reached. These set passages were of about 100 words. The child then reads the passage with the teacher recording incorrectly read words, omissions, self-corrections, words the teacher had to provide and phonic attempts at unfamiliar words. This provides a simplified form of a miscue analysis.

This test broke new ground in several ways. First, it is very unusual in allowing a range of stimulus material in order to allow a reflection of children's interests and to allow them to show 'best performance'. As such it was an attempt to meet the prevailing theories of assessment of the 1980s, enunciated first by Wood (1986). Educational assessment should:

- deal with the individual's achievement relative to himself rather than to others

- seek to test for competence rather than for intelligence

- take place in relatively uncontrolled conditions and so not produce 'well-behaved' data

- look for 'best' rather than 'typical' performances

- be most effective when rules and regulations characteristic of standardised testing are relaxed

- embody a constructive outlook on assessment where the aim is to help rather than sentence the individual.

This though gives rise to a conflict between validity and reliability. With the use of differing passages, a variety of answers, an interactive and relaxed format for the child and reliance on teacher judgement, the key stage 1 reading tasks seemed not to be the type of assessment which would survive in a high-stakes accountability regime (as became the case in England). In the early years, they were attacked in both the press ('a woolly-minded fudge' – *TES*, 1991) and by academic psychologists (Pumphrey and Elliott, 1991). Yet, they have survived from 1991 through to 2004. Over this period, there have been changes. The initial tasks were tied closely to the criterion-referenced statements of the first incarnation of the National Curriculum, but from 1996 the task was updated to reflect a more holistic approach of the revised National Curriculum. The need for standardisation, heightened by accountability was met through the introduction of a formal written test, at first taken voluntarily, at the choice of teachers, then becoming compulsory. In 2004, a pilot of key stage 1 assessments allowed greater flexibility in the timing and conduct of the tasks, taking them back to their origins. This is to become the procedure for all schools from 2005.

In some ways, the task with its running records and miscue analysis was a continuation of the approach in the Neale Analysis and other reading-aloud tests. Such a running record approach was not new and was widely recommended before the introduction of the National Curriculum. It was not, however, widely used. In the first pilots for the National Curriculum tests, its use was emphasised and it received a great deal of attention at training sessions. As a result, most infant teachers became proficient at using the running record and its diagnostic value was recognised by teachers and LEA advisers. This helped the task to survive, rather than being replaced completely by a simple written test.

The importance of the key stage 1 reading task for level 2 is in its authenticity for the classroom environment. It allows choice and endeavours to allow children to show their best attainment. It provides some diagnostic information, yet functions in a high-stakes environment. All schools in England must use it, so it has had a wide impact in terms of training teachers and forming their attitudes to the assessment of reading. For all these reasons, it has to be seen as an important contribution to current understandings of the concept of reading, for young children.

Conclusion

This listing of significant reading tests has spanned about ninety years of educational assessment. It has included tests intended for screening, supporting teaching, diagnosis, surveys and monitoring and, eventually, accountability. The tests themselves have moved from word-level through sentence level to whole texts.[3] In their scope and demand on students they are very different. Yet some characteristics remain fairly constant. Throughout, from Burt onwards through to the key stage tests there is an overt desire to be fair to the children. Material, whether it is words, sentences or texts, was selected to be familiar to the children and to be accessible to them. In all cases, the educational purpose of the tests was laudable, from Burt's desire to prevent misplacement of children in schools for the mentally deficient through desires to improve the teaching of reading (Schonell, Neale, Edinburgh) to attempts to support the curriculum (APU tests) and provide information to parents and schools (key stage tests). Where they differ is in the approach taken to reading as a construct. They move from attempts to simplify and break up the reading process, a psychological approach, to attempts to have naturalistic texts with purpose to the reading, a constructivist and literary approach. These reflect the needs of the education systems of the times and also the view of those controlling the test construction. This gradually moved from individuals (often psychologists) like Cyril Burt, Fred Schonell and Marie Neale to representatives of government, committees and society's representatives (Edinburgh, APU and key stage tests).

The tests included in this account vary a great deal, in a sort of progression. Yet, they are all called reading tests and considered to be so. In each case, their longevity and wide use demonstrates that they have been accepted as measuring reading. In terms of validity (as elaborated by Sainsbury in this volume), they all represent some construct which is or was acceptable to society of the time. It could be argued that the essential process of reading has not changed over this time. At each stage, it still demanded decoding of symbols, recognition of words and extraction of meaning from sentences and texts. But in different ages the emphasis has been on different parts of this process leading the tests to change over the eighty years. What was measured may well have been related to the capabilities of the majority of children at the time, but this in itself was a reflection of the established curriculum and its teaching. This chapter has attempted to show that the acceptability of the construct (in its own time) arises from its adoption by individuals or groups empowered by society to devise or accept the prevailing notion of reading. Such a notion can come from careful academic study, referenced and scientific in nature, or from the spirit of the times, the current view among those interested in the question. That seems to be the case to a greater extent with the later tests, defined and controlled by committees established by governments.

The significant assessments of reading in the UK over the last century each reflect a prevailing definition of reading reflecting the needs of society of the time, as perceived by some empowered individual(s). This is the essence of their construct validity.

References

Brooks, G., Foxman, D. and Gorman, T. (1995). *Standards in Literacy and Numeracy: 1948–1994* (NCE Briefing New Series 7). London: National Commission on Education.
Burt, C. (1921). *Mental and Scholastic Tests*. London: King and Staples.
Department of Education and Science (1975). *A Language for Life* (Bullock Report). London: HMSO.

Department of Education and Science and Welsh Office (1989). *English in the National Curriculum*. London: HMSO.

Elliott, C. with Smith, P. and McCulloch, K. (1997). *British Ability Scales II*. Windsor: nferNelson.

Gorman, T.P. *et al.* (1988). *Language Performance in Schools: Review of APU Language Monitoring, 1979–1983*. London: HMSO.

Hagley, F. (1987). *Suffolk Reading Scale*. Windsor: nferNelson.

Hearnshaw, L. (1979). *Cyril Burt: Psychologist*. London: Hodder and Stoughton.

La Fontaine, D. (2004). 'From comprehension to literacy: thirty years of reading assessment.' In: Moskowitz, J. and Stephens, M. (Eds) *Comparing Learning Outcomes: International Assessment and Education Policy*. London: RoutledgeFalmer.

Macmillan Test Unit (1997). *Group Reading Test II (6–14)*. Windsor: nferNelson.

McLeod, J. and Anderson, J. (1970). 'An approach to the assessment of reading ability through information transmissions', *Journal of Reading Behavior*, **2**, 116–43.

Miliband, D. (2003). 'Don't believe the NUT's testing myths', *Times Educ. Suppl.*, 4558, 14 November, 19.

Morris, J. (1959). *Reading in the Primary School: an Investigation into Standards of Reading and their Association with Primary School Characteristics*. London: Newnes Educational Publishing.

Pumphrey, P. and Elliott, C. (1991). 'A house of cards?' *Times Educ. Suppl.*, 3905, 3 May.

Sainsbury, M. (1996). 'Assessing English.' In: Sainsbury, M. (Ed) *SATS the Inside Story: The Development of the First National Assessments for Seven-year-olds, 1989–1995*. Slough: NFER.

Stibbs, A. (1984). 'Review of Schonell Reading Tests.' In: Levy, P. and Goldstein, H. (Eds) *Tests in Education: A Book of Critical Reviews*. London: Academic Press.

Taylor, W.L. (1953). 'Cloze procedure: a tool for measuring readability', *Journalism Quarterly*, **30**, 415–33.

Turner, M. (1990a). 'A closed book', *Times Educ. Suppl.*, 20 July.

Turner, M. (1990b). *Sponsored Reading Failure*. Warlingham: Warlingham Park School, IPSET Education Unit.

Vincent, D. and Cresswell, M. (1976). *Reading Tests in the Classroom*. Slough: NFER.

Wood, R. (1986). 'The agenda for educational measurement.' In: Nuttall, D.L. (Ed) *Assessing Educational Achievement*. London: Falmer Press.

Reading tests

Burt Word Reading Test

Burt, C. (1921). *Mental and Scholastic Tests*. London: King and Staples.

Scottish Council for Research in Education (1976). *The Burt Word Reading Test 1974 Revision*. London: Hodder and Stoughton.

Schonell Reading Tests

Schonell, F.J. and Goodacre, E. (1974). *The Psychology and Teaching of Reading*. Fifth edn. Edinburgh: Oliver and Boyd.

Reading Test AD

Watts, A.F. (1955). *Reading Test AD*. Windsor: NFER.

Neale Analysis of Reading Ability

Neale, M.D. (1958). *Neale Analysis of Reading Ability*. Basingstoke: Macmillan Education.
Neale, M.D. (1988). *Neale Analysis of Reading Ability – Revised Australian Edition*. Melbourne: Australian Council for Educational Research.
Neale, M.D. (1989). *Neale Analysis of Reading Ability: Revised British Edition* (British Adaptation and Standardization by Una Christophers and Chris Whetton). Windsor: nferNelson.

Gap and Gapadol Tests

McLeod, J. (1970). *Gap Reading Comprehension Test*. London: Heinemann.
McLeod, J. and Anderson J. (1973). *Gapadol Reading Comprehension Test*. London: Heinemann.

Edinburgh Reading Tests

Moray House College of Education (1981). *Edinburgh Reading Tests Stage 3*. Second edn. London: Hodder and Stoughton.
University of Edinburgh, The Godfrey Thomson Unit (1977). *Edinburgh Reading Tests Stage 1*. London: Hodder and Stoughton. (Third edn. 2002).
University of Edinburgh, The Godfrey Thomson Unit (1977) *Edinburgh Reading Tests Stage 2*. London: Hodder and Stoughton. (Second edn. 1980, fourth edn. 2002).
University of Edinburgh, The Godfrey Thomson Unit (1977). *Edinburgh Reading Tests Stage 3*. London: Hodder and Stoughton. (Third edn. 2002).

APU Reading Assessment National Surveys

The APU Tests were not published as separate entities. Extracts appear in the following reports, together with commentaries on pupils' performances.

Gorman, T.P. *et al*. (1981). *Language Performance in Schools: Primary Survey Report No. 1* (APU Survey). London: HMSO.

Gorman, T.P. *et al*. (1982). *Language Performance in Schools: Primary Survey Report No.2* (APU Survey). London: HMSO.

Gorman, T.P. *et al*. (1983). *Language Performance in Schools: Secondary Survey Report No.1* (APU Survey). London: HMSO.

Gorman, T.P. *et al*. (1983). *Language Performance in Schools: Secondary Survey Report No.2* (APU Survey). London: HMSO.

Gorman, T.P. *et al*. (1988). *Language Performance in Schools: Review of APU Language Monitoring 1979–1983*. London: HMSO.

Key Stage 1 Reading Tasks

Key stage 1 National Curriculum Reading Assessment – new tasks published every year.

School Examinations and Assessment Council (SEAC) (1991–1993).

School Curriculum and Assessment Authority (SCAA) and Curriculum and Assessment Authority for Wales (ACCAC) (1994–1995).

Qualifications and Curriculum Authority (QCA) and Curriculum and Assessment Authority for Wales (ACCAC) (1996–1999).

Qualifications and Curriculum Authority (QCA) (2000–2004).

Notes

1. Strangely, for such an important test, it is never referenced in full, and no publication details can be given.

2. During research for this paper, the author examined Cyril Burt's 1921 edition of *Mental and Scholastic Tests*. This includes many psychological and educational tests and techniques. Among these is a type of tests called by Burt 'Completion' which required the entry of words into blanks in a piece of continuous narrative text. This is used as a measure of intelligence rather than reading. Unfortunately without a reference, Burt attributes the style of test to Ebbinghaus the German psychologist (1850–1909). It seems that the basic technique of cloze tests was familiar at least forty years before its generally ascribed invention and possibly long before that.

3. This survey describes the popular tests, that is those mostly used. In fact many of the styles of test which followed (Schonell, Neale and Edinburgh) were included in Burt's *Mental and Scholastic Tests*, but were not widely taken up. The progression referred to was not one of invention but of use.

9 Lessons of the GCSE English '100 per cent coursework' option, 1986–1993

Paul Thompson

Many schools, particularly those with a poor academic track record, have opted for 100 per cent course work. The replacement of formal examinations by 100 per cent course work is surely the heart of the corruption.

(Stoll, 1988, p.34)

In 1986, a new kind of public examination was launched for all 16-year-olds in England and Wales. Neither the introduction of the General Certificate of Secondary Education (GCSE), nor the abolition of its 100 per cent coursework options in 1993, escaped controversy. Responding to allegations that GCSE 100 per cent coursework was subject to abuse, exam boards in England and Wales were required in 1993 to introduce 'a more reliable system of assessment'. The 1988 Education Reform Act had introduced a higher degree of 'public accountability'. Nationally published league tables were instated for the purpose of school comparison. Those at the bottom would be publicly 'named and shamed'. In the particular field of GCSE assessment, policymakers in the early nineties argued that the abolition of 100 per cent coursework would increase test reliability through a higher quality of standardisation in terms of questions asked, time allocated for answers and mark schemes.

Two decades later, the prospect for high stakes testing is far less positive. It is conventional wisdom within the profession that 'teaching to the test' skews the curriculum. Many educationalists consider that the tail of assessment is wagging the curriculum dog. There is also a major crisis in the recruitment of markers: Edexcel, for example, one of England's biggest exam boards, admitted that it regularly used non-teaching staff to mark papers where there was a shortage of practitioners (Curtis and Smithers, 2005).

On the website of English 21, which hosts a consultation by the Qualifications and Curriculum Authority (QCA) on the possible shape of English in 2015, English Officer Paul Wright comments:

The current high-stakes position of exams rests on the assumption that they deliver the most reliable comparability of standards and are easily understood by the public. Yet there remains a widespread perception that standards are falling. It may be time to re-examine the idea that examinations are the only way to ensure credibility with the public and media.

(Wright, 2005)

Until fairly recently, it looked as though high-stakes testing was a fixture in English education. Today the picture is changing. A QCA and DfES-funded project, 'Monitoring Pupils' Progress in English at KS3', has been working since 2003 to 'improve the quality, regularity and reliability of teacher assessment throughout KS3' through the development of diagnostic approaches which are based on the principle of portfolio assessment (QCA, 2004). Enthusiasm for formative assessment has never apparently been greater. In the first year of its introduction as a strand in the KS3 National Strategy (2004–5), 'Assessment for Learning' was chosen by 80 per cent of schools as their key whole school priority, suggesting considerable hunger for a more responsive assessment approach, no doubt partly in order to counteract the negative, constraining backwash of summative National Curriculum tests.

Reflecting the urgency of this debate, Paul Wright's introductory statement to the assessment section of the English 21 website calls for a reassessment of the teacher's position in the assessment process and seeks to re-evaluate the sharp prevailing distinction between formative and summative assessment practices:

> *Are there ways of making formative and summative assessment more complementary, rather than seeing them in opposition? We need to explore ways to harness the detailed knowledge teachers have of their pupils as learners in ways that will help them progress as well as being accountable to national standards.*

Many older English teachers would argue that it was precisely this productive balance which we had twenty years ago in GCSE English 100 per cent coursework assessment. In fact, '100 per cent coursework' was something of a misnomer: all such schemes actually included at least one assignment conducted under controlled conditions and all syllabuses were subject to internal and external moderation procedures. Of course, the system had weaknesses as well as strengths. The purpose of this chapter is to review them in order to draw some lessons for the future of assessment at GCSE level in English and English Literature. What was the nature of this assessment approach and how did it impact on candidates' learning experiences? What lessons can be learned from a system of assessment and a curriculum which were primarily in the hands of teachers?

Principles of 100 per cent coursework

GCSE English adopted a unitary approach. It replaced the General Certificate of Education (GCE) 'O' level English and Certificate of Secondary Education (CSE) English which had examined the top 60 per cent of the school population. The bottom 40 per cent had not been entered for examinations at all. GCSE, by contrast, aimed to accommodate all candidates. The earliest GCSE English syllabuses offered both 100 per cent coursework and 50–50 options (i.e. 50 per cent examination and 50 per cent coursework). Neither emerged 'out of the blue' in 1986. Both represented the culmination of developments which had been taking place in English throughout the 1970s and early

1980s, particularly in lower school English. The introduction of GCSE English allowed teachers to extend some of the good practice current in the lower school syllabus into examination work:

> *Methods of cooperative study, the focus on oral communication, drafting and editing of written assignments and the emphasis on the individual selection of reading matter, for example, are common experiences for many pupils in the early years of the secondary school. GCSE has encouraged teachers to experiment further with such approaches with all age groups, with the result that the secondary English course should become a coherent whole; GCSE will not be seen as a bolt-on necessity but a natural development of what has preceded it.*

(Wainhouse, 1989, p.80)

'Whole language' approaches to literacy education and a spirit of integration had been paramount in the eighties (Newman, 1985). GCSE English and English Literature came to be regarded as a single unified course which could nevertheless lead to a grade in two separate subjects. The GCSE English Criteria explained that English should be regarded as 'a single unified course' in which spoken and written work blended seamlessly. Assessment objectives in English were considered to be interdependent and could be tested both through speech and writing. (Although students could study the same texts for both subjects, the same pieces of work could not be submitted for both 'exams'.) The aim was to establish an integrated course which did not artificially separate the four language modes – speaking, listening, reading and writing. It was hoped that this would enable a wider range of integrated, realistic and purposeful classroom activities. There was a renewed emphasis on English as meaningful communication, carried out for genuine purposes.

Candidates were expected to produce a folder of work over the five terms of the course which involved both formal and informal speaking and listening, study of a wide variety of reading (including complete non-literary as well as literary texts) and a wide range of writing (including stories, reports and letters). 'The writing must include written response to reading and this must range from the closed response of ... a report of some kind to the more open-ended response of a piece of imaginative writing' (Chilver 1987, p.9). All syllabuses included an element of wider reading. Although coverage of Shakespeare was not compulsory, study of a minimum of five or six texts in three genres was expected. Some response to unseen texts was required under controlled conditions although structured tests could not account for more than 20 per cent of the syllabus.

The approach was positive. Teachers were encouraged to differentiate by task where necessary in order to give candidates every chance to display their ability. A range of assignment choices was often offered to students who also had a certain amount of freedom in deciding which evidence would be submitted for their final 'folder'. The notion of 'differentiation by outcome' was used to explain how candidates of differing levels of ability could respond to a common question in a variety of different ways, ranging from the basic to the advanced. This seemed to be particularly suitable in English where, given careful thought, it seemed relatively easy to design common tasks which gave candidates across the whole range of ability the opportunity to do their best.

The end of set-text prescription and the broadening of the canon was a particular source of anxiety for traditionalists who were concerned that GCSE English criteria required literature during the course to reflect 'the linguistic and cultural diversity of society'. The proposition in the GCSE General Criteria that the teacher must 'make sure ... that the range of texts offered relates equally to the interests and experiences of girls and boys and meets the requirements for ethnic and political balance' (SEC, 1986, p.14) was seen by some as a threat: 'Education is the transmission of culture and the public has the right to expect that British culture is being transmitted in British schools' (Stoll, 1988, p.35).

There was also anxiety that the 'best authors' – especially Shakespeare – would inevitably be ignored within GCSE's mixed ability teaching approach. Worthen (1987, p.32) feared that traditional literary study would soon be phased out by 'the egalitarians' and replaced with a 'mish-mash of other "ways of responding" to literature' (p.32). Indeed, prefiguring dual accreditation, he also predicted that English Literature could soon be abolished as an area of study in its own right and diluted into a programme of 'general English'. What arguably materialised under the Dual Award, however, was a greater breadth of study within which the literary heritage remained largely intact. According to an Assistant Chief Examiner, Shakespeare, Dickens, Hardy and Owen were still studied in most centres. He stated that candidates

no longer have to pretend that they are incipient literary critics, at least in the stylised literary form of the discursive essay and equipped with the appropriate tools for the dissection of literary bodies. They can now be frankly and expressively what literature requires them to be – readers.

(Thomas, 1989, pp.32–3)

The staple diet of reading development in the old GCE 'O' level and mode 1 CSE exams had been the comprehension test in which a short extract was followed by a sequence of questions requiring short written answers. Critics had argued that such exercises often required little more than literal paraphrasing of words and phrases. Many 'progressive' English teachers at this time treated 'the extract' with great caution on the grounds that its de-contextualisation distorted authorial intention and weakened the quality of the reading experience (e.g. Hamlin and Jackson, 1984). There was a particular emphasis on the need to read whole texts which were thought to serve the purposes of active reading and critical engagement more effectively than short passages. More purposeful approaches to reading comprehension were now preferred. Directed Activities Related to Texts (DARTs), for example, enabled the reader to actively construct meaning, undermining the authoritarian notion which was implicit in traditional comprehension testing – that it, is the writer of the mark scheme who 'owns' the correct textual interpretation; in DARTs, the reader was empowered (Lunzer and Gardner, 1984).

What 100 per cent coursework approaches aimed to do was move beyond the artificiality and mundanity of traditional approaches to reading and writing by asking teachers themselves to design assessment tasks which embodied genuine purposes and audiences. It was felt that GCSE assessment should reflect the wide range of purposes for which language was used outside school. Teachers tried to establish a greater degree of task authenticity, often through use of drama and role play in the setting up of assignments. Part of the purpose was to motivate students but the deeper aim was to capture, as closely as possible, the elusive quality of reading response. Authenticity was considered to be as much about the quality of response as the quality of the task. By allowing teachers to use popular modern literature to help students to explore issues and ideas that were important in their own lives, the new GCSE syllabuses aimed to release students' own voices:

> *The possibilities opened up by the GCSE syllabuses mean that the authentic voice in pupils' writing ought to be much more prevalent than was ever possible under the old system of timed essays in response to given and often sterile topics. It remains to be seen how capable we are as teachers of releasing this voice.*

(Walker, 1987, pp.45–54)

Central to this new approach was the idea that students should feel passionately about their work. Particularly in the reading of literature, the National Criteria for English (section B, para. 1.1.1) recognised that students' own personal responses were valuable and important. Whereas GCE 'O' level had been concerned overwhelmingly with literary knowledge and the development of comprehension skills, GCSE English objectives repeatedly alluded to the need for candidates to be able to communicate sensitive and informed personal response.

In GCSE English, candidates were expected 'to understand and respond imaginatively to what they read, hear and experience in a variety of media; enjoy and appreciate the reading of literature'. In GCSE English Literature, candidates were required 'to communicate a sensitive and informed personal response to what is read' (DES, 1985).

As well as encouraging more active reading, GCSE English demanded more imaginative frameworks for the study of literature. Whereas CSE English literature coursework had basically required the repetitive production of assignments of essentially the same discursive type, GCSE promoted a much wider range of writing and teachers were encouraged to devote quality time to the discussion of drafts as well as to finished pieces. Literature was no longer to be regarded as an object for memorising and classification but rather as a medium for reflection and the expression of personal experience. Whereas GCE 'O' level had concentrated on the text as an object of study, 100 per cent coursework approaches in GCSE English foregrounded the reader and the process of reading itself.

GCSE English aimed not to deliver the 'canon' but to teach students *how* to study literature. This 'liberation' from prescribed set texts meant that candidates could now be offered opportunities both for detailed study and wide reading. The coursework folder was expected to include both detailed study of a small number of texts and wider reading of a broader range of texts. The GCSE syllabus recognised the diversity inherent in language use, encouraging a much wider range of types of writing and reading response. In so doing, it particularly aimed to support less able students who might have struggled in the past with the narrower range of academic forms. The study of women novelists, dramatists and poets was particularly recommended.

It was hoped that teachers' selection of texts would include a balance of genres so that students could acquire as varied a reading experience as possible. Both literary and non-literary material was required for study. Some works of translation could be included. There was also a greater stress on the range of purposes for reading. Candidates were encouraged to read for pleasure, look for information, explore underlying assumptions, compare texts on the same topic and become familiar with new kinds of writing such as biography, travel writing and scientific accounts. There was an enormous widening of the subject matter of English lessons. Films were 'read' in class for the first time. Film versions might be compared with the original or studied in their own right. Media studies and theoretical ideas about how films could be analysed began to pervade the English classroom.

For many English teachers, the new approach seemed to offer greater rigour and opportunities for a higher level of literary appreciation than the earlier examinations. By broadening the range and depth of study, the GCSE course created the potential for increased challenge and higher standards. Additionally, the freedom given to English teachers to choose their own assignments and texts was highly empowering. They were offered greater responsibility than ever before for the structuring, assessment and moderation of candidates' work. Many consequently felt that 100 per cent coursework was both fairer and more satisfying as a method of assessment, both for students and teachers (Walker, 1987, p.45). By 1993, when the 100 per cent coursework option was scrapped, only 20 per cent of candidates were following the alternative, more traditional 50–50 (i.e. 50 per cent examination/ 50 per cent coursework) syllabuses (Leeming, 1994).

Activity theory

Havnes (2004) uses activity theory to theorise the 'backwash' of assessment on learning, aiming to understand how assessment affects education at the level of 'system' (Engestrom, 1987, 2000). He argues that any form of testing and examination must fundamentally influence how teachers teach and their students learn. Any particular form of formative or summative assessment will also systemically influence other aspects of the educational process such as the production of textbooks, learning materials and the design of the learning environment.

Black and Wiliam (2005) also suggest that a helpful way of understanding the impact of formative assessment approaches in subject classrooms is through the medium of activity theory (Engestrom, 1987, 1993, 64–103). Using Engestrom's theoretical model, they show how the enhancement of the formative aspects of assessment interaction can radically change classroom relationships and the quality and culture of learning. Speaking about the King's, Medway and Oxfordshire Formative Assessment Project, they comment:

> *Using this framework, the course of the project can be seen as beginning with* tools *(in particular findings related to the nature of feedback and the importance of questions) which in turn prompted changes in the relationship* between the subjects *(i.e. in the relationship between the teacher and the students) which in turn prompted changes in the* subjects *themselves (i.e. changes in the teachers' and students' roles). These changes then triggered changes in other tools such as the nature of the subject and the view of learning. In particular, the changes prompted in the teachers' classroom practices involved moving from simple associationist views of learning to embracing constructivism, taking responsibility for learning linked to self-regulation of learning, metacognition and social learning.*

(Black and Wiliam, 1998, pp.12–3)

They explain that the *subjects* of the activity system are teacher and students: the *tools* (or cultural resources) which appeared to be significant in the development of formative assessment in the classrooms which they researched were the views held by students and teachers about the nature of the subject and the nature of learning; the *object* of each classroom activity system was 'better quality learning' and improved test scores; its *outcome* included changes in expectations and also changes 'towards assessments that could be formative *for the teacher*'.

Using Engestrom's theoretical model (see Figure 9.1), they show how the enhancement of the formative aspects of assessment interaction can radically change classroom relationships and the quality and culture of learning.

Figure 9.1 Activity triangle (adapted from Engestrom, 1987)

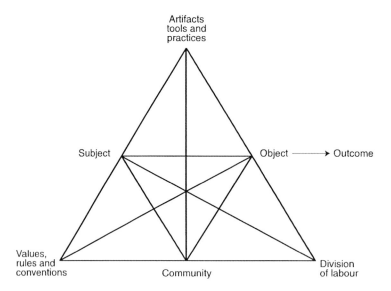

I would suggest that a similar framework of activity analysis can be used to retro-spectively understand changes which took place in GCSE English classrooms in the late eighties and early nineties when the 100 per cent coursework folder became a new *tool* or instrument of classroom activity. Because the syllabus-driven *rules* of year 10 and 11 classroom activity systems changed so radically in 1986 with the introduction of GCSE, so did their *division of labour*; teachers and students worked much more collaborative-ly. Students began to share greater ownership of their work. Their roles and social relationships became transformed. At the time, these changes were seen quite negatively from the standpoint of the traditionalist wing of educational opinion:

> *Traditionally, individual pupils faced a teacher and listened. Now groups of pupils face each other around tables and talk. The devaluing of the teacher as an authority (both on his subject and as a controller of classroom discipline) is implicit in the new classroom arrangement and in the whole GCSE style. Implicit also is the idea that the GCSE is an examination which will make mixed-ability teaching a widespread practice.*

(Worthen, 1987, p.41)

Traditionalists had maintained since the abolition of grammar schools and the introduc-tion of comprehensives that the 'pseudo-egalitarianism' of mixed ability teaching would lead to an erosion of the authority of the teacher's voice and an inevitable decline in standards. Mixed ability organisation often did involve students being seated around tables for the purposes of small group discussion. In GCSE English, since the early sev-enties, there had also been the growth of the 'oracy movement' through which talk had been increasingly regarded within English as an important medium of good learning; the classroom activity systems instigated by the arrival of GCSE in 1986 would, in many cases, have foregrounded small group discussion as a feature of their pedagogy. In the view of most English specialists, however, this did not by any means devalue the role and authority of the teacher: quite the opposite. The teacher in the typical mixed ability, GCSE English classroom now became a resource – much more a source of sup-port and scaffolding than an oracle of subject knowledge. Students, with the help of their teachers, were now expected to actively construct their own understanding of literature and language. The basic learning paradigm had changed.

Especially through classroom talk activity, the roles of students and teachers them-selves could be transformed. In his account of the National Oracy Project (NOP) whose timespan coincided almost identically with that of 100 per cent coursework, project director, John Johnson, explained that 'children did good and important, work in small-group activities, particularly if they had or established fairly clear roles and purposes for their individual contributions and for the whole-group activities' (Johnson, 1994, p.35). Teachers also gradually realised over the course of the NOP that 'putting children and students into new roles also gave them the opportunity to take on new roles' (Johnson, 1994, p.37). Of course, the NOP covered the whole age continuum but it was equally true of the 100 per cent coursework GCSE classroom that students were able to adopt a much wider range of classroom roles through the medium of group talk and that the teacher's role, (e.g. as organiser, provider, collaborator, expert, listener) became much more diversified.

As for the idea that the introduction of GCSE subverted discipline, my own experience, as Head of English in what were regarded as two of the most challenging schools in Nottingham, was that the new paradigm quite clearly *enhanced* the quality of learning and the quality of classroom relationships between 1986 and 1993; it was actually during the mid nineties that classroom discipline began to seriously deteriorate as league table anxiety and Ofsted oppression created a paradigm of mundane, objectives-led English lessons, subverting teacher autonomy, student motivation and general interest. By comparison, in the 100 per cent coursework years, the feeling of many colleagues was that classroom relationships had become much more intimate and cooperative. Through imaginative assignments, students became inspired and engaged and it was possible, for the first time, to work collaboratively and build trust.

One chief examiner argued that the new approach made it 'possible to release English Literature from the clutches of an elitist concept of Literary Criticism and to make the study of books, plays and poetry into an open engagement for all rather than a sterile pursuit for the chosen few' (Sweetman, 1987, p.62).

As in the classrooms studied by Black and Wiliam (2005), new theories of learning developed from the changes in teachers' classroom practices. Teachers and students were able to move beyond transmission approaches towards a more constructive methodology of literary study. Traditionalists had argued that the new GCSE practice of allowing students access to their texts when writing under controlled conditions minimised the importance of memory and textual knowledge:

> *The progressives, who now have in the GCSE the encapsulation of their doctrines, would claim to lay stress on understanding rather than knowledge. But the fact is that knowledge is the necessary prerequisite to understanding.*

(Worthen, 1987, p.35)

Worthen believed that to know a text is an indispensable basis for understanding it because memory trains the mind and allows students to internalise by committing to heart an area of valued knowledge. Pupils consequently needed to be taught the fundamentals of literary study before they could branch out into speculation and independent research. He maintained that, although coursework folders may have promoted 'breadth of study', they did not make students think with any rigour, often demonstrating superficiality and a lack of focus.

The experience of teachers in GCSE classrooms was quite different: one Assistant Chief Examiner (writing towards the end of the 100 per cent coursework period) stated that he had found more evidence of thinking about reading and enjoyment in reading during six years of examining 100 per cent coursework than had ever been the case during GCE 'O' level study – and far greater evidence of 'sustained application of intelligence to fiction':

> *The question to me seems simple: Do we want people who think and feel passionately about Literature and its connection to life as it is lived around them? If we do, then*

> *GCSE Coursework schemes offer enormous benefit. If not, then a restoration of the norm-referenced, externally-set and assessed will soon put Literature back in its place as a marginal subject useful in testing comprehension and memory.*
>
> (Thomas, 1989, p.41)

The restoration of the examination as the primary medium of GCSE assessment in 1993 did not quite marginalise literature but it did lead to the development of a newer, different kind of activity system which continues to prevail: although the content and emphasis of the examination has rarely remained static since 1993, the basic combination of 60 per cent examination and 40 per cent coursework (including 20 per cent speaking and listening) has been the standard format across syllabuses for over ten years. The classroom dynamic which has emerged from these more recent arrangements seems to many older teachers to be much more transmissive and hierarchical than the collaborative, mixed ability classrooms of the late eighties and early nineties.

Assessment issues

A great strength of the assessment system in GCSE English 100 per cent coursework lay in the fact that it depended upon and directly involved classroom teachers who worked in local consortia (which often included quite different types of school) to develop a shared expertise in the marking of candidates' writing. Although consensus marking is time-consuming, it has great in-service education and training (INSET) potential and the local consortia acted as INSET networks through which assignments could be shared and good practice collaboratively developed. Through group marking and moderation, a guild knowledge was rapidly accumulated of the key features of different levels of performance and there was an emerging awareness of what was needed to move on from one level to the next. Although assessment was made holistically and there were few detailed mark schemes, teachers believed that they were able to offer reliable summative judgements as well as ongoing formative advice which involved students themselves in assessment and target setting.

Teachers worked hard in their consortia to create systems of continuous assessment which monitored the development of coursework over the five terms of the course. There was extensive debate about the possible shape of assessment proforma. Review sheets were designed for use at the end of each unit. Student self-assessment sheets were also developed. It was during this period that self-assessment approaches were introduced for the first time into many English classrooms.

However, it was the assessment of GCSE 100 per cent coursework in particular which many politicians and policymakers targeted for criticism. The central issue was 'consistency'. At the root of perceived inconsistency lay a general weakness in mark schemes and some fairly underdeveloped grade descriptions. For example, the Midlands Examining Group (MEG) GCSE English syllabus grade criteria for reading performance at Grade D required that 'students will understand and convey information at a straightforward and occasionally at a more complex level'; one grade higher at C required that 'students will understand and convey information at a straightforward and at a more complex level'; at grade B '… at a straightforward and a quite complex level'; at grade A '… at both a straightforward and a complex level' (MEG, 1986). Such bland generalities did not encourage either public or professional confidence.

Although examination results did improve year on year, critics argued that this was only as a result of an absence of proper checks and balances within the moderation system. 'Controlled conditions' did not seem to be controlled in the way that examinations had been; candidates could use prepared material and would often know the question in advance. Work started at school under controlled conditions could be completed at home without supervision or time limit. The problem of plagiarism and the danger of excessive parental or teacher support for particular assignments was also identified by some commentators.

There was a deep-seated political belief that 100 per cent coursework assessment was beyond most teachers' professional capacity because assessors needed training, time and a distance from their students to enable objective comparison of different levels of performance. It was felt to be inherently problematic to place such great importance on teachers' own assessments of their students. Proper and fair comparison of a final grade based entirely on coursework with a grade based on the 50 per cent coursework and 50 per cent exam option was considered to be inherently difficult. The possibility of a legitimate comparison between work handed in at the beginning of year 10 with work completed at the end of the course in year 11 was also questioned. How could a teacher assessor easily and fairly evaluate the standards appropriate at each extreme? Another problem lay in the fact that students had opportunities to edit their work in successive drafts. At what point in the process did assessment occur? To what extent should formative evaluation be taken into consideration? What is the ideal balance between formative and summative assessment? These questions were certainly broached both by politicians and by English educators at this time.

Reading assessment also presented particular opportunities for debate and improvement. Both comprehension testing and responsiveness to literature were issues of concern. MacLure (1986) argued that assessment of the language modes should be holistic, opposing moves in one Examining Group to artificially distinguish between expression, understanding and response to reading. Since the teaching of reading, writing, speaking and listening are coordinated, she maintained, assessment should equally be conducted in the spirit of integration.

Of course, the reading process is particularly difficult to isolate. Although teachers have several possible ways of discovering information about students' reading performance (e.g. reading aloud, reading logs, library issue statistics), written and oral response to text are usually the primary sources. Several arguments have recently been advanced in favour of placing greater value on speaking and listening as a medium for assessment, especially for the assessment of children's reading responses (e.g. Coultas, 2005).

In fact, oral response to reading was encouraged in several 100 per cent coursework syllabuses. This aimed to address the problem of the 'double transformation', i.e. when the first mental reading response undergoes further transformation into writing. Oral responses were felt to be more authentic and closer to the original act of cognition. Interviews and role plays based on candidates' reading were consequently recorded in many classrooms. This especially supported students who read well but wrote badly, particularly disadvantaged if the exclusive medium of reading response was written.

The traditional form of written response to text had been either the comprehension test or the discursive essay. By encouraging a much wider variety of extended written forms, GCSE English broadened the range of reading assessment information potentially available to teachers. Students might be asked to write a newspaper account of an incident from a novel. They might be asked to reformulate a textual incident for a younger audience. They could be asked to create a script of a radio interview with the novel's characters. An incident might be reconstructed dramatically or in the form of a television documentary. Such assignments required completely new forms of interpretive and linguistic ability. This broader range of possible reading response made texts much more accessible to the full ability range than the traditional discursive assignment which had typically asked for an 'account of an incident' or the extent to which a candidate agreed or disagreed with a particular statement. However, this richness of potential reading assessment information was not always realised by teachers because the task of inferring reading ability from written and oral response is complex. The act of writing or speaking about text inevitably modifies the nature of the response itself, making the reading process correspondingly less accessible:

> It could be argued that there has been a tendency for discussion and experimentation to be focused on the more obviously assessable aspects of the course, that is on the products of written and oral work rather than on the receptive processes. A great deal more practical exploration is needed to find ways of encouraging an active and involved pupil response to all aspects of reading.

(Wainhouse, 1989, p.68)

Particularly after 1990, examiners worked hard to encourage teachers to develop their understanding of 'reading response through writing' by requiring, for all assignments, the formulation of mark schemes which included a reading assessment framework. There was, within the 100 per cent coursework movement, an advanced form of self criticism which was beginning to address the inevitable problems and anomalies posed by this new approach.

Another area of contention lay in the increasingly popular genre of 'empathy assignment' through which candidates were asked to assume the viewpoint of a fictional character in order to demonstrate textual comprehension at a variety of levels. Several commentators were dubious about the notion of empathy as a medium of response, (Worthen, 1987; Stoll, 1988). It was suggested that empathy was being used as a short cut for the expression of basic textual knowledge which was held to be pointless, offering few advantages over direct statement. In a very constructive article on this subject in *English in Education*, Thomas (1989) argued that, in writing an empathy assignment, the candidate enters into a purposeful dialogue with the text, not merely as a passive recipient but actively engaged in the construction of personal meaning. 'The task does not require a straightforward description of character as the *reader* understands it, but a partial and possibly distorted one as the *character* sees it' (Thomas, 1989, p.36). He argued that a successful empathy assignment should replicate 'perceptions consistent with the perspective of the persona chosen for empathetic identification' (p.36) and suggested that a pair of descriptions from different character viewpoints, together with a brief postscript explaining the key features of the text under focus, could help to deepen the quality of assignments of this kind.

Validity or reliability?

The strongest argument that can be advanced in favour of any form of assessment is that it raises standards at the same time as reporting efficiently on performance. What many argue that we have today is a system of assessment that reports on performance without raising standards (e.g. Black and Wiliam, 1998). Was the GCSE English 100 per cent coursework option any better? There is no doubt that it had strengths. For example, the early GCSE English syllabuses required candidates to read far more widely than had been the case before 1986 and there are strong arguments for believing that candidates at that time read more extensively than they have done since. Warner (2003) compares the richness of GCSE candidates' reading experiences in the late eighties and early nineties with 'the suffocating effect of genre theory and literacy strategy' on students' reading today. He maintains that 'centralised attempts to widen the reading curriculum have narrowed it' (p.13). Despite some patchiness and inconsistency in curriculum coverage, there was a breadth and range built into 100 per cent coursework syllabuses certainly not evident today.

The system of teacher assessment itself has many advantages. Observations made by a range of people over a range of authentic situations must be fairly reliable. There is an inherent advantage for an assessment system when teachers themselves are involved in its creation and development. When 100 per cent coursework was abolished in 1993, improvements in external moderation procedures and teacher assessment techniques were already under way. Many older English teachers would still maintain that regional consortia are quite capable of establishing a reliable and valid form of national assessment through improved training and the accrediting of appropriate personnel. External moderation can validate teacher assessment while particular aspects of the course are tested under strictly maintained controlled conditions. With the support of external validation, it ought to be possible to mark formal tests fairly within schools.

Nevertheless, the difficulties of generalising from assessment data which have been collected at a local level should not be underestimated either. It may well be that there is a fundamental incompatibility between developmental and high-stakes assessment. Part of the problem is that no single form of assessment can meet the requirements of both teacher and state. Teachers need assessment to formatively evaluate and diagnose whereas policymakers and government require assessment to compare and predict. After 1993, the formative assessment approaches which had helped teachers during the early GCSE years were supplanted by comparative 'league table' approaches which primarily supported the government's accountability agenda. In retrospect, it might be argued that public accountability is not simply a matter of test and exam results. In any case, the media pour doubt on every annual improvement. What is surely needed is a higher level of public understanding of the examination system. This could be achieved through a closer involvement of parents and employers in assessment processes.

Accountability has many facets. As well as being accountable to the public, governments are also accountable to the need for national competitiveness in the world economy. It seemed to politicians in the early nineties that, in educational terms, global solutions required greater norm-referencing. As the world economic paradigm became more cut-throat, the assessment paradigm had to follow suit. However, the consequence was that, in order to 'raise standards', teachers were forced to increasingly concern themselves with exam technique and the art of dissimulation. In many ways, the testing process came to predominate over – and even, at times, impede – the development of good practice.

Many of the most vital qualities of teaching and learning arise out of teaching situations in the classroom which are unlikely to be captured in an examination setting. The current assessment of writing, for example, tends to be based on the evaluation of sentence structure and use of connectives. It is much more difficult for an examination system to make satisfactory judgements about candidates' engagement, passion or quality of communication with the reader. Equally, many aspects of the reading process, such as the ability to participate in a group discussion about a novel or the ability to sustain a detailed reading journal over several months, are best assessed by teachers in classrooms. It is easier for a classroom teacher than an external examiner to measure the quality of a candidate's personal response to a novel or poem. Because it is so difficult to measure the quality of personal response in an examination setting, that quality became increasingly unassessed after 1993. Because it was not assessed, it was correspondingly less likely to be encouraged and taught.

On the QCA English 21 website, Caroline Gipps explains that they key issue in this debate is fitness for purpose: although high-stakes assessment is appropriate under certain limited circumstances, it should not impede the need for more subtle or critical curricular objectives: for example, 'more standardised and controlled approaches to assessment generally restrict the degree to which the meanings of texts can be challenged'. She maintains that any system of assessment is underpinned by a particular model of learning:

> *In the traditional model of teaching and learning the curriculum is seen as a distinct body of information, specified in detail, that can be transmitted to the learner.*

Assessment here consists of checking whether the information has been received and absorbed... By contrast, constructivist models see learning as requiring personal knowledge construction and meaning making and as involving complex and diverse processes. Such models therefore require assessment to be diverse ... intense, even interactive.

(Gipps, 2005)

It seems that a consensus is developing within the profession around a view that a greater degree of flexibility is necessary and that there is room in the future for both paradigms. In order to match the type of assessment as closely as possible to its specific learning objective, we need a wider range of assessment forms. The use of external assessment should be sparing and thoughtful – appropriate when valid but that is not likely to be often. Neither should assessment any longer be allowed to distort the curriculum. It should be part of the process of planning, teaching and learning and ought to be able to give students the best chance of performing well. Assessment in English needs to be directly relevant to pupils themselves. It needs to reflect pupils' authentic experiences of reading, writing, speaking and listening.

Conclusion

The main problem in reintroducing a significant amount of teacher assessment might well lie in the issue of workload. The 100 per cent coursework option was very demanding on the time of both teachers and students. The NUT and NAS/UWT had opposed the introduction of the GCSE in 1986 because of the limited time that had been allowed by the government for planning schemes of work and developing resources. Their view of the ending of 100 per cent coursework in 1993 was ambivalent. On the one hand, there were serious fears about the narrowing of the curriculum with the return of examinations. On the other, there was some relief that workload issues were finally being addressed. Some schools had already begun to develop whole school policies, appointing coordinators who were responsible for synchronising coursework requirements and deadlines. In other schools, this problem was being addressed through a cross-curricular approach. The exam boards had agreed to allow students to submit a piece of writing from, for example, Science or Humanities to the English coursework folder if it met assessment objectives. For the purposes of dual submission, barriers were lifted on the photocopying of assignments.

This concern about workload reflects the need for any national assessment system to be manageable. The demands made on the time of teachers and students should not be excessive if the system is to be effective. In the final analysis, there has to be an acceptable balance between the principles of manageability, reliability and the requirements of validity or task authenticity. Since the introduction of GCSE twenty years ago, this balance has swung like the proverbial pendulum. In 1986, 'validity' was the universal watchword. Ten years later, there remained a considerable outcry among many English teachers about the abolition of 100 per cent coursework and the sacrifice of the principle of task authenticity. Due to the proliferation of new educational initiatives and their associated workload over the past decade, it could prove quite difficult in the future to reintroduce a national coursework-based system of teacher assessment in English. Nevertheless, the pendulum, which had seemed to be swinging away from the principle of validity towards a requirement for greater manageability and test reliability, is now swinging back again. It is clear that several aspects of the current examination arrangements have had a pernicious backwash effect upon the English curriculum and that 'something needs to change'. This chapter has sought to inform the change process by reviewing significant features of the rise and fall of 100 per cent coursework assessment between 1986 and 1993.

References

Black, P. and Wiliam, D. (1998). *Inside the Black Box: Raising Standards through Classroom Assessment*. London: School of Education, King's College.

Black, P. and Wiliam, D. (2005). 'Developing a theory of formative assessment'. In: Gardner, J. (Ed) *Assessment for Learning: Practice, Theory and Policy*. London: Sage Books.

Chilver, P. (1987). *GCSE Coursework: English and English Literature. A Teacher's Guide to Organisation and Assessment*. Basingstoke: Macmillan Education.

Coultas, V. (2005). 'Thinking out of the SATs box – Assessment through talk.' Available: http://www.late.org.uk/English21OralAssessment.htm

Curtis, P. and Smithers, R. (2005). 'GCSE papers marked by admin staff', *The Guardian*, 22 August, 1.

Department of Education and Science (DES) (1985). *GCSE: The National Criteria: English*. London: HMSO.

Department of Education and Science (DES) and Welsh Office (1989). *English for Ages 5 to 16*. London: DES and Welsh Office.

Engestrom, Y. (1987). *Learning by Expanding. An Activity-Theoretical Approach to Developmental Research*. Helsinki, Finland: Orienta-Konsultit Oy.

Engestrom, Y. (1993). 'Developmental studies of work as a testbench of activity theory: the case of primary care in medical education.' In: Chaiklin, S. and Lave, J. (Eds) *Understanding Practice: Perspectives on Activity and Context*. Cambridge: Cambridge University Press.

Engestrom, Y. (2000). 'Activity theory as a framework for analyzing and redesigning work', *Ergonomics*, **43**.7, 960–74.

Gipps, C. (2005). 'Assessing English 21: some frameworks'. Available: http://www.qca.org.uk/13008.html

Hamlin, M. and Jackson, D. (1984). *Making Sense of Comprehension*. Basingstoke: Macmillan Education.

Havnes, A. (2004). 'Examination and learning: an activity-theoretical analysis of the relationship between assessment and educational practice', *Assessment and Evaluation in Higher Education*, **29**, 2, 159–76.

Johnson, J. (1994). 'The National Oracy Project.' In: Brindley, S. (Ed) *Teaching English*. London: Routledge.

Leeming, D. (1994). *A Report on Coursework Examinations in English and English Literature*. Northern Examinations and Assessment Board.

Lunzer, E. and Gardner, K. (1984). *Learning from the Written Word*. Edinburgh: Oliver and Boyd.

MacLure, M. (1986). 'English'. In: Horton, T. (Ed) *GCSE: Examining the New System*. London: Harper & Row.

Midlands Examining Group (1986). *GCSE English Syllabus*. Midlands Examining Group.

Newman, J.M. (Ed) (1985). *Whole Language Theory in Use*. Portsmouth, NH: Heinemann Educational Books.

Qualifications and Curriculum Authority (QCA) (2004). *Introducing: Monitoring Pupils' Progress in English at KS3*. London: QCA.

Secondary Examinations Council (SEC) (1986). *English GCSE: A Guide for Teachers*. Secondary Examinations Council.

Stoll, P.A. (1988). 'Two into one does not go: GCSE English is mostly CSE English'. In: Sexton, S. (Ed) *GCSE. A Critical Analysis*. Warlingham: IEA Education Unit.

Sweetman, J. (1987). 'Examining literature through the creative response.' *English in Education*, **21**, 1, 55–62.

Thomas, P. (1989). 'Empathy, wider reading and response'. *English in Education*, **23**, 1, 32–41.

Wainhouse, V. (1989). *Coursework in GCSE. English Planning and Assessment*. London: Hodder and Stoughton.

Walker, P. (1987). 'Assignments for GCSE English: finding an authentic voice,' *English in Education*, **21**, 2, 45–54.

Warner, L. (2003). 'Wider reading', *English in Education*, **37**.3.

Worthen, J. (1987). 'English'. In: North, J. (Ed) *The GCSE: An Examination*. London: The Claridge Press.

Wright, P. (2005) 'Ways ahead in assessment' [online]. Available: http://www.qca.org.uk/11782_11910.html

[Part 3]
Theory into practice: current issues

10 Postmodern principles for responsive reading assessment: a case study of a complex online reading task

Colin Harrison, Nasiroh Omar and Colin Higgins

Introduction: the need for intelligent adaptive online assessment

This chapter develops the theme of postmodern assessment of reading presented in chapter 5 in this volume, but with a different emphasis – an artificial intelligence approach to evaluating online reading activity and introduces an exploratory case study of a complex internet research and essay – writing task. The six imperatives of post-modern assessment presented in the earlier chapter are explored in a practical context, that of computer-based assessment of reading. The six imperatives (the first three derived from a scientific perspective on postmodernism, the second three from a literary perspective), were as follows:

1. we acknowledge the potential of local systems solutions

2. we acknowledge the importance of the subjective

3. we accept a range of methodologies

4. we recognise a polysemic concept of meaning

5. we privilege the role of the reader

6. we acknowledge a diminution of the authority of the author and of the text.

Currently, many commercial test development companies, states and governments are moving into computer-based assessment of reading and this is hardly surprising: computers and especially computers connected to the internet, offer the promise of instant data on reading achievement, based on centrally standardised and uniformly administered tests. Computers also offer commercial developers the promise of instant sales of test instruments, with minimal printing and distribution costs. To make online assessment appear more sensitive to the individual, an increasing number of states in the USA are declaring that their tests are 'adaptive': the computer tailors the items to the achievement level of the child taking the test, thereby, it is argued, increasing validity and reliability, while reducing stress, anxiety and a possible sense of failure.

'Idaho to adopt "adaptive" online state testing' ran the headline in *Education Week* (Olson, 2002), over a story that saw the chair of the state board of education saying 'We wanted an assessment system that would provide data first and foremost to improve instruction, which in turn, would improve accountability.' But if assessment is to improve instruction, then the nature of the data is critical and in the case of most online reading assessment the most common data source is that generated by multiple-choice test results and it is by no means clear just what 'data to improve instruction' is available from these scores. The question of the ways in which the tests are 'adaptive' is also somewhat problematic: broadly speaking, the computer takes multiple-choice items from an item bank and if the reader gets the question wrong, offers an easier one and if the reader gets the item correct, selects a harder one. The bonus for the testee and test developer is shorter tests and fewer items (though drawn from a large item bank); the bonus for the state is online access to statewide data on reading or maths achievement that is updated hourly. However, if we consider for a moment what is happening here, the gains for the individual student are negligible – if the student receives no useful feedback an online test is no different from the old pencil-and-paper tests that have been taken for decades. In most cases such tests provide no developmental profile, no diagnosis of reading errors and no recommendations for the individual's future pedagogy.

The question that drove the present study was whether it was possible to design a reading test that was based on a more authentic and ecologically valid task than a multiple-choice comprehension test, one that also made better use of the massive increases in computing power that are now available – advances so great that what was twenty-five years ago a whole university's computing power is now compressed into a single desktop computer. The challenge we set ourselves was to consider, as a desk study initially, the extent to which it might be possible to evaluate a reader's skilled behaviour in carrying out a complex research task using the internet.

To begin with, let us consider for a moment how good readers behave when carrying out such a complex research task. Good readers do more than just read: we suggest in the list below that they carry out eight related sets of behaviours. Clearly there is a massive set of research studies that one might call upon in drawing up such a list and we have necessarily been selective, but while the individual studies that we have cited might not necessarily be the ones that other researchers (or indeed the authors themselves) would choose, we suggest that our eight areas themselves are less contentious.

In carrying out a complex reading task, good readers:

- set themselves purposeful reading and writing goals (O'Hara, 1996)

- decide where they need to look for multiple reading resources (McGinley, 1992)

- navigate effectively towards those resources (Wright and Lickorish, 1994)

- adjudicate thoughtfully between possible sources of information: rejecting, selecting, prioritising (Pressley *et al.*, 1992).

- decide which parts of the chosen sources will be useful: rejecting, selecting, prioritising (Pearson and Camperell, 1994)

- decide how to use the sources: to edit, order, transform, critique (Duffy and Roehler, 1989; Stallard, 1974; Kintsch and van Dijk, 1978)

- produce a text that takes account of its audience (Hayes and Flower, 1980)

- evaluate the adequacy of their performance, revising and looping back to earlier stages of the process as appropriate (Rudner & Boston, 1994).

The first point to make is that a reading task that offered an opportunity to demonstrate these behaviours would also provide a close mapping onto our six practical imperatives for postmodern assessment, in that evidence of a student's performance on these tasks would be valuable for both student and teacher (a 'local systems solution' – Imperative 1); the task could readily accommodate self-assessment (acknowledging 'the importance of the subjective' – Imperative 2); it would be based on a range of reading skills and behaviours (accepting 'a range of methodologies' – Imperative 3); it would make use of a massive range of potentially conflicting data sources in a highly authentic environment (recognising a 'polysemic concept of meaning' – Imperative 4); it would invite a dynamic, critical reading response (privileging 'the role of the reader' – Imperative 5) and would do so in a context that clearly puts an emphasis on the authority and autonomy of the reader (thereby diminishing 'the authority of the author and of the text' – Imperative 6). Such an approach would therefore offer in principle a comprehensive basis for a postmodern and responsive assessment of reading.

The second issue is to consider whether it possible for a computer to assess automatically such authentic reading behaviour. Our answer is – yes, in principle, but it would be incredibly challenging, for not only would it be dauntingly difficult to attempt to write an intelligent adaptive program that would capture and evaluate some of the behaviours listed above; in reality, as Spiro *et al.* (1994) have reminded us, actual online behaviours are even more complex than is indicated in the list. For a good reader, goal-setting is provisional and the task being executed is therefore provisional; resource selection is provisional and evaluation at the local level is carried out incredibly rapidly, on the basis of partial information (fluent readers can evaluate and reject potential web sites at the rate faster than one per second, under certain conditions); finally, a good reader assembles information from diverse sources, integrates it with what is already known, mapping it into a new, context-sensitive situation-specific adaptive schema, rather than calling up a precompiled schema.

But if we are interested in pushing forward the use of the computer into this area then we would want to suggest that reading specialists and test developers need to work with cognitive scientists and artificial intelligence specialists and to begin to take reading assessment into this new and exciting domain. The case study reported in the remainder of this chapter represents the first fruits of such a collaboration, in a project that we call Intelligent Online Reading Assessment (IORA). We are possibly a decade away from having anything approaching online reading assessment of the sort that is envisioned here, but we want to suggest that if we put online multiple-choice tests at one end of the continuum and fully fledged IORA at the other, then we can at least use the two as reference points and measure the progress in intelligent online assessment against a challenging and more worthwhile target than that offered by 'adaptive' instruments that do little more than put multiple-choice reading tests onto the internet.

The study that we report was preliminary and exploratory and no more than an indication of the direction that IORA might take. It makes use of Latent Semantic Analysis (LSA) (Landauer, 2002), an interesting but somewhat contentious computer-based approach to evaluating the semantic content of texts. We are currently embarking upon a more extensive series of studies, using seventy readers, a new set of tasks and our own (rather than the University of Colorado's) LSA program which will be based on the 100-million-word British National Corpus; we are also trialling a plagiarism detection tool to give those taking the test constant information about the relative amounts of verbatim and non-verbatim content in their essays.

Investigating an approach to Intelligent Online Reading Assessment – an overview

The exploratory study that we report here aimed to explore an alternative to multiple-choice online reading comprehension tests, which may have high construct validity, but which also have low ecological validity and negative backwash effects at the system level. Our aim was to investigate an approach that might capture and evaluate some of the complex cognitive processes that are involved in authentic web-based research tasks. Eight fluent readers participated and for each participant, files were generated based on the search terms used, the URLs visited and the text of a final essay. Each participant's evidence (i.e. the search terms they entered into Google and the text of their final essay) was evaluated using LSA to produce an indication of five factors:

1. the degree of match between participant's search goal and the lexical items in the given task

2. the degree of match between the participant's Google search terms and an expert's Google search terms

3. the degree of match between the participant's essay task output and lexical items in the given task

4. the degree of match between the participant's essay task output

5. an expert's written task output and the overall coherence of essay task output.

Background – determining online reading complexity

Emerging technologies have changed the ways we read and write. Readers are not only often confronted with a potentially vast amount of online text but also with web technologies which introduce new research tools, while preserving much of the old ways of reading in traditional print. In addition, online texts link a variety of media and sources that challenge readers to locate the information they need, decide which pieces of text to view and in what order and relate this information to other facts also found among the thousands of millions of web pages available via the internet (Charney, 1987). Reading online text involves handling multiple texts displayed concurrently, sorting, navigating, responding (summarising or copying and pasting the text) and filing (Schilit *et al.*, 1999).

Figure 10.1 is a flow chart based on actual reader behaviour and outlines the nature of the observable online reading process, starting from when readers are given an online reading task until they produce a written output.

Defining online reading comprehension

Reading is an extremely complex process (Pressley, 1997, p.248) with a number of products (Dreyer and Nel, 2003; Snow, 2002, p.15) and there have been many attempts to define the term. A study by Harrison (2004, p.51) on reading definitions concluded that there exist two types of definition: definitions that describe the products of reading and definitions that describe the reading processes. Despite the complexity of the reading process, it consists of only three elements: the reader, the text and the activity (Snow, 2002, p.11). The activity, which is based on visual inputs, involves transactions between the published text and the reader (Goodman, 1994, p.1124). Also, reading requires readers to think (Pumpfrey, 1977) and actively construct meaning as they read (Rose and Dalton, 2002, pp.257–74) and to integrate information from a variety of sources (Goodman, 1994, p.1118). The existence of the worldwide web presents a number of new opportunities to research how information is accessed and integrated. A large volume of reading materials is accessible constantly and from all over the world. As a result, reading and technology are converging in new ways in online reading (Schmar-Dobler, 2003; McEneaney 2000, 2001; Burniske, 2000; Eagleton, 2002). Figure 10.2 depicts the definition of online reading comprehension used in this study.

In Figure 10.2, online reading comprehension is partitioned into two groups of processes – offline (inferred) and online (observed) reading processes. The online reading processes are partitioned into three groups: input, process and output. The offline reading processes (the generally inaccessible processes of cognition), are shown in the figure, but are not our primary focus. Our aim is to place primary emphasis on observed rather than inferred processes. Based on the online reading comprehension model in

Figure 10.1 What happen when a reader performs a complex search task? (Derived from Harrison *et al.*, 2004)

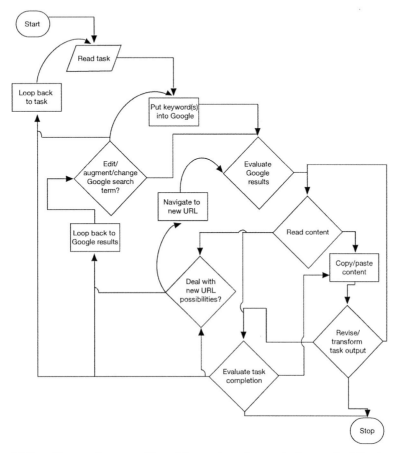

Figure 10.2, online readers are affected by various factors before and while the online reading take place. Readers' reading skills, vision skills, web skills, reading styles, goals and strategies, prior knowledge and belief will guide them while reading and comprehending the current online text.

Pilot work with adults in a higher education setting led us to the following reading activity cycle. In reading online, readers will first determine a search goal. To determine the search goal, parts of the Comprehending procedure are called up and readers will check their current knowledge state against the potential areas for searching out new knowledge and the search terms that might lead them to that knowledge.

Readers will then attempt to reach a search goal and search the web by using a search engine. Then, readers will activate the Online Reading procedure, which is to navigate the search list provided by the search engine. In the next step, readers will select a web page and read. Upon reading, readers will call up the Reading procedure, in which readers will integrate word, phrase and sentence while at the same time checking for local

Figure 10.2 The input, process and output of online reading comprehension (derived from Omar *et al.*, 2004)

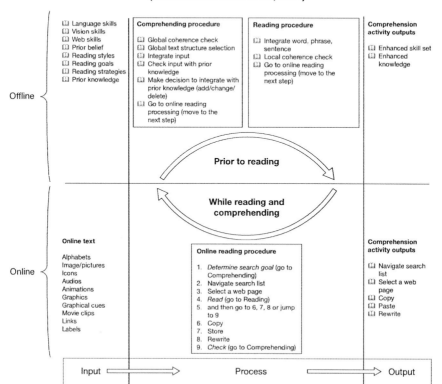

reading coherence. After reading the selected web page, readers will decide whether to accept the content (copy and paste or summarise the content in the working document) or to reject the content and activate the Comprehending procedure again in order to check their current comprehension and to come up with a revised search goal. The activation cycles of Online Reading, Reading and Comprehending procedures will continue until the online readers are satisfied with their reading comprehension in order to produce reading comprehension activity outputs: navigation search lists, selected web pages, copy, paste and rewrite activities.

A simplified computer-based online reading process model

The computer-based model of readers' online reading behaviour as presented in Figure 10.3 depicts the observed procedures in Figure 10.2 collapsed into seven computer-based processes.

Figure 10.3 presents the key elements of a low-inference model of reading, one which focuses on the observable. It is this model (see Harrison *et al.*, 2004) for details on how the reading and research captured from the searching or writing tasks are related) whose usefulness we aim to explore in this paper.

Latent Semantic Analysis (LSA)

LSA is a technique using a vector-based approach to automatically construct a semantic representation of a text (Schunn, 1999; Landauer *et al.*, 1998). The procedure for conducting LSA is not simple: broadly speaking, LSA begins by using a technique similar to factor analysis to construct, based on a very large text corpus, a mathematical model of the semantic universe, in which a text's meaning is plotted as a vector in n-dimensional semantic space. What makes LSA attractive to researchers is that the relationship between two texts (a source text and a summary of that text, for example) can be represented very simply: because each text produces a vector, a simple cosine (which can be

Figure 10.3 The flowchart representation of the online reading behaviour starting from the web sites (source file) to the output file (the product) (Omar *et al.*, 2004)

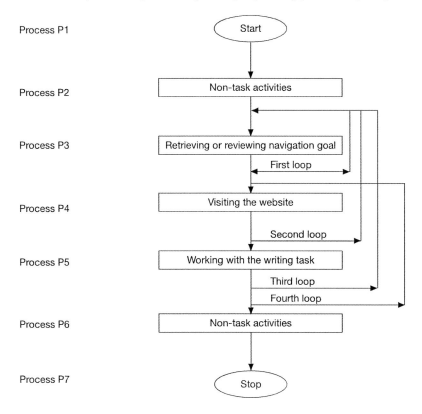

treated as a score in the range 0.0–1.0) can tell us how similar one text is to the other. A cosine of 0.6, for example, would suggest that the texts are very similar; a cosine of 0.2 would suggest that they have some similarities, but are not closely related. LSA has been widely used in the evaluation of written answers (Kintsch *et al.*, 2000; Lemaire and Dessus, 2001; Kanijeya, Kumar and Prasad, 2003) and also has been found useful in assessing online reading behaviour (Juvina *et al.*, 2002; Juvina and van Oostendorp, 2004). Since online reading involves online reading comprehension and online web navigation, our research used LSA in a two-pronged evaluation: of online reading comprehension and online web navigation outputs.

The experiment

In this study, we were interested in what kind of data we might capture concerning readers and their interaction with online text so that we could have a detailed understanding of their online reading behaviour. Eight participants who were regular computer users took part in the experiment. Six participants, who were also students or student teachers, were paid to participate. All participants were given one hour to complete the task of defining Socialism, using web resources, in not more than 500 words, of which up to 300 could be verbatim quotation from sources. The search task was defined as follows:

> *The web offers many definitions of the term Socialism. Perhaps this is because it is a term that produces strong emotions and it is a word that is considered important by groups as well as individuals. Your task is to spend an hour looking at the information available to you using whatever internet resources you are able to locate, to produce a document in Word that presents and comments on some definitions of Socialism.*

Every participant used the same hardware: a computer – a Pentium 4 desktop with 2.66GHZ CPU, 40G hard disk storage, network connection, sound system, head set microphone, external CD writer and external hard disk (for backup purposes), CDs – 700 MB capacity (for backup purposes) and Camcorder, tripod and Mini DVs – to capture observable behaviour) and software (Internet Explorer and Netscape Navigator to make online reading possible, Camtasia (Camtasia) to record audio of the participant's verbal comments and interview and to capture screen and online activities, Squid-NT – to capture visited URLs with time stamp and Beeper – to beep every 2 minutes so that the participant was alerted to comment on his or her work). The experiment took place in a quiet area where only the online reader and the observer/technician were allowed to be present and all the software and hardware were as depicted in Figure 10.4.

Before the experiment took place, the technician turned on the computer, deleted the previous cache file written by the Squid-NT, ran the batch file – to activate the Squid-NT, checked the internet connection, started Word and created a new document, started the browser, checked that the participant knew how to quickly switch between Word

Figure 10.4 Combinations of methodologies for capturing online reading data

Web logging – to capture web data

Video camera – to capture observable behaviour

Audio recorder – to capture 'talk aloud' and short interview

Screen recorder – to capture screen content and activities

and the Browser (using the Taskbar or Alt-Tab), did a sound check to ensure the speech recording was working properly, turned on the camcorder, started the beeper and arranged windows (beeper and browser so that both would appear on the screen) and last, asked the participant not to move around too much in order to make sure the video recorder managed to capture a clear view of the participant and his/her online activities. Once the participant was ready, he or she was given the written task and reminded to respond (explain on what they were doing) when the beeper beeped. Then the technician started recording audio, video and screen.

After the experiment, the technician would stop Camtasia; stop Squid-NT, move and rename its *var* directory; stop the beeper, turn off the camcorder and microphone and copy the *history.dat* in the browser to a file, video tape from camera and the .avi (camtasia file) to CD. Then, the observer would have a short interview with the participant. The camcorder would be on once again. The following were the prompts for the interview:

Thank you very much indeed for helping us.

Please talk to us about how you felt you tackled this task.

Did you feel happy about any things you did?

Were you unhappy about anything?

How would you comment on your own searching and navigation strategies?

What can you tell us about how you selected the sources that you decided were useful?

Have you anything to say about how you carried out the written task?

Thank you very much indeed for all your help.

Once the observer finished the interview, the technician would turn off the camcorder and copy the captured interview to videotape.

Initially, all the data captured by video, audio and screen recorder were transcribed manually. However, the screen captures were the primary source of interest, as they explicitly and implicitly revealed online reading progress. Collecting data from various sources was valuable, despite the fact that transcribing the audio/video of the screen capture file was very time consuming. Combining different data sources allowed triangulation of different data sources, which provided a fuller data picture of users' reasoning and interactions during reading online.

Each participant produced two types of data files: 1. A text file consisting of all the visited URLs. 2. A document file consisting of an essay. The document file needed only a few modifications (delete blank lines in between paragraphs) in order to be used by the LSA system. However, the text file (these were identified and analysed in more detail, e.g. by examining the log file, audio and screen recording), which contained the visited URLs, needed to be processed by a specific Java program to differentiate which URLs were to be considered as the navigation page (referred to as P3 in Figure 10.3) and which as websites (referred to as P4 in Figure 10.3) and to identify the navigational goals used. Figures 10.5, 10.6, 10.7 and 10.8 show the URLs collected from one participant, the search terms used, the URLs of the page returned by the Google search term call and finally the websites visited as a result of navigating away from the Google-supplied links.

Figure 10.5 Part of the participant's collected URLs

http://www.google.com

http://www.google.co.uk/search?q=socialism&ie=UTF-8&oe=UTF-8&hl=en&btnG
   =Google+Search&meta=

http://www.google.co.uk/search?q=socialism&ie=UTF-8&oe=UTF-8&hl=en&btnG
   =Google+Search&meta=

http://home.vicnet.au/~dmcm/

http://www.socialism.com/

http://www.socialism.com/whatfsp.html

Figure 10.6 Part of the participant's navigational goals

   socialism

   socialism

   socialism

   dictionaries

   dictionaries

   dictionaries

   dictionaries

   online charles kingsley

   political dictionary

   political dictionary

Figure 10.7 Part of the participant's associated navigational search list

   http://www.google.co.uk/search?q=socialism&ie=UTF-8&oe=UTF-8&hl=en&btnG

=Google+Search&meta=

http://www.google.co.uk/search?q=dictionaries&ie=UTF-8&oe=UTF-8&hl=en
&meta=

http://www.google.co.uk/search?q=dictionaries&ie=UTF-8&oe=UTF-8&hl=en
&meta=

Figure 10.8 Part the participant's associated of visited websites

http://home.vicnet.au/~dmcm/ , http://home.vicnet.au/~dmcm/,

http://www.socialism.com/whatfsp.html ,http://www.socialism.com/whatfsp.html ,

http://www.socialism.com/ ,http://www.google.com

Once all the participants' files had been collected, the data were evaluated by using LSA data obtained from the www.lsa.colorado.edu website. Table 10.1 shows the degree of similarity (i.e. cosine scores) for the seven participants based on the following five factors:

1. the degree of match between participant's search goal and the given task

2. participant's search goal and an expert's internet search goal

3. participant's written task output with the given task

4. participant's written task output with an expert's written task output

5. the overall coherence of written task output.

The eighth participant was an expert historian and his responses were used as a basis for comparison (see factors 2 and 4 in Table 10.1).

Table 10.1 Latent Semantic Analysis cosine scores of all participants

		Participants						
	Factors	1	2	3	4	5	6	7
1	Google search terms vs task terms	0.34	0.24	0.08	0.10	0.29	0.16	0.42
2	Google search terms vs expert's	0.58	0.75	0.68	0.71	0.79	0.55	0.19
3	Essay output vs task terms	0.37	0.28	0.26	0.26	0.32	0.37	0.41
4	Essay output vs expert's essay	0.95	0.95	0.95	0.96	0.93	0.94	0.94
5	Coherence of essay output	0.68	0.83	0.71	0.77	0.92	0.11	0.10

The result in row 1 of Table 10.1 shows that all the participants received an LSA cosine score (indicating the degree of similarity with a source text) of less than 0.5 when their search terms (as used in Google) were compared with the words in the research task. This is because, while navigating the web, participants 1–6 tended at times to enter tangential search terms (e.g. participant 1 put 'Charles Kingsley' and 'political', participant 2 put 'emotion' and 'Nouveu Cristianity' [sic], participant 3 put 'Communism' and 'democracy'). However, participant 7 scored the highest degree of match when he just used two search terms: 'Socialism' and 'Oxford Dictionary', which seemed to agree more with the given task. However, the LSA values in row 2 (which computes the LSA score between participants' and expert's Google search terms) have higher values. Participants 1–6 scored more than 0.5. This showed that, the participants used search terms similar to those of an expert, those of participant 5 being the most similar.

Rows 1 and 3 show LSA similarity scores on the search terms used by participants and on the lexical items in their essays, as compared to the lexical items in the research task. Even though the scores in row 1 vary, the LSA score in row 3 does not follow the same pattern. However, neither sets of scores is high, which suggests that using the task prompt as a basis for LSA comparisons is not particularly illuminating.

Rows 2 and 4 present LSA similarity scores on the Google search terms used by participants and on their written output, the essay. Row 2 shows a good deal of variation; participants 2 and 5 are very similar and participant 7 is quite distant. However, the LSA scores based on the participant's essay as compared with the expert's essay were in the range 0.93 to 0.96, which suggests that for these participants, at least, variation in search term did not lead to variation in overall content and in terms of what LSA can measure, there was high degree of agreement between the non-expert and expert.

Row 5, however, shows clear differences between participants. The coherence score is based on the mean of cosine scores from pairs of adjacent sentences in the final essay (i.e. an LSA score is computed for each pair of sentences in the essay: 1 v 2, 2 v 3, 3 v 4, 4 v 5, etc.; the mean of these cosine scores is taken as an indication of the overall coherence of the text). Participants 1–5 have more writing experience background when compared to participants 6 and 7. Therefore, while summarising, copying and pasting from the web pages to their document, they were aware of their own writing coherence. Whereas, participants 6 and 7 were concerned with getting the materials pasted in their documents without thinking much about the coherence between the selected sources. However, participant 5 has an exceptionally high value of coherence because she copied or summarised from a single well-organised web page.

Our current research is still at an early stage and will be used as the basis of the next stages of our investigation. There are still many angles to explore on the online reading assessment horizon especially in the aspect of psychology (Juvina and Oostendorp, 2004) and web navigation (McEaney, 1999a). The correlation statistical analysis made between the expert's mark for all the participants and the five factors in Table 10.1 showed that there were positive correlations between the expert's scores with factors 2, 3 and 5. In our next experiment we will further investigate these three factors by increasing the number of participants and collecting our data automatically by using

Real-time Data Collection (RDC) (McEaney, 1999b) since the data collection method significantly enhances the potential to contribute to investigations of reading.

The five factors used in the evaluation did not penalise those who copied verbatim from the source web pages more than they were allowed to. Therefore, in the next stage of our experiment, a verbatim detection method will be included. Another matter that we have to think about is the number of web pages visited and referred to. Our thinking here is that if the participant visited and referred to only a one or two web pages, they might score higher in factor 5 but defeat the main purpose of evaluating the whole perspective in online reading, that is, to gain as much information as possible from a variety of sources.

Conclusions

As we have already stated, our work is at an early stage, but we are clear about a number of issues: we want to research online reading using complex, purposeful and authentic tasks; we want to continue to use the whole internet, rather than a limited subset of web pages, as the basis for those tasks; we are interested in assessment using artificial intelligence approaches and we feel that these may well continue to exploit LSA approaches (though we also believe that our LSA scores will be more valid when they are based on a much larger and UK-derived corpus).

As we have indicated, we now have our own LSA engine, which is capable of delivering online LSA text matching data and we also have a beta version of an online plagiarism detection tool. We anticipate using both tools as part of a kit that would be capable of not only assessing online reading activity, but of providing real-time online support for readers tackling complex research tasks. Over the next two years, therefore, we expect to be developing programs that will both deliver both assessment tools and online reader support tools.

References

Burniske, R.W. (2000). 'Literacy in the cyber age', *Ubiquity* – an ACM IT Magazine and Forum.

Camtasia, 'TechSmith Corporation' [online]. Available: http://www.techsmith.com.

Charney, D. (1987). 'Comprehending non-linear text: the role of discourse cues and reading strategies.' Paper presented at the Hypertext 87 Conference, New York.

Kanijeya, D., Kumar, A. and Prasad, S. (2003). 'Automatic evaluation of students' answers using syntactically enhanced LSA.' Paper presented at the HLT-NAACL 2003.

Dreyer C. and Nel, C. (2003). 'Teaching reading strategies and reading comprehension within a technology-enhanced learning environment', *System*, **31**, 3, 349–65.

Duffy, G.G. and Roehler, L.R. (1989). 'Why strategy instruction is so difficult and what we need to do about it.' In: McCormick, C.B., Miller G. and Pressley M. (Eds) *Cognitive Strategy Research: From Basic Research to Education Applications*. New York: Springer-Verlag.

Eagleton, M.B. (2002). 'Making text come to life on the computer: toward an understanding of hypermedia literacy', *Reading Online*, **6**, 1, 2002.

Goodman, K.S. (1994). 'Reading, writing and written text: a transactional sociopsycholinguistic view.' In: Singer, H. and Ruddell, R.B. (Eds) *Theoretical Models and Processes of Reading. Fourth edn*. Newark, DE: International Reading Association.

Harrison, C. (1995). 'The assessment of response to reading: developing a post-modern perspective.' In: Goodwyn, A. (Ed) *English and Ability*. London: David Fulton.

Harrison, C. (2004). *Understanding Reading Development*. London: Sage.

Harrison, C., Omar N. and Higgins, C. (2004) 'Intelligent Online Reading Assessment: capturing and evaluating internet search activity.' Paper presented at the Beyond the Blackboard: Future Direction for Teaching, Robinson College, Cambridge, 3–4 November.

Hayes, J.R. and Flower, L.S. (1980). 'Identifying the Organization of Writing Processes.' In: Gregg, LW. and Steinberg, E.R. (Eds) *Cognitive Processes in Writing*. Hillsdale, NJ: Lawrence Erlbaum Associates.

International Reading Association (1999). 'High Stakes Assessments in Reading.' Available: http://www.reading.org/pdf/high_stakes.pdf [9 July, 2003].

Juvina, I., Iosif, G., Marhan, A.M., Trausan-Matu, S., van deer Veer, G. and Chisalita, C. (2002). 'Analysis of web browsing behavior – a great potential for psychology research.' Paper presented at the 1st International Workshop on Task Models and Diagrams for user Interface Design Tamodia 2002, Bucharest, 18–19 July.

Juvina, I. and Van Oostendorp, H. (2004). 'Predicting user preferences – from semantic to pragmatic metrics of web navigation behaviour.' Paper presented at the Dutch Directions in HCI, Amsterdam, June 10.

Kintsch, E., Steinhart, D., Stahl, G., Matthews C. and Lamb, R. (2000). 'Developing summarization skills through the use of LSA-backed feedback', *Interactive Learning Environments*, **8**, 2, 87–109.

Kintsch, W. (1998). *Comprehension: A Model for Cognition*. Cambridge: Cambridge University Press.

Kintsch, W. and van Dijk, T.A. (1978). 'Toward a model of text comprehension and production', *Psychological Review*, **85**, 363–94.

Landauer, T. K. (2002). 'On the computational basis of learning and cognition: Arguments from LSA.' In: Ross, N. (Ed) *The Psychology of Learning and Motivation*, **41**, 43–84.

Landauer, T.K., Foltz, P.W. and Laham, D. (1998). 'An introduction to latent semantic analysis', *Discourse Processes*, **25**, 2 and 3, 259–84.

Lemaire, B. and Dessus, P. (2001). 'A system to assess the semantic content of student Essays', *Journal of Educational Computing Research*, **24**, 3, 305–20.

McEneaney, J.E. (1999a). 'Visualizing and assessing navigation in hypertext.' Paper presented at the 10th Hypertext Conference of the Association for Computing Machinery, Darmstadt, Germany, February.

McEneaney, J.E. (1999b). 'New approaches to data collection and analysis in online reading studies.' Paper presented at the Annual Meeting of the National Reading Conference, Orlando, FL USA, 3 December.

McEneaney, J.E. (2000). 'Learning on the web: a content literacy perspective', *Reading Online*.

McEneaney, J.E. (2001). 'The Language Arts Dilemma.' Paper presented at the 51st annual meeting of the National Reading Conference, San Antonio, 5 December.

McGinley, W. (1992). 'The role of reading and writing while composing from multiple sources', *Reading Research Quarterly*, **27**, 227–48.

Omar, N. Harrison, C. and Higgins, C. (2004). 'Online reading and web navigation: a computer-based low inference model of expert reader behaviour.' Paper presented at the 5th International Conference on Recent Advances in Soft Computing, Nottingham, UK, 16– 18 December.

O'Hara, K. (1996). 'Towards a Typology of Reading Goals.' Technical Report EPC-1996-10. Cambridge, England: Rank Xerox Research Centre [online]. Available: http://www.xrce.xerox.com/publis/cam-trs/pdf/1996/epc-1996-107.pdf [9 September, 2003].

Olson, L. (2002). 'Idaho to adopt 'adaptive' online state testing', *Education Week*, 23 January, 2002, **21/19**, 6–7.

Pearson, P.D. and Hamm, D.H. (in press). *The Assessment of Reading Comprehension: A Review of Practices – Past, Present and Future.*

Pressley, M. (1997). 'The cognitive science of reading', *Contemporary Educational Psychology*, **22**, 2, 247–59.

Pressley, M., El-Dinary, P.B., Gaskins, I., Schuder, T., Bergman, J., Almasi, L. and Brown, R. (1992). 'Beyond direct explanation: Transactional instruction of reading comprehension strategies', *Elementary School Journal*, **92**, 511–54.

Rose, D. and Dalton, B. (2002). 'Using technology to individualize reading instruction.' In: *Improving Comprehension Instruction: Rethinking Research, Theory and Classroom Practice*. San Francisco: Josey Bass Publishers.

Rudner, L.M. and Boston, C. (1994). 'Performance assessment', *The ERIC Review*, **3**, 1, Winter, 2–12.

Schilit, B.N. *et al.* (1999). 'As we may read: the reading appliance revolution', *IEEE Computer*, **32**, 1, 65–73.

Schmar-Dobler, E. (2003). 'Reading on internet: the link between literacy and technology', *Journal of Adolescent and Adult Literacy*, **47**, 1, 80–85.

Schunn, C.D. (1999). 'The presence and absence of category knowledge in LSA.' Paper presented at the 21st Annual Conference of the Cognitive Science Society.

Snow, C.E. (2002). 'Reading for understanding: toward a research and development program in reading comprehension.' RAND Reading Study Group, Santa Monica, CA and Washington.

Spiro, R., Rand J., Coulson, R.L., Feltovich, P.J. and Anderson, D.K. (1994). 'Cognitive flexibility theory: advanced knowledge acquisition in ill-structured domains.' In: Singer, H. and Ruddell, R.B. (Eds) *Theoretical Models and Processes of Reading. Fourth edn*. Newark, DE: International Reading Association.

Stallard, C. (1974). 'An analysis of the writing behaviour of good student writers', *Researching the Teaching of English*, **8**, 206–18.

Wright, P. and Lickorish, A. (1994). 'Menus and memory load: navigation strategies in interactive search tasks', *International Journal of Human-Computer Studies*, **40**, 965–1008.

Further reading

AEA (2003). 'American Evaluation Association Position Statement on high stakes testing in pre K-12 Education' [online]. Available: http://www.eval.org/hst3.htm.

BBC (2003a). Tests 'cause infants stress'. BBC News online, 25 April.

BBC (2003b). Teacher jailed for forging tests. BBC News online, 7 March. Available: http://news.bbc.co.uk/1/hi/england/2829067.stm.

Cronbach, L.J., Linn, R.L., Brennan, R.L. and Haertel, E.H. (1997). 'Generalizability analysis for performance assessments of student achievement or school effectiveness', *Educational and Psychological Measurement*, **57**, 3, 373–99.

Derrida, J. (1976). *Of Grammatology*. Trans. Spivac, G.C. Baltimore: The Johns Hopkins University Press.

Eagleton, T. (1983). *Literary Theory*. Oxford: Basil Blackwell.

Fullan, M. (2000). 'The return of large scale reform,' *Journal of Educational Change*, **1**, 15–27.

Harrison, C. (1995). 'The assessment of response to reading: developing a post-modern perspective.' In: Goodwyn, A. (Ed) *English and Ability*. London: David Fulton.

Harrison, C., Bailey, M. and Dewar, A. (1998). 'Responsive reading assessment: is postmodern assessment possible?' In: Harrison, C. and Salinger, T. (Eds) *Assessing Reading 1: Theory and Practice*. London: Routledge.

Harrison, C. and Salinger, T. (Eds) (1998). *Assessing Reading 1: Theory and Practice*. London: Routledge.

Hayward, L. and Spencer, E. (1998). 'Taking a closer look: a Scottish perspective on reading assessment.' In: Harrison, C. and Salinger, T. (Eds) *Assessing Reading 1: Theory and Practice*. London: Routledge.

Hellman, C. (1992). *Implicitness in Discourse*. International Tryck AB, Uppsala. Available http://lsa.colorado.edu/papers/Ross-final-submit.pdf [22 November, 2002].

Jacob, B.A. and Levitt, S.D. (2001). 'Rotten apples: An investigation of the prevalence and predictors of teacher cheating' [online]. Available: http://economics.uchicago.edu/download/teachercheat61.pdf

Kibby, M.W. and Scott, L. (2002). 'Using computer simulations to teach decision making in reading diagnostic assessment for re-mediation', *Reading Online*, **6**, 3. Available: http://www.readingonline.org/articles/art_index.asp?HREF=kibby/index.html

Kintsch, W. (1998). *Comprehension: A Model for Cognition*. Cambridge: Cambridge University Press.

Lyotard, J.-F. (1984). *The Postmodern Condition: A Report on Knowledge*. Trans. Bennington, G. and Massumi, B. Manchester: Manchester University Press.

Medvedev, P.N. and Bakhtin, M. (1978). *The Formal Method in Literary Scholarship*, trans. Wehrle, A.J. Baltimore: Johns Hopkins University Press.

Pearson, P. D. and Hamm, D.H. (in press). *The Assessment of Reading Comprehension: A Review of Practices – Past, Present and Future*.

Pumpfrey, P.D. (1977). *Measuring Reading Abilities: Concepts, Sources and Applications*. London: Hodder and Stoughton.

Salinger, T. (1998). 'Consequential validity of an early literacy portfolio: the "backwash" of reform.' In: Harrison, C. and Salinger, T. (Eds) *Assessing Reading 1: Theory and Practice*. London: Routledge.

Valencia, S. and Wixon, K. (2000). 'Policy-oriented research on literacy standards and assessment.' In: Kamil, M. *et al.* (Eds) *Handbook of Reading Research: Volume III* Mahwah, NJ: Lawrence Erlbaum Associates.

Vincent, D. and Harrison, C. (1998). 'Curriculum-based assessment of reading in England and Wales.' In: Harrison, C. and Salinger, T. (Eds) *Assessing Reading 1: Theory and Practice*. London: Routledge.

11 Automated marking of content-based constructed responses

Claudia Leacock

Introduction

Educators and assessment specialists would like to increase test validity by replacing, as much as possible, multiple-choice assessments with constructed responses. However, scoring or marking these assessments is time consuming and therefore costly. As an example, Vigilante reports that '25 percent of online faculty time [is] currently spent on grading written assignments and examinations' in the New York University Virtual College (Vigilante, 1999, p.59). To date, most of the research in automated marking has focused on grading essay-length responses (Burstein, 2003, pp.113–22; Landauer *et al.*, 2003, pp.87–112).

However, much of the teacher's time is spent on grading short content-based responses such as those that appear in in-class tests or quizzes or homework assignments, such as those found in a textbook's end-of-chapter review questions. There is a growing interest in automated marking of fairly brief content-based responses (Penstein-Rosé and Hall, 2004; Perez *et al.*, 2004; Sukkarieh *et al.*, 2004). An automated marking engine, *c*-rater™, is being developed at the Educational Testing Service (ETS), to measure a student's understanding of specific content material. *c*-rater is designed to measure a student's understanding of specific content in free responses – and assigns full, partial or no credit to a response. It uses automated natural language processing (NLP) techniques to determine whether a student response contains specific linguistic information that is required as evidence that particular concepts have been learned.

If responses can be marked automatically, then a natural extension of *c*-rater would be to provide automatically generated feedback for the student as to why a response received the mark that it did. That is, *c*-rater could identify which part of the response it recognized as being correct and also identify the concept(s) that it did not find in the student response.

A question can be scored by *c*-rater if there is a fixed set of concepts that satisfy it. An open-ended question asking for an opinion or for examples from personal experience is not a question for *c*-rater. A sample of questions that *c*-rater has scored successfully appears in Table 11.1. As can be seen, the questions are varied – over science, math and reading comprehension – and open-ended enough to admit a variety of responses. However, there is a limited number of possible correct answers. Consider the 11th grade reading comprehension question. This particular question requires the student to identify four concepts, in order for a response to get full credit: (1) what is important to Walter, (2) a supporting quote from Walter, (3) what is important to his mother and (4) a supporting quote from her. In this particular rubric, partial credit is assigned if the response contains only one, two, or three of these concepts. Otherwise, no credit is assigned.

Table 11.1 Questions that *c*-rater has successfully marked

Grade	Assessment	Question
4	Reading Comprehension: National Assessment of Educational Progress (NAEP)	Give two reasons stated in the article why the hearth was the center of the home in colonial times.
8	Reading Comprehension: National Assessment of Educational Progress (NAEP)	How did 'Oregon fever' influence westward movement?
8	Science	Explain how you would design an experiment that would investigate the importance of light to plant growth. Include the type of organisms required, the control and the variable and the method of measuring results.
8	Math: Reading Comprehension: National Assessment of Educational Progress (NAEP) (This is an approximation of the prompt used in the study.)	A radio station wanted to determine the most popular type of music among those in the listening range of the station. Would sampling opinions at a Country Music Concert held in the listening area of the station be a good way to do this? Explain your answer.
11	Reading Comprehension: Indiana Core 40 End-of-Year Assessment	Compare and contrast what Mama and Walter in A Raisin in the Sun believe to be the most important thing in life or what they 'dream' of. Support your choice for each character with dialogue from the excerpt of the play.

c-rater marks a response by matching it to a set of model answers that have been generated by a content expert using a graphical user interface that is described in Leacock and Chodorow (2003). In order for these models to be robust, the person who is generating it needs to have access to about 50 human-scored responses for each score point.

The system recognises when a response is equivalent to a correct answer that is represented in the model or, in other words, *c*-rater recognises paraphrases of the correct answer or answers. In order to recognise a paraphrase, *c*-rater normalises across the kinds of variation that typically occur in paraphrases: syntactic and morphological variation, use of words that are synonymous or similar in meaning and the use of pronouns in the place of nouns.

How *c*-rater works

A single concept can be expressed in many different ways. One of the concepts that is required in order to get full credit for the 11th grade reading comprehension item is that 'money is important to Walter'. Below are some of the ways the students expressed this concept:

1. Walter thinks that it is money.

2. ... but to Walter money is almost everything.

3. He mostly believes that money is important.

4. Walter is concerned with money.

5. ... he wants material things.

6. ... the son tries to tell his mom that money is the most important thing.

Although these sentences and thousands of other variants differ in a number of ways, they all convey the same concept. It is *c*-rater's task to recognise that these responses are correct while distinguishing it from incorrect responses that contain very similar language, such as '*Walter cares* about his dignity and his mother worries about *money*.'

Much of the variation among the student's responses is due to surface syntactic differences. For example, in the question about photosynthesis, one student may write an active sentence such as, 'water them both' while another may choose to use the passive voice as in 'they both should be watered'. To recover the underlying syntactic form, *c*-rater generates a syntactic analysis (Abney, 1996) from which it extracts each clause's predicate argument structure – such as its subject, verb and object. When the predicate argument structure is extracted, much of the surface syntactic difference among the responses is eliminated.

c-rater then normalises across word variation due to inflected and derived word forms using a morphological analyser that was developed at ETS. Inflectional normalization removes the differences due to number, tense or agreement (*dreamed* and *dreams* are normalised to *dream*). Normalising across derived forms allows verbs like *measure* and the derived noun *measurement* to be collapsed when one student uses the noun in 'Take their *measurements*' while another use the verb in '*Measure* the plants' growth.'

c-rater's pronoun resolution module is a version of Morton (2000) that has been specifically trained on student responses to essays and short-answer question. It identifies all of the noun phrases that a pronoun could refer to and automatically selects the most likely one. In the examples we have seen, *he* and *she* refer unambiguously to Walter or to his mother. However, when *c*-rater was used to mark a question that involved comparing three former US presidents, the pronoun *he* provided no clue as to which president was being discussed. The most frequently used pronoun in these responses is *it*, which similarly gives little clue as to its referent.

The system also needs to recognise lexical substitution – when students use words that are synonyms of, or have a similar meaning to, words in the model answer. To this end, the system uses a *word similarity matrix* (Lin, 1998) that was statistically generated after training on more than 300 million words of current American and British fiction, nonfiction and textbooks. Table 11.2 shows the words that are closest to 'important', 'humorous' and 'light'.

Table 11.2 Example word similarity matrices

Word	Words closest in meaning
important	crucial, significant, vital, useful, essential, interesting, difficult, valuable, key, necessary, critical, urgent, beneficial, indispensable, relevant, decisive, positive, exciting, major, fundamental …
humorous	amusing, witty, hilarious, comic, satirical, funny, ironic, wry, droll, mocking, sardonic, autobiographical, lighthearted, entertaining, insightful, comical, satiric, tongue-in-cheek, amused, irreverent, sarcastic …
light	sunlight, glow, yellow light, sun, lamp, sunshine, brightness, sunlit, darkness, daylight, ray, beam, sun …

Generating the predicate argument structure, pronoun resolution and morphological normalisation is all fully automated – and out of the hands of the content expert who builds the *c*-rater models. However, it has not been possible to automate the inclusion of similar words into the model. The assumption behind the word similarity matrices is that words with similar meanings appear in the same contexts. However, inappropriate words can be generated by the word similarity matrix. It is easy to see how 'important' and 'difficult' occur in similar contexts, but they bear quite different meanings, as do 'humorous' and 'autobiographical'. An even more important problem is that antonyms, such as 'light' and 'darkness' often appear in identical contexts and so can usually be found as high ranking words in the matrices. In order to prevent antonyms from getting into the model, the content expert who is building the model needs to select those words from the matrices that are appropriate for the model answer.

Morphological and syntactic variation and the use of synonyms and pronouns are well understood commonly associated with paraphrases while spelling is not. However, as *c*-rater developed, it became apparent that spelling errors are a very important source of variation when marking responses to test questions. In order for *c*-rater to be effective, it must recognise words that are spelled incorrectly – and correct them 'behind the scenes'.

Typically spelling correction is an interactive process – when a word processor does not find a word in its dictionary, it displays a menu of possible words and the user chooses to appropriate word. However, when *c*-rater is marking a response, the student who generated the response is no longer available. Therefore, *c*-rater needs both identify and correct spelling errors.

As do other spell correction systems, *c*-rater's spelling correction module identifies a word as being misspelled when it cannot find the word in its dictionary. It then uses a standard edit distance algorithm to count the number of keystrokes that separate the unrecognised word from the words in a dictionary. When the minimum edit distance is small, the unrecognised word is replaced with the closest word in the dictionary.

When marking content-based short answer questions, the domain of discourse is highly restricted – consisting of the test question, the model answer and the reading passage or the content on which an assessment is based. This restricted domain enables c-rater to perform accurate highly spelling correction because it uses only the discourse as its dictionary. For example, one of the questions that c-rater marked was looking to see whether President Reagan was identified in the response. We identified 67 distinct mis-spellings of 'Reagan' in the student responses, one of the most frequent being 'Reagons'. My word processor suggests replacing 'Reagons' with 'Reasons'. However, since 'reasons' does not appear in the domain of that question, it was not considered as a possible correction at all. Using this method, 84 per cent of the variants of 'Reagan' were correctly identified.

The c-rater answer models consist of a set of relations that represent the components of a correct answer. Then, for each relation that is represented in that model, c-rater attempts to identify a comparable relation in a student's response by extracting and normalising verbs and their arguments.

Case studies

In the Spring of 2003, the State of Indiana Commission for Higher Education, the Indiana Department of Education, ETS and a subcontractor, Achievement Data, Inc., collaborated to develop and field test an administration of an online end-of-course test for 11th grade students. The two courses selected for this pilot study were 11th grade English and Algebra I. All of the prompts were marked on a three-point scale, with zero for no credit, one for partial credit and two for full credit. There was a six-week period from when testing began in May to reporting all of the scores. During these six weeks, c-rater scoring models were deployed for 17 reading comprehension and five algebra questions. By the middle of June, c-rater had scored about 170,000 11th grade student responses to the reading comprehension and algebra questions.

In order to estimate how accurate the scoring was, 100 responses to each question were selected from the pool and scored by two readers. These data were used to calculate inter-reader agreement, as well as c-rater agreement with reader 1 and with reader 2. The average agreement rates and kappa values for the five algebra models and 17 reading comprehension models are shown in Table 11.3. On these responses, c-rater agreed with the readers about 85 per cent of the time for both the reading comprehension and algebra questions, whereas the readers agreed with each other 93 per cent of the time for reading comprehension and 91.5 per cent of the time for algebra.

Table 11.3 Results for the Indiana 2003 pilot

	Reading comprehension percent agreement (kappa)	Algebra percent agreement (kappa)
c-rater and reader 1	84.7 (.78)	85.8 (.74)
c-rater and reader 2	85.1 (.78)	84.9 (.74)
reader 1 and reader 2	93.0 (.90)	91.5 (.86)

A subsequent pilot test of the system took place in May 2004, in which eight of the *c*-rater models were reused – two of the algebra models and six of the reading comprehension models. Again, to estimate the scoring accuracy, 100 responses to each question were scored by two readers used to calculate inter-reader agreement, *c*-rater agreement with reader 1 and with reader 2, as shown in Table 11.4. The *c*-rater models remained stable and the results have remained consistent with a previous *c*-rater study (Sandene *et al.*, 2005).

Table 11.4 Results for the Indiana 2004 pilot

	Reading comprehension percent agreement (kappa)	Algebra percent agreement (kappa)
c-rater and reader 1	82.3 (.72)	86.0 (.73)
c-rater and reader 2	83.0 (.73)	82.5 (.68)
reader 1 and reader 2	91.2 (.86)	93.5 (.88)

Sources of error

c-rater/reader agreement is consistently lower than reader/reader agreement. There are several reasons for this. First, there are borderline responses – where on inspection of the *c*-rater errors, it is not clear whether or why the *c*-rater score is wrong. Another reason is that humans are far better at recognising spelling errors than *c*-rater is. For example, one question requires mentioning the concept of *repetition* as a literary device. Both readers accepted *repation* as a variant of *repetition*, whereas the *c*-rater spelling correction program did not. In addition, some misspellings happen to be perfectly good English words. For example, in looking for the concept of an *odd number* in a response, the readers accepted *add number*. But since *add* is a correctly spelled English word, *c*-rater did not attempt to 'correct' it so that it would match a word in the model.

There are also times when the response is truly original. One accurate response is that a certain kind of window is *too expensive* or *too costly*. One student wrote, idiomatically, that the windows would '*take a chunk of change*'. Of course, the model can be modified to include *chunk of change*, but the chances of that particular idiom ever being encountered again is slight. More importantly, the more open-ended a question is, the more difficult it is to build a model. When the concept being looked for is imprecise, then there are sure to be ways of stating it that are not found in the range-finding sets.

Usually when *c*-rater errs, it assigns a score that is too high rather than one that is too low, thereby giving more credit than is deserved. This often occurs because a response can contain the appropriate language even though its meaning differs from the concept required by the model. As an example, a concept that *c*-rater tries to identify is '*it is an old house*'. One student wrote that 'the author is telling you how *old the house* is', which was not credited by either reader. This becomes more problematic as a model is adjusted to accept sentence fragments as being correct answers. In this adjustment, *c*-rater imposes fewer requirements in order to allow syntactically incomplete forms that nonetheless embody the elements of the model. The problem seems unavoidable because human readers consistently accept sentence fragments – even very ungrammatical ones.

In general, if a distinction between partial or no credit is difficult for humans to make, as shown by inter-rater agreement, then that distinction is even more difficult for *c*-rater to make. The same holds for distinctions between partial and full credit.

Feedback to students

Since *c*-rater can recognise which concepts appear in a student response and which do not, a natural extension for *c*-rater is to give feedback as well as a score. For example, suppose a prompt asks for an explanation and an example in order to receive full credit. If *c*-rater finds neither example nor explanation and zero is assigned to the response, it is clear that neither was found. Similarly, if it assigns a 2 to the response, obviously both concepts were identified. However, when *c*-rater assigns partial credit, it can return a score and along with it a feedback message such as: *c*-rater *has identified your explanation but cannot find your example* or, conversely, *c*-rater *has identified your example, but cannot find your explanation.*

Of course, when partial credit is assigned, *c*-rater may have assigned the correct score for the wrong reason. For example, it is possible that the response contains an explanation but no example and that *c*-rater has inappropriately recognized an example but not the explanation. In this case, the score is correct but the feedback would be in error. Table 11.5 shows the cross tabulation table for *c*-rater and one of the readers for the eight reading comprehension questions. Table 11.6 shows the cross tabulation for the two Algebra questions. The boldface cells show the number of responses where both *c*-rater and the reader assigned partial credit. It is these responses where *c*-rater and the reader agree – but the score may not have been assigned for the same reason.

Table 11.5 Cross-tabulation for the eight reading comprehension questions

	c-rater: no credit	c-rater: partial credit	c-rater: full credit
Reader: no credit	**95**	30	2
Reader: partial credit	10	**215**	26
Reader: full credit	1	31	**188**

Table 11.6 Cross-tabulation for the two algebra questions

	c-rater: no credit	c-rater: partial credit	c-rater: full credit
Reader: no credit	**114**	8	4
Reader: partial credit	8	**46**	4
Reader: full credit	1	3	**12**

The scoring rubrics for the prompts in the 2004 pilot have three structures:

Structure 1. *Full credit:* 2 concepts

Partial credit: 1 concept

No credit: 0 concepts

Structure 2. *Full credit:* any 2 examples (out of 3 in the reading passage)

Partial credit: 1 example (out of 3 in the reading passage)

No credit: 0 examples

Structure 3. *Full credit:* 2 examples and 1 explanation

Partial credit: 2 examples and no explanation

1 or 2 examples and no explanation

0 or 1 example and 1 explanation

No credit: no examples and no explanation.

Six of the prompts have structure 1 (the two algebra items and four reading comprehension items), one reading comprehension prompt has structure 2 and another has structure 3.

For the 100 examples from each prompt that were scored by two readers, we generated feedback of the sort:

Structure 1:   *C*-rater has identified the concept that … you have not answered the question completely.

Structure 2:   *C*-rater has found only one example, that … you should give two examples.

Structure 3:   *C*-rater has identified one example, that … you need to give another example and an explanation.

… and so on.

These messages were inspected, along with the response to determine the accuracy of the feedback. As can be seen from the three structures, there are many ways to get partial credit. In structure 1, there are two ways, in structure 2 there are three ways and structure 3 there are six. When *c*-rater and the reader both assigned partial credit, *c*-rater gave about 4 per cent inappropriate feedback on both the Algebra test (2 out of 46 responses) and the Reading Comprehension test (9 out of 215 responses). These cases represent only about 1 per cent and 1.5 per cent of all responses, respectively. As expected, the prompt with structure 3 had the highest level of inaccurate feedback. Often, disagreement between the readers and *c*-rater was caused by spelling errors that *c*-rater could not correct (the readers are extraordinarily good at interpreting spelling errors) or to very ungrammatical responses. In many cases, *c*-rater/reader agreement would improve if the student were to revise the response by fixing these errors.

Conclusion

When *c*-rater agrees with readers on a partial-credit score, it may do so for the wrong reasons. These reasons are revealed in its feedback comments so the accuracy of the feedback is a higher standard of measure than simple score agreement. However, experimental results show that only a small proportion of partial credit score agreement is for the wrong reasons. If these cases are added to the score disagreements, the overall error rate increases only 1–1.5 per cent.

Author's note

This chapter describes work that was done by the author when she was at Educational Testing Service.

References

Abney, S. (1996). 'Partial parsing via finite-state cascades.' In: *Proceedings of the ESS-LLI '96 Robust Parsing Workshop*.

Burstein, J. (2003). 'The E-rater scoring engine: automated esscay scoring with natural language processing.' In: Shermis, M.D. and Burstein, J. (Eds) *Automated Essay Scoring: A Cross-Disciplinary Perspective*. Mahwah, NJ: Lawrence Erlbaum Associates.

Landauer, T.K., Laham, D. and Foltz, P.W. (2003). 'Automated scoring and annotation of essays with the Intelligent Essay Assessor.' In: Shermis, M.D. and Burstein, J. (Eds) *Automated Essay Scoring: A Cross-Disciplinary Perspective*. Mahwah, NJ: Lawrence Erlbaum Associates.

Leacock, C. and Chodorow, M. (2003). 'c-rater: Automated scoring of short-answer questions', *Computers and the Humanities*, **37**, 4.

Lin, D. (1998). 'Automatic retrieval and clustering of similar words.' In: *Proceedings of the 35th Annual Meeting of the Association for Computational Linguistics,* Montreal, 898–904.

Morton, T.S. (2000). 'Coreference for NLP applications.' In: *Proceedings of the 38th Annual Meeting of the Association for Computational Linguistics*, Hong Kong.

Penstein-Rosé, C., and Hall, B.S. (2004). 'A little goes a long way: quick authoring of semantic knowledge sources for interpretation.' Paper presented at the 2nd International Workshop on Scalable Natural Language Understanding (ScaNaLU 2004) at HLT-NAACL 2004.

Perez, D., Alfonseca, E. and Rodriguez, P. (2004). 'Upper Bounds of the Bleu algorithm applied to assessing student essays.' Paper presented at the 30th annual conference of the International Association for Educational Assessment (IAEA), Philadelphia, PA.

Sandene, B., Horkay, N., Bennett, R.E., Allen, N., Braswell, J., Kaplan, B. and Oranje A. (2005). *Online Assessment in Mathematics and Writing: Reports From the NAEP Technology-Based Assessment Project, Research and Development Series*. Washington, DC: National Center for Education Statistics.

Sukkarieh, J.Z., Pulman, S.G., and Raikes, N. (2004). 'Auto-marking 2: an update on the UCLES-Oxford University research into using computational linguistics to score short, free text responses.' Paper presented at the 30th annual conference of the International Association for Educational Assessment (IAEA), Philadelphia, PA.

Vigilante, R. (1999). 'Online computer scoring of constructed-response questions', *Journal of Information Technology Impact*, **1**, 2, 57–62.

12 The role of formative assessment

Gordon Stobart

The role of formative assessment

Assessments of reading, particularly reading tests, are typically used to determine where students are in their reading at a given point in time – assessment *of* learning. This chapter concentrates on how assessment can become part of the learning process – assessment *for* learning. The approach is took review some general principles of formative assessment rather than focus on the specifics of a particular reading assessment – which Andrew Watts does in his chapter (see chapter 13). It seeks to clarify what is involved in formative assessment and the relationship between formative and summative assessments. Taking a view of learning as an active, meaning-making process which involves changes to capabilities or understanding, a distinction is made between deep approaches to learning and surface approaches reflected in improved test taking techniques. Validity in formative assessment is considered in relation to 'consequential validity'. This means that if there is no further learning as a result of the assessment it is not valid formative assessment. The focus then shifts to feedback, one of the core concepts of formative assessment. The forms of feedback that lead to further learning are discussed, along with practices that may discourage learning.

Purpose in assessment

Two key questions of any assessment are:

- What is the purpose of this assessment?

- Is the form of assessment fit-for-purpose?

If the purpose of an assessment is not clear, or there are multiple, and sometimes competing, purposes then there is the potential for confusion about what inferences can be drawn from that assessment. One broad classification of purpose distinguishes between *summative* and *formative* assessments. Summative incorporates assessments which 'sum up' at a given point in time where students are in their learning. End of course examinations would be an obvious example of this, with the results used for managerial purposes such as selection or reporting progress.

Far more problematic is the definition of formative assessment. Formative has proved so elastic in its usage that many have stopped using it and have switched to 'assessment *for* learning' (e.g. Assessment Reform Group, 1999, 2002). This switch emphasises that 'formative' is part of the learning process, so that to be formative an assessment has to lead to learning (Wiliam and Black,1996). Increasingly the focus in the British formative assessment literature has been on student learning (Torrance and Pryor, 1998; Assessment Reform Group (ARG) 1999, 2002; Black *et al.*, 2003) with the ARG 2002 definition widely accepted:

> *Assessment for Learning is the process of seeking and interpreting evidence for use by learners and their teachers to decide where the learners are in their learning, where they need to go and how best to get there.*

Evidence in this definition is construed generously: anything from formal written to recognising bemused looks provides evidence. What it understates is that learning also applies to the teacher, so that an assessment can be formative if a teacher learns from it, for example by modifying the curriculum or teaching methods. This is particularly relevant where an attempt is made to use formatively the outcomes of a summative assessment such as a beginning, or end, of year reading test.

The relationship of formative and summative assessments

Much reading assessment will have a summative function, reporting what stage or level a student has reached at a given point in time – often at the beginning or end of a school year. The task is therefore how to make formative use of this summative information.

The relationship between formative and summative assessment is far from straight-forward (Wiliam and Black, 1996; Harlen and James, 1997; Wiliam, 2000). If summative assessment is only formative when further learning takes place then a reading test, on this definition, is not formative unless it is used to move learning on. A paradox here is that even a diagnostic reading test may not be formative if the results are used for selection and placement purposes (i.e. summatively) rather than for informing learning (see Kyriakides, 2004).

Timing

It is an oversimplification to claim that the difference is essentially one of timing. Timing simply offers more or less potential for learning from an assessment, it does not define which kind of assessment it will be. Robert Stake's often quoted 'when the cook tastes the soup it's formative, when the customer tastes the soup, it's summative' is potentially misleading if the impression is given that it's the timing that makes the difference rather than the purpose and consequence of tasting.

Timing is not the difference between formative and summative assessments, but is often an expression of it. Summative assessment can be used formatively when there is subsequently time to learn from the responses and act upon them. Thus summative assessment used before the end of a course or phase has clearly more potential to be formative for students. Would not classroom assessment undertaken two thirds of the way through a course provide a better basis for learning?

This may sound a bit idealistic (how will their further learning be recognised if they've already done the test?). However, the Daugherty Assessment Review Group in Wales (2004) recommended something similar for the national tests. At present the National Curriculum tests are taken at the end of primary school (year 6). The results have no impact on secondary school selection, that is decided prior to the tests, and secondary schools make little systematic use of the information. Daugherty has recommended that the tests (or modified versions which look at broader skill areas) should be taken at the end of year 5 so that teachers can use them formatively during the next year. The end of primary school assessment will then be a summative teacher assessment. What has made this possible for Wales is that primary school performance tables have been abolished, so the distorting role of this form of accountability is removed. Another variation of this is found in France where the pattern is to test students at the beginning of secondary school, rather than the end of primary, so that the teacher can use the information formatively.

More emphasis on teacher learning

The current emphasis in formative assessment is on student learning. In earlier formulations more attention was paid to the feedback to teachers allowing them to adjust their teaching to aid student learning, though not necessarily the students who had been assessed. So this year's summative assessment may be formative for next year, especially for the teacher.

One issue is what use teachers actually make of summative evidence. In the National Curriculum tests in England, the students' marked scripts are sent back to the schools. However the evidence suggests that little formative use is made of this data. It seems that most teachers use it as an opportunity to check the reliability of the marking (they also have the mark schemes) with around a third giving them back to the students and only a third of these using them formatively (Stobart, 2001). A concern here is that the focus is on the data – patterns of results, comparison with others and previous years – rather than on relative strengths and weaknesses in understanding and attainment.

Learning

One further definitional point needs to be made – that we also need a working definition of learning. How we view learning impacts on how we approach assessment. The assumption here is that learning is an active, meaning-making process (see chapter 4) which is most effective when it builds on what is already known and makes connections with other learning. I am adopting Eraut's 'strong' definition of learning as *'a significant change in capability or understanding'* which excludes 'the acquisition of further information when it does not contribute to such changes' (Coffield, 1997, p.5). The spirit of this is also captured in Harlen and James' (1997) distinction between deep and surface learning (see Table 12.1). They seek to reduce polarities with the introduction of the concept of strategic learning in which the learner seeks optimal combinations of deep and surface learning – the problem being that much current assessment encourages only surface learning.

Table 12.1 The distinctions between deep and surface learning

Deep learning approach	Surface learning approach
An intention to develop personal understanding	An intention to be able to reproduce content as required
Active interaction with content, particularly relating new ideas to previous knowledge and experience	Passive acceptance of ideas and information
Linking ideas together using integrating principles	Lack of recognition of guiding principles and patterns
Relating evidence to conclusions	Focusing learning on assessment requirements

While some of the polarities between learning and performance orientations have been overplayed, I would not wish to identify learning directly in terms of tests scores, especially where the tests may show limited construct validity. Good scores do not necessarily mean that effective learning has taken place, as evidenced by Gordon and Reese's (1997) conclusions on their study of the Texas Assessment of Academic Skills (TAAS) which students were passing

> *even though the students have never learned the concepts on which they are being tested. As teachers become more adept at this process, they can even teach students to correctly answer test items intended to measure students' ability to apply, or synthesise, even though the students have not developed application, analysis or synthesis skills.* (p.364)

That test scores may, in part, be the result of training in test-taking techniques independent of an understanding of the subject matter may be self-evident to practitioners, this is not always how policy makers see it. For many of them the relationship is unproblematic: test scores are a direct representation of learning standards. If more 11-year-olds reach level 4 for reading on the National Curriculum assessment in England, then reading standards have risen, with no acknowledgement that there may be an 'improved test taking' factor in this. Tymms (2004) has demonstrated this effect in relation to National Curriculum assessment of literacy in England, where progress on other independent assessments of literacy has been far more modest. Linn (2000) has shown how there is a regular pattern of substantial early improvements in scores on a new high-stakes test, as teachers improve their preparation of their students, followed after about four years by a flattening out of scores (which then comes as a shock to these same policy makers).

So if evidence from a reading assessment is used to identify misunderstandings and leads to a clearer conceptual understanding, then this is formative. If it simply improves test taking techniques, with no need for changes in mastery of the concept or skill, then this learning does not meet the definition. While I recognise there will be some grey zones between understanding and technique, I want to signal that improving scores is not automatically a formative learning process.

The evidence from Andrew Watts' research in chapter 13 illustrates just such concerns. While the use of Assessment Focuses offers the potential for formative feedback from reading assessments they also run the risk of being used as micro-teaching techniques which focus on gaining extra marks ('knowledge in bits') rather than increasing understanding.

Validity in formative assessment

One of the central themes of this book is validity. Critical to any discussion of the assessment of reading is making explicit the construct of reading that is being tested and evaluating the extent to which an assessment represents this. This approach sits well with recent formulations of validity in which it is no longer seen as a static property of an assessment (e.g. predictive/concurrent/face validity) but is based on the inferences drawn from the results of an assessment. It is treated as:

- an integrated concept, rather than a variety of approaches, organised around a broader view of construct validity (Shepard, 1993, pp.405–50)

- a property of the test scores rather than the test itself. The 1985 version of the American Standards was explicit on this: 'validity always refers to the degree to which … evidence supports the inferences that are made from the scores' (AERA, 1985, p.9).

This approach was championed by Samuel Messick (1989):

Validity is an integrated evaluative judgement of the degree to which empirical evidence and theoretical rationales support the adequacy *and* appropriateness *of* inferences *and* actions *based on test scores or other modes of assessment.* (1989, p.13)

The more recent debate has been about whether the concept of validity should also include the *consequences* of an assessment. This was the position adopted by Messick:

For a fully unified view of validity, it must also be recognised that the appropriateness, meaningfulness and usefulness of score-based inferences depend as well on the social consequences of the testing. Therefore, social values cannot be ignored in considerations of validity. (1989, p.19)

It is this *consequential validity* that is central to the validity of formative assessment.

If formative assessment is to be valid it must lead to further learning (Wiliam, 2000). The assumption is that the assessment includes information which enables this further learning to take place – the 'how to get there' in the definition of assessment for learning.

Unlike in summative assessment, reliability is of less concern in formative assessment. This is because consistency across students is unimportant, different students with similar outcomes may need different feedback to 'close the gap' in an individual's learning and part of the teacher's skill is deciding what feedback is most likely to do this. And given feedback is repeated and informal, errors in interpretation will, ideally, be self-correcting. This, however, is problematic when attempts are made to use formative assessment as the basis for summative judgements since the formative is likely to become a series of mini-summative assessments, with the emphasis on reliability rather than further learning. For this reason I am very wary of schemes of continuous assessment which claim to be formative, since it is often meant in terms of 'forming' the final mark rather than informing learning.

Where these difficulties are not appreciated we may see threats to the validity of both formative and summative assessments. Harlen and James (1997) propose that:

> *The alternative to using the same* results *of assessment for both purposes is to use relevant* evidence *gathered as part of teaching for formative purposes but to review it, for summative purposes, in relation to the criteria that will be used for all pupils ... In other words, summative assessment should mean summing up* the evidence, *not summing across a series of judgements or completed assessments.* (p.375)

Given the complexity of the formative/summative relationship, how can assessments be used to help learning? The rest of this chapter will focus on a central aspect of this process: the quality of feedback and how this may encourage or discourage further learning.

Effective feedback

Feedback is a defined as 'closing the gap' between current and desired performance (Sadler, 1989). Some of the key features of effective feedback are:

- it is clearly linked to the learning intention

- the learner understands the success criteria/standard

- it focuses on the task rather than the learner (self/ego)

- it gives cues at appropriate levels on how to bridge the gap:

    - self-regulatory/metacognitive

    - process/deep learning

    - task /surface learning

- it challenges, requires action, and is achievable. (Stobart, 2003, pp.113–22)

If the gap is not closed (that is, learning has not taken place) then what has been done does not qualify as feedback. In their meta-analysis of feedback studies Kluger and DeNisi (1996) concluded:

> *In over one third of the cases Feedback Interventions reduced performance ... we believe that researchers and practitioners alike confuse their feelings that feedback is desirable with the question of whether Feedback Intervention benefits performance.* (pp.275, 277)

Some of the main causes of feedback failure are appear to be:

- feedback cues are given at the wrong 'level'

- the learners do not understand the standard ('desired performance') so cannot fully make sense of the feedback

- feedback is 'too deeply coded' to close the gap

- the learner has choices over what to do with feedback.

Feedback cues are given at the wrong 'level'

Kluger and DeNisi argue that if feedback is pitched at a particular level then the response to it is likely to be at that level. For example, feedback is most powerful when it is provided at the process level and seeks to make connections and grasp underlying principles. Feedback at the task level is productive when it deals with incorrect or partial information, though less so when the task/concept is not understood. If feedback is in terms of encouraging perseverance with task ('self-regulation') the response will be in terms of more effort. While this in itself will not lead to new learning it will provide the context for seeking feedback at the process or task level.

The most unproductive form of feedback is that addressed at the self or 'ego' level because the gap that is to be closed is less to do with learning than with self-perception, it will be seen through a 'reputational' lens (Hattie, 2002). If I am given feedback that my work has disappointed my teacher – 'you can do better than this'– I will seek ways of reconciling these judgements to my own self-perception. Thus I may attribute the quality of my work to lack of effort, protecting my view of myself as having the ability to do it if I chose to (a favourite attributional trick for many boys). However, if the teacher's judgement was on a task on which I had done my best I may begin to doubt my ability – a process which if continuously repeated (as it is for many students) may lead to a state of 'learned helplessness' (Dweck, 1986). In this I declare 'I am no good at this' and avoid further exposure to it. Reading tests which stop after repeated failure (e.g. Schonell's Graded Word Reading Test) may also play into this attitude.

Research into classroom assessment (Gipps et al., 2001) has shown that even with expert primary teachers most feedback is 'evaluative' and takes the forms of the teacher signalling approval or disapproval, with judgements focusing on, for example, attitude or the effort made. Relatively little process or task focused 'descriptive' feedback, which attempts to provide the next learning steps, takes place. This raises issues for star and smiley faces cultures in schools, since these are essentially 'ego-related' (for being good, trying hard etc.) rather than task focused.

The learners do not understand the standard ('desired performance') so cannot fully make sense of the feedback (Sadler, 1989)

For Sadler, one of the key theorists of feedback, this is the missing link in understanding 'the common but puzzling observation that even when teachers provide students with valid and reliable judgements about the quality of their work, improvement does not necessarily follow' (p.119). If students do not understand the purpose of what they are doing and have no clear sense of the quality of performance needed, then feedback will make little sense.

There are two main, and inter-related, strands to addressing this issue. The first involves making the intended level of performance more explicit to the student. This may involve making the 'learning intention' explicit as well as the 'success criteria' (Clarke, 2001). This is something that has been addressed in materials that accompany National Curriculum reading assessment, though the critical issue is the extent to which teachers have 'downloaded' them to their students. Two key teaching and learning approaches are the use of *exemplars* and *modelling*, both of which are familiar to most practitioners and part of the primary and secondary teaching and learning strategies in England. It is through the active use of exemplars ('what make this response better than that one') that learners begin to appreciate the differences in the quality of performance and may begin to articulate what would be needed to improve a piece of work (Sadler, 1989). Modelling involves demonstrating how to approach a question, for example 'drawing inferences' from a reading passage will mean nothing to, or be completely misunderstood by, some students until there is a practical demonstration of how to go about this task (made more active when students are able to improve on the teacher's draft).

The second, and closely linked, strand involves students in peer- and self-assessment. The rationale here is that if students are being asked to assess each other and themselves they will have to actively develop a sense of the success criteria/standard against which their work is to be evaluated. At the heart of this is the teacher handing over the control and authority which assessment brings, something which teachers often find very anxiety provoking (Black *et al*., 2003). This is also a student skill which has to be developed rather than assumed (Black *et al*., 2003). This is a long way from the common 'peer assessment' practices of marking each other's work using answers provided by the teacher.

Feedback is 'too deeply coded' to close the gap (Sadler, 1989)

If feedback does not provide enough information to move learning on then it is going to be ineffective. Where feedback is in terms of grades or marks or levels, these coded responses fail to offer the 'and how to get there' element of formative assessment (Assessment Reform Group, 2002). To know I am at reading level 4 does not help in what to do next. The solution appears to be to offer additional comment about what to do next. The problem with this is that research shows a grade accompanied by more explicit advice may not be much more successful. The widely quoted work of Butler (1988) has shown that, in many learning contexts, the presence of a grade appears to negate the value of accompanying comments, which Kohn (1999) captures with his 'when a grade is given, learning stops'.

I think recent developments to articulate in far more detail the standard that a grade or level represents may help to ease this situation. The move to fuller specification of both learning and assessment objectives offers possibilities for better de-coding of results, particularly with more authentic assessments. This is particularly the case where reporting is in terms of a profile rather than just a single grade. The assumption is that this provides increasingly rich detail about what needs to be done and so next steps can be made explicit. I am not as optimistic about the potential from feedback on fixed response/multiple-choice tests, where information is generally in terms of numbers of correct responses.

The learner has choices over what to do with feedback

A further, and salutary, factor in feedback not leading to learning is that the learner has a choice as to what to do with it. If 'learners must ultimately be responsible for their learning since no-one else can do it for them' (Assessment Reform Group, 1999, p.7) then how they use feedback is part of this. The risk of only making limited use increases when it is given in the form of a 'gift' – handed over by the giver to the recipient – rather than as part of a dialogue (Askew and Lodge, 2000). If the gap between current and desired performance is perceived as too great the learner may modify the desired standard or abandon it altogether ('retire hurt') – or reject the messenger.

A recognisable experience that parallels those of many students may be that of taking a course for which there is certification at the end. We may start with intentions of getting the highest grade but then modify our standards in the light of disappointing feedback ('all I want to do now is get through'). We may even drop out because we decide we don't now really need this qualification ('abandon') or because it was so badly taught and organised ('reject').

Conclusion

Assessing reading provides complex information about where students are in their learning. Formative assessment seeks to move this learning on by providing feedback which will encourage such movement. This chapter has illustrated that this is not a simple teacher led process. For learning to take place the student must also understand what is being learned and what successful performance entails. Similarly feedback has to be geared to the task or process and be realistic and informative to the learner. Formative assessment in reading offers the potential to improve as well as monitor reading skills.

Author's note

This chapter draws on the author's paper, 'The formative use of summative assessment', presented at the 30th Annual IAEA Conference, June 2004, Philadelphia, USA.

References

APA/AERA (1985). *Standards for Educational and Psychological Tests*. Washington, DC: American Psychological Association.

Askew, S. and Lodge, C. (2000). 'Gifts, ping-pong and loops – linking feedback and learning.' In: Askew S. (Ed) *Feedback for Learning*. London: RoutledgeFalmer.

Assessment Reform Group (1999). *Assessment for Learning: Beyond the Black Box*. Cambridge: Cambridge Institute of Education.

Assessment Reform Group (2002). *Assessment for Learning: 10 Principles*. Cambridge: Cambridge Institute of Education.

Black, P., Wiliam, D., Harrison, C., Lee, C. and Marshall, B. (2003). *Assessment for Learning: Putting it into Practice*. Buckingham: Open University Press.

Butler, R. (1988). 'Enhancing and undermining intrinsic motivation: the effects of task-involving and ego-involving evaluation on interest', *British Journal of Educational Psychology*, **58**, 1–14.

Clarke, S. (2001). *Unlocking Formative Assessment*. London: Hodder and Stoughton.

Coffield, F. (1997). 'Nine learning fallacies and their replacement by a national strategy for lifelong learning.' In: Coffield F. (Ed) *A National Strategy for Lifelong Learning*. Newcastle: University of Newcastle.

Daugherty Assessment Review Group (2004). 'Learning Pathways through statutory assessed stages 2 and 3' [online]. Available: http://www.learning.wales.gov.uk.

Dweck, C.S. (1986). 'Motivational processes affecting learning', *American Psychologist*, **41**, 1040–8.

Gipps, C., McCallum, B. and Hargreaves, E. (2000). *What Makes a Good Primary School Teacher? Expert Classroom Strategies*. London: Falmer.

Gordon, S. and Reese, M. (1997). 'High stakes testing: worth the price?' *Journal of School Leadership*, **7**, 345–68.

Harlen, W. and James, M. (1997). 'Assessment and learning; differences and relationships between formative and summative assessment', *Assessment in Education*, **4**, 4, 365–79.

Hattie, J. (2002). The power of feedback for enhancing learning (personal communication).

Kluger, A.V. and DeNisi, A. (1996). 'The effects of feedback interventions on performance: a historical review, a meta-analysis, and a preliminary feedback intervention theory', *Psychological Bulletin*, **119**, 2, 252–84.

Kohn, A. (1999). *Punished by Rewards: The Trouble with Gold Stars, Incentive Plans, As, Praise and Other Bribes*. Boston: Houghton Mifflin.

Kyriakides, L. (2004). 'Investigating validity from teachers' perspectives through their engagement in large-scale assessment: the Emergent Literacy Baseline Assessment project', *Assessment in Education*, **11**, 2, 143–65.

Linn, R.L. (2000). 'Assessment and Accountability', *Educational Researcher*, **29**, 2, 4–16.

Messick, S. (1989). 'Validity.' In: Linn R.L. (Ed) *Educational Measurement*. Third edn. New York: American Council on Education and Macmillan.

Sadler, R. (1989). 'Formative assessment and the design of instructional systems', *Instructional Science*, **18**, 119–44.

Shepard, L. (1993). 'Evaluating test validity.' In: Darling-Hammond, L. (Ed) *Review of Research in Education*, Vol. 19.

Stobart, G. (2001). 'The Validity of National Curriculum Assessment', *British Journal of Educational Studies*, **49**, 1, 26–39.

Stobart, G. (2003). 'Using assessment to improve learning: intentions, feedback and motivation.' In: Richardson, C. (Ed) *Whither Assessment*. London: QCA.

Torrance, H. and Pryor, J. (1998). *Investigating Formative Assessment: Teaching, Learning and Assessment in the Classroom*. Buckingham: Open University Press.

Tymms, P. (2004). 'Are standards rising in English primary schools?' *British Educational Research Journal*, **30**, 4, 477–94.

Wiliam, D. (2000). 'Recent development in educational assessment in England: the integration of formative and summative functions of assessment.' Paper presented at SweMaS, Umea, Sweden.

Wiliam, D. and Black, P. (1996). 'Meanings and consequences: a basis for distinguishing formative and summative functions of assessment?' *British Educational Research Journal*, **22**, 5, 537–48.

13 Using assessment focuses to give feedback from reading assessments

Lorna Pepper, Rifat Siddiqui and Andrew Watts

Background and aims

While it is generally acknowledged that reading is an holistic process, defining goals for improving pupils' reading often depends on the identification of discrete skills. Such categorisations are an integral part of the process of planning, teaching and assessment, as teachers may target particular areas of reading by drawing on their assessments of pupils' performances in the discrete skills.

In the mark schemes for the National Curriculum tests of reading in England, an explicit statement about the focus of each test item is made. Six 'assessment focus' (AF) categories are presented to make clearer to markers of test papers and to teachers, the aspect of reading being tested by each question. This information is not given explicitly to the pupils: it is the questions which tell them what to focus on and the AFs are not printed on the test paper. However, schools have been encouraged to undertake self-evaluative activities with pupils, exploring their performance at question level and discussing targets for improvement. An article in *'On Track' The Secondary English Magazine* in April 2004 described such a use of AFs with year 10 pupils. It concluded that for reading they produced useful information from the assessment, but for writing they were 'of very limited help in providing pupils with specific targets for future improvement' (Matthews, 2004, pp.12–14).

Drawing on these areas of current practice, a study was planned to explore the usefulness of the AFs in giving feedback to year 9 pupils from a reading test. The study aimed to investigate pupils' understanding of the AFs, and the degree to which knowledge of the focus of each question might help them in successfully understanding and then answering reading test questions. If it is successful, this process could be said to follow what Brookhart says is the key to the formative process, which is 'having a concept of the goal or learning target, which originally is the teacher's, but which ideally the student will internalise' (Brookhart, 2001, p.153). This echoes the Assessment Reform Group's prescription that if assessment is to lead to learning it should 'help pupils to know and to recognise the standards they are aiming for' (Assessment Reform Group, 1999, p.7).

The assessment focuses that apply to reading tests at KS3 are:

AF2 understand, describe, select or retrieve information, events or ideas from texts and use quotation and reference to text

AF3 deduce, infer or interpret information, events or ideas from texts

AF4 identify and comment on the structure and organisation of texts, including grammatical and presentational features at text level

AF5 explain and comment on writers' uses of language, including grammatical and literary features at word and sentence level

AF6 identify and comment on writers' purposes and viewpoints and the overall effect of the text on the reader (QCA, 2003).

Procedure

An experienced English teacher, who was teaching several classes of year 9 pupils, agreed to participate in the research. While a mixed-ability group was considered beneficial for the research aims, the teacher felt that the procedure would prove challenging for some pupils with lower attainment levels in English. It was agreed that as the pupils were organised in ability groups for English, a class of average to above-average ability would take part. This group consisted of 31 pupils (although not all pupils were present during all research sessions).

A sequence of teaching sessions was agreed as part of the project, with the administration of a KS3 reading test (the 2003 test, QCA 2003) being the starting point. The research was completed during four teaching sessions, within a three-week period.

A number of questionnaires and tasks were developed to capture pupils' reflections on the process, and their understanding of assessment focuses. The following list summarises the procedure and instruments.

1. Pupils completed a KS3 reading test paper (the 2003 paper).

2. The teacher marked the pupils' test papers.

3. The teacher introduced pupils to the idea of assessment focuses and together they discussed the application of AFs to questions in a different KS3 reading paper.

4. Pupils received their marked 2003 test papers along with a bar graph of their performance on each AF, including comparisons with 'pre-test' average scores (taken from a representative sample who trialled the test paper). This was designed to focus their attention on potential for improvement in their own scores.

5. Pupils were asked to consider their results, and their areas of strength and weakness, using prompts on *Questionnaire 1*.

6. Pupils then received different copies of the original test paper, on which the relevant assessment focus was printed under each question. They were asked to amend or rewrite their answers in order to improve their scores, using the AFs to help them.

7. After amending their papers, pupils were asked to complete *Questionnaire 2* in order to give their opinions about the helpfulness of AFs to the process of revision. They were also asked to indicate the types of changes they had made to their answers.

8. The teacher marked pupils' amended answers, and added these marks to their original scores.

9. Pupils received a bar graph showing their original and revised marks.

10. Using *Questionnaire 3*, pupils were asked to rank the different factors that they found helpful as they revised their answers, choosing from 5 options, with 1 the highest and 5 the lowest. 0 was also offered as an option, in cases where a particular factor was not at all helpful.

11. In *Questionnaire 4*, pupils were asked to rewrite each assessment focus in their own words, to make it as simple as possible for younger pupils to understand. This was aimed at capturing those aspects of the AFs that pupils found particularly difficult to interpret.

12. Finally, pupils considered three specific questions from the test again, in *Questionnaire 5*. They were asked to describe how they might use the assessment focus to help them answer more effectively at the first attempt, or how the AF might prove helpful in answering similar questions. This task was designed to record the extent to which pupils could extract and apply aspects of the AFs to questions.

13. The teacher's views on the value and impact of assessment focuses on pupils' performances were captured through a semi-structured interview.

Findings

How far did pupils understand the assessment focus categorisations?

During the classroom-based research, pupils engaged in many activities that involved reading and interpreting the assessment focuses. Particularly, they were asked to rewrite each focus in simpler language, and to apply the skills described within the AFs as they tried to improve their answers to the reading test paper.

Data from these different tasks suggests that aspects of the AFs were recognised by all pupils and some were able to understand most of each AF. But it appears that most pupils do not fully understand the language of the assessment focuses. In their rewriting of the AFs, the majority showed partial understanding, but particular concepts were consistently omitted.

AF2 was most successfully paraphrased by pupils, emphasising as it does the straightforward retrieval of content and use of quotation. Successful attempts included:

> Use quotations and refer to the text in your answer by collecting information from the text, making sure that you understand it.

> Take bits out of writing and talk about it, and use parts of the writing to show you know about it.

> Understand describe or take information, events or ideas from the text and use pieces of the text to back up or explain things.

Where pupils were unsure about this AF, observations demonstrated that 'retrieve' and 'reference to text' proved difficult for them to comprehend, although all pupils' attempts were close to the meaning of the AF.

AF3 was challenging for pupils to interpret (and paraphrase), primarily because of the terms, *deduce* and *infer*. During their writing, two pupils sought the teacher's help with the definition of these words. Many others wrote descriptors of this AF that focused on understanding events or ideas, but did not touch on the meaning of *deduce* or *infer*. In a few cases, pupils appeared to relate these terms to the need for personal opinion in answers. Some partially accurate attempts included:

> In depth describe the text, what is it saying in detail.

> Use your own ideas to explain the text. Don't just write about the text, write about what the text makes you think.

> Write what you see in the text in your own words and how you see it.

A few pupils seemed to grasp the focus on 'reading between the lines' in the AF:

> To be able to understand the text and what is behind it.

> Use the text and find the meanings hidden in it.

AF4 also prompted writing that demonstrated pupils' partial understanding of the focus. *Structure and organisation* were relatively well presented, while *grammatical and presentational features at text level* proved more problematic. A few pupils referred to grammar or punctuation in their descriptions, but it is clear that the majority found these difficult or unfamiliar concepts. Attempts included:

> Find and talk about the way the writing is set out and look at the sort of punctuation used, on your point of view.

> Point out how grammar/composition is used to improve the text.

> Look at and make a comment on the way the text is written and organised make sure you include grammar at the same level as the text.

AF5 also posed difficulties for pupils in understanding *grammatical and literary features*. Many pupils demonstrated understanding of the general focus on use of language, and sometimes related this to *word and sentence level*, although the terms themselves may not have been familiar.

> Use the writer's use of language and explain and comment on it at a higher level.

> Explain and make comments on how the[y] written the text eg what language use in full worded sentences.

Some successful renderings of this assessment focus showed good understanding of the skills involved.

> Explain and comment on writer's use of language, including grammar, e.g. exclamation marks and literary features, eg metaphors.

> Write about what words the writer uses and why, what parts the words play in each sentence.

AF6 gave rise to many partially successful definitions. While handling the writer's views or intentions pupils often failed to include the *effect of the text on the reader*.

> Look at what the writers [are] saying and their opinions about the topic.

> Explain parts of the story and why the writer has chosen to do that.

> Find what point the writer is trying to get across.

Successful attempts included:

> Comment/describe how the writer looks at certain things. What effect does this have on the reader?

> Create your own opinions on what the writer has given you as a viewpoint and the effect that it had on you as a reader, how it made you feel.

Pupils' responses provide rich data for further exploration and they suggest that the starting point for developing a more meaningful processes of feedback could be the pupils' own definitions of the assessment focuses.

What impact did the introduction of AFs have on pupils' responses to questions?

After completing their first attempts at the reading test questions, pupils explored each assessment focus with their teacher and looked through a different reading paper, assigning AFs to questions. They were encouraged to make links between question wordings and the wordings of the AFs. Pupils were then presented with their original answers for the reading test, their marks and a version of the paper that included the relevant assessment focus printed beneath each question. They were asked to make improvements to their answers and to refer to the AFs in order to understand better what elements might be lacking in their original responses.

An analysis of the revised answers revealed improved scores in all but one case, though one must bear in mind the small numbers of total marks involved. The largest percentage increase for any individual was 28 per cent (two cases) and the smallest (excluding the pupil who made no improvement) was 3 per cent. The average increase for the whole group was 15 per cent. Scores on six of the 20 questions in the test improved by 35–45 per cent. It is notable that all of these were one-mark items. (The majority of questions in the test carried one mark.) Looking at scores for particular assessment focuses (that is, for the group of questions in each AF category), there were some noticeable differences (see Table 13.1).

Table 13.1 Changes in average class performance by AF

AF	1st attempt %	2nd attempt %	Improvement %
AF2	91	98	7
AF3	62	81	19
AF4	71	74	3
AF5	48	67	19
AF6	50	80	30

It is clear that performance on questions in the AF6 category rose most sharply but, in common with the other categories that saw large improvements (AF3 and AF5), initial scores for AF6 questions were among the lowest. There was, therefore, greater scope for pupils to make gains in these categories. Questions addressing AF4 saw the smallest improvement, which may confirm the difficulties noted during pupils' attempts to interpret and re-express this focus (discussed above).

While the data provide much information about performance on the test, changes in the pupils' scores cannot be attributed to any single factor. This research did not establish a control group with which comparisons could be drawn. The support and teaching pupils received between their first and second attempts, aimed to introduce and explain assessment focuses. They were encouraged to make an explicit connection between questions in reading test papers and the AFs. This targeted intervention may have influenced the success of pupils' revised responses. However, other factors were also, inevitably, influential in their performance.

During the process of revising their answers, the researchers noted the high degree to which pupils sought help from others. In order to interpret the accuracy of their original answers and understand which elements were lacking, pupils looked to their peers. They also asked for clarification and help from the teacher and researchers, primarily because they had tried unsuccessfully to use the assessment focus as a prompt, and were genuinely nonplussed by the question concerned. For some pupils, a further unassisted attempt to answer the questions seemed de-motivating.

How useful did pupils find the assessment focuses?

Having had the opportunity to amend their test answers using the assessment focus of each question to help them, pupils were asked to rate the usefulness of the AFs for this purpose.

As Table 13.2 shows, immediately after revising their answers, the majority of pupils felt that the AFs had been somewhat useful to them. Their comments highlighted some perceived benefits of using the focuses.

Table 13.2 Pupil ratings of the helpfulness of AFs when revising answers

Response	Frequency
Didn't help me at all	4
Helped me a little	14
Helped me quite a lot	10
Helped me a lot	1

The assessment focuses gave interesting 'educational' words for us to put in our answers. It also helped us to understand the questions and what type of answers we should put.

It obviously didn't tell me what to do, but I also basically knew what the questions were looking for, but it helped distinguish between different ideas I had about answering some questions.

Because I knew what the markers were looking for in the answer, and helped understand how to put more detail in what areas.

Because I knew the outlines to put in the questions, I knew the outline for the answers instead of more or less flailing for the answers and getting lucky guesses.

A few pupils, while they felt the AFs had helped them, noted other factors.

The fact that we got to do it again and knowing what we got wrong helped. Plus knowing what area our answer should be in and seeing if the answer that was wrong was in that category.

Among those pupils who stated that the AFs were unhelpful, comments were also revealing.

I didn't understand the description. I didn't think that knowing what type of question it is would help me answer it.

It doesn't explain the answers.

Following their second attempts, pupils were also asked to consider the kinds of changes they had made to their answers and to comment on whether they felt their answers had improved. The vast majority of the group felt that they had increased their score, and once again, pupils' explanations referred to different factors. The benefits of re-reading both the questions, and their original answers, were mentioned several times.

Yes, because I have read them more carefully and I can see where I went wrong.

I think that I have put better answers to some difficult questions. I did this by reading the questions well.

I think so, looking through it I made a few stupid mistakes. I added more information in some particular answers and I saw my particular areas I was struggling on.

Some pupils felt the assessment focuses had been helpful and a few mentioned using the language of the assessment focuses in their answers (the latter had been listed as a possible strategy in a different part of the questionnaire, so may have influenced some responses).

> *I think I have improved my answers in particularly the 1 or 2 mark questions. After reading the questions again I was able to look at the question from another angle. The assessments [sic] focuses did help too, they told me what type of things I needed to put in my answer, whether it be about language, structure or writer's purposes.*

> *I think I have improved my answer to Question 13 a lot because I wrote more about the general language and why he chose words. I also improved question 10 by talking about the reasons for language and structure that the writer chose, and the effect of them.*

> *Yes, because in some of them [the first time] I had 'alternative' answers, but I didn't put them down. The sad thing is was [sic] that they were right! Also the assessment focuses gave 'educational' words to include in my answers.*

The process of revision, involving interaction with a number of different sources of information (including assessment focuses), seemed to the pupils to have been useful.

In the next session, pupils were asked to rank a range of factors for their helpfulness during the process of revision. Table 13.3 shows frequencies for the highest rating.

Table 13.3 The most helpful factors for pupils when revising answers

Factor	Number of '1' ratings
Having time to reread the text	2
Having time to reread the questions	7
Looking at the Assessment Focus for each question	2
Discussing the questions with others	8
Looking at how other pupils answered the questions	9

Three of the five factors from which pupils could choose were clearly viewed as being more useful than others: *Looking at how other pupils answered the questions; Discussing the questions; Having time to reread the questions.* This is unsurprising in some ways, but nevertheless revealing. For the majority of pupils, the process of reviewing their performance was most fruitful when it involved interaction with others. As discussed above, in many cases pupils were uncertain about: why their initial answers were inaccurate; the precise demands of the question (and mark scheme) and the meaning of the AFs themselves. Comparing their responses with those of others offered immediate insight into some of these unknowns. Similarly, discussing and comparing their interpretations of questions supported their understanding of how an answer might be refined.

Pupils had the opportunity to add comments to explain their rankings, providing some useful insights into their thinking.

Being able to discuss different questions with people enabled me to understand the things I didn't when we done [sic] *the first test. It also helped re-reading the question, in case you missed anything. The AFs helped when you had no idea what to write.*

I found that being able to look at how others answered some of the questions was very helpful because if you had no idea about how to go about answering the question it gave you a good idea starter.

As observed by the teacher and researchers during this session, the opportunity for pupils simply to re-read the questions and their own answers was, in itself, an important factor in improving responses. Pupil ratings confirmed this. However, referring to the assessment focus for each question was not rated highly by pupils in this exercise (in contrast to some of their positive ratings in the questionnaire discussed above).

Table 13.4 Pupil rankings of the usefulness of AFs when revising answers

Factor	Ranking	Frequency
	1	2
	2	2
Looking at the Assessment	3	5
Focus for each question	4	10
	5	7
	0	1

As Table 13.4 shows, pupils predominantly ranked use of the AFs as '4' and '5', the lowest points on the 5-point scale, with one assigning '0', to signify the AFs were not at all useful.

An important point that emerged from the sessions was that pupils' claimed that they rarely received detailed information about their performance following summative assessments. Black and Wiliam's review of the literature on classroom assessment, *Assessment and Classroom Learning*, reported that 'there is little reflection on what is being assessed' even among teachers (Black and Wiliam, 1998), so the pupils' perception above is perhaps not surprising. For them the study provided an unusual and welcome opportunity to re-read, review and revise their answers, as part of a feedback process. The role of the assessment focuses in this process was, however, not easy to isolate.

What is the teacher's view of the effectiveness of this use of assessment focuses?

Following the research sessions, the teacher's views were sought through an interview covering the following areas: the usefulness of assessment focuses to her practice; the strengths and limitations of the AFs; pupils' understanding of the AFs; the impact of the research on pupils' learning; possible uses that teachers might make of the AFs.

Overall, the teacher commented positively on the assessment focuses and the experiences of the research project. As an experienced marker of the KS3 reading tests, she was already very familiar with the assessment focuses as a guide to marking, but this knowledge had not automatically been transferred into her teaching practice. To support pupils' skills in interpreting and answering reading questions, she would focus on the language of the question itself, asking them to highlight key words; as she put it: 'I would always start with the question.' She felt that, as the assessment focuses are drawn from the National Curriculum for English, teachers often work in harmony with them, even if they are unaware of this. The way in which the AFs are expressed is important in this respect. She identified several terms that are not in common usage among teachers (in her experience):

> We don't tend to think in terms of 'text-level', 'sentence-level', 'grammatical features'. We think: 'this is in exam-speak'. We tend to say [to the pupils]: 'pick out the words that suggest ... to you' [for 'use of language' questions].

Particular terms (for example, *show, express, reveal*) were highlighted for pupils (at KS3 and GCSE level) as signifiers of specific requirements in a question. Teachers used language that they knew would be familiar and comprehensible to pupils.

Looking at each AF, the teacher felt that AF2 was 'not a problem' for pupils to understand, with *describe, select* and *retrieve* being familiar terms. AF3 was considered a little more difficult, particularly as *deduce* and *infer* are 'not really used' by teachers and she felt pupils would find it difficult to work out their meaning unaided. (This is consistent with pupils' own lack of familiarity with these terms, discussed above.) For AF4, she identified *structure* and *organisation* as easier elements for pupils to understand and to 'do on their own'. AF5 was considered more challenging, particularly because of the phrase, *grammatical and literary features at text level*. This 'defeats' pupils because of the unfamiliarity of the language. While she felt that AF6 was generally well understood by pupils, a weakness was their lack of awareness of the writer's identity or existence beyond the text. Some pupils read texts (fiction in particular) as 'real', rather than as constructed works. Explicitly mentioning the author's name in questions could support them.

Focusing on the impact of the research project, the teacher felt that the process of feedback and review had a positive impact on pupils. Seeing a graph of their performance on the test helped to give a 'confidence boost' to some pupils and to stimulate those who were unfocused or careless. The teacher felt there were some differences between the attitudes of girls and boys, and that the graphical data would prompt some boys to put greater effort into their work. She felt that the opportunity to amend their answers was valuable and that the pupils had gained much from their discussion of answers and of the assessment focuses. Looking at other pupils' answers and making judgements about degrees of success in different answers was also helpful. She felt it would be useful to formalise this task by providing pupils with a range of answers and asking them to explain why each answer was awarded a particular mark.

The teacher described plans to use assessment focuses with the same group in the following half term, before they complete their next reading test; she expected their performances to have improved. In addition, collaborating with colleagues, she intended to carry out a sequence of lessons with other year 9 classes as part of their preparation for KS3 assessments, looking at the different kinds of questions in reading tests. She intended to translate 'AF-speak' into her language, and then, through discussion with the pupils, to transform it into 'kid-speak'. They would then look at a question paper and assign AFs to each question, before answering the questions. Drawing on the experiences of the project, she was also considering using a 'control' group, who would complete the same paper without additional input on assessment focuses.

Some weeks later, she wrote a report after running a similar sequence of lessons with a 'less able group' (target levels 4–6 but mostly 5, as compared to the 5–7 range of the previous group, who are mostly target level 6). She commented that, 'The outcome of all this actually turned out to be an increase in confidence; they felt that knowing what the AFs were enabled them to know what the questions wanted.'

Commentary

The purpose of feedback from assessment should be further learning. Cowie and Bell described formative assessment as, 'The process used by teachers and students to recognise and respond to student learning in order to enhance that learning, during the learning' (Cowie and Bell, 1999). In the case reported above, however, one might easily say that what was happening was that the pupils were merely trying to up their marks in the test, a task involving little worthwhile learning. One boy in the study captured well a cynical view of what was going on: 'During the time we were "rewriting" the test, people copied answers from other people who got them right. This is why some people got a higher level than they had done recently.' There is certainly evidence that some pupils saw what they were doing merely in terms of gaining more marks.

Some might say that the possibility of using such feedback for a more educational purpose – for example, to enable pupils to learn more about what it means to read and understand a text – was lost at the start. This was because the feedback was explained in terms of asking pupils to say how they might improve their answers in a test. This involved a consideration of the marks they had scored, which according to the work cited by the Assessment Reform Group 'encourages pupils to concentrate on getting better grades rather than on deeper understanding' (Assessment Reform Group, 2002, p.6). Sadler also says that, 'where a grade or a score assigned by the teacher constitutes a one-way cipher for students, attention is diverted away from fundamental judgements and the criteria for making them.'(Sadler, 1989, p.121). Brookhart, however, argues that our view of the implications of the use of summative assessment models need not be so negative. Her study of students in English and Anatomy classes led her to suggest that for those students 'summative judgements were temporary stops along a learning path' (Brookhart, 2001, p.157). She quotes Biggs in order to make the point that what matters is how 'deeply criterion-referenced' the exercise is (Biggs, 1998). We would argue that the teacher in the study reported here was, in her use of AFs, putting her emphasis on the underlying criteria for more successful reading, except that instead of discussing criteria the class discussed focuses.

We must look more closely at the concept of focuses, or focusing, in reading. There are two kinds of focusing going on here. One is the focusing done by the pupil on the text to be read. The second is the focus of the assessor. For the national tests the assessors fall into two categories: the test developers, for whom the AFs serve to clarify the writing of questions and the markers, for whom the AFs guide decisions about what credit to give. When the teacher is the assessor he or she usually plays both these roles.

The focus that is relevant to the pupils, however, is the focus of the reader. It is important to be clear when we talk about AFs, that both kinds of focusing are caught up in the phrase and that we are not asking the pupils to be assessors, but readers.

As readers, we can approach texts in a variety of ways, particularly when we reflect on what we have read. We sometimes look closely at the text, at a particular word or phrase; sometimes we stand back from it, and think about the structure. Sometimes we think about the ideas in the text, sometimes about the feelings. Sometimes we think about the writer and his or her point of view, sometimes we think about the text as it appears to us as readers. Such a process in reading, which is part of our trying to make sense of the text for ourselves, could be described as 'focusing'. To become reflective readers, pupils need to learn to be able to do this.

It is more appropriate to talk about *focusing* in reading, as we have just done, than *focuses*. To choose *a* focus is a legitimate thing to do, but it can distort the whole picture. If we take a close-up photograph of one flower, the picture of the garden becomes blurred. To get the full picture we must be able to move forwards and backwards. This illustration suggests why too hard and fast an interpretation of AFs can become problematic. Our definition of reading focuses must capture the fact that they are part of a living experience of reading, and that they change and blend into a process. Focusing as a metaphor for what is happening when we read, reminds us of the possibility of blurring what we see. A reading focus does not have a hard edge, it can be imprecise, but that doesn't invalidate its use.

These points raise a fundamental question, which is: Can we validly describe and use focuses, or assessment objectives, when we seek to assess and improve pupils' reading? We believe we can. Sadler describes a 'progression in which criteria [in our case for successful reading] are translated for the students' benefit from latent to manifest and back to latent again' (Sadler, 1989, p.134). But we think that we have not been good at describing why it is that attempts to sharpen the focus, or make the criteria manifest, (for example in mark schemes for tests of reading) are problematic and do not produce clear-cut answers. The use of AFs is made problematic when the process of reading is lost sight of. And the process of using AFs well is made problematic by their only appearing in tests, especially tests which have public implications for the pupils, teachers and schools involved. If the AFs were seen more in the context of learning, and particularly of self-assessment, it would be the perspective of the readers that became more prominent, above that of the assessors.

In this study, the aim was to find out what feedback might help pupils understand more the reading skills that they need to deploy in order to understand a text. They wrote very positively about the benefits of interacting with others, but were they merely looking for 'the correct answers'? And they tended not to value the work with AFs. Many of the quotations from pupils do appear to be very test-bound, and one wonders how far they would be able to generalise from working on the answers to these questions to the underlying educational aim of the exercise.

QCA has proposed the above kind of use of AFs as 'diagnostic feedback'. It would be however a mistake to see what is happening during such feedback on a reading exercise as a series of diagnoses into strengths and weaknesses in the pupils' overall performance in reading. To treat this as a diagnostic exercise would indeed push the outcome towards a series of narrow hints about how to get more marks on one particular test, and possibly on how to improve your performance in a future test. What underlies this misconception is the fact that 'diagnostic' feedback refers to the kind of focuses that interest the assessor (the test marker, or the teacher who is possibly too focused on the product), whereas it is the focusing of the reader that needs to be addressed.

From the perspective of the creative activity of reflecting on our reading, the use of AFs with pupils does indeed appear to have some possibilities. Sadler (1989, p.134) claims that 'Knowledge of the criteria is 'caught' through experience, not defined' (Sadler, 1989, p.135). Pupils in their feedback for this study wrote of understanding more what lay behind the questions, once they had thought about the AFs. They had used in their activities some of the vocabulary and concepts which underlie the subject 'English'. For example, at the very least they had identified concepts like 'deduce and infer' and acknowledged that there was something about these that they needed to understand better. Some of their comments on what they needed to learn next relied heavily on repetition of the, perhaps, unfamiliar vocabulary of the AFs. But in using this vocabulary, they found a language to go beyond this test and these questions to an underlying purpose. The fact that they grasped that there was a bigger picture into which their efforts could fit would have been an empowering exercise for them, as the teacher described. In Sadler's interesting term they were becoming part of 'the guild' of readers.

With greater familiarity with the vocabulary of the subject's underlying aims leading to an increasing understanding of its concepts, the pupils' pursuit of higher level reading skills becomes a possible one. The pursuit involves purpose and successes rather than pessimistic cries of 'I must try harder', which imply little hope of knowing where to make the effort. We could say that what the teacher was doing was, in Sadler's words, 'providing guided but direct and evaluative experience for students, which enables them to develop *their* evaluative knowledge, thereby bringing them within the guild of people who are able to determine quality using multiple criteria' (Sadler, 1989, p.139). Further study would be needed to assess whether this generally is the case for classes which are given feedback in terms of the AFs. This was a small preliminary study which we hope will lead to a clearer definition for a larger study in future. But the use of AFs in this exercise appeared to create a positive experience for the pupils, to which the teacher strongly responded. It was not a diagnostic exercise, or indeed an exercise in increasing the pupils' marks in tests, but an exercise in talking about reading, and in expanding the vocabulary in which the pupils could do this.

Implications and areas for further research

This preliminary study has yielded a number of insights into the usefulness of assessment focuses in providing feedback to KS3 pupils on their reading performance. In their present form, the assessment focuses are not wholly effective tools for communicating skills and concepts to all year 9 pupils. Some words and phrases are unfamiliar, and pose particular difficulties if pupils attempt to apply them (for example, to reading tasks or questions). Pupils' own suggestions of alternative ways to express the AFs could prove very useful starting points for any work on re-framing the focuses.

In order to give pupils meaningful information about their performance, it is also important to consider the process of feedback. This study suggests that activities and contexts in which pupils interact with others (or with others' ideas and written responses) could be particularly successful. Sadler points out that students not only need to know the criteria by which they are assessed but 'an equally important need is for students to know what the standards to be used are' (Sadler, 1996). Thus, following a test, pupils would benefit from the opportunity to read and assess a range of answers, alongside their own, to determine how the standards have been applied in each different case.

Some interesting questions about the significance of assessment focuses in schools have also been raised. Many teachers may be unfamiliar with the AFs, but existing assessment and feedback processes draw on similar principles. Would pupils gain from one particular framework for feedback, or are there a number of ways that the skills within the assessment focuses could be structured and expressed?

To extend these initial findings, a number of areas could be investigated further. Possible activities include:

- a larger study of the impact of using AFs to provide feedback on test performance (this could look more closely at groups of pupils according to ability, sex and other characteristics)

- a longitudinal study investigating the impact of using AFs across years, or across key stages

- a larger study of teachers' existing methods for providing feedback on reading performance and their use of assessment focuses or the equivalent

- a re-framing of the existing assessment focuses to increase their accessibility for pupils.

References

Assessment Reform Group (1999). *Assessment for Learning: Beyond the Black Box*. Cambridge: Cambridge Institute of Education.

Assessment Reform Group (2002), *Testing, Motivation and Learning*. Cambridge: Cambridge Institute of Education.

Biggs, J. (1998). 'Assessment and classroom learning: a role for summative assessment?' *Assessment in Education*, **5**, (1), 103–110.

Black, P. and Wiliam, D. (1998). 'Assessment and classroom learning', *Assessment in Education*, **5**, 1, 7–74.

Brookhart, S.M. (2001). 'Successful students' formative and summative. Uses of assessment information', *Assessment in Education*, **8**, 2, 153–169.

Cowie, B. and Bell, B. (1999). 'A model of formative assessment in science education', *Assessment in Education*, **6**, 101–116.

Matthews, S. (2004). *'On Track?' The Secondary English Magazine*. London. NATE.

Qualifications and Curriculum Authority (2003). Key Stage 3 English: Teacher Pack 1 (QCA/03/988), London: QCA.

Sadler, D.R. (1989). 'Formative assessment and the design of instructional systems', *Instructional Science*, **18**, 121 and 134–5.

Sadler, D.R. (1996). '"Criteria and standards in student assessment", different approaches: theory and practice in higher education.' Proceedings of the HERDSA Conference. Perth, Western Australia, 8–12 July.

[Part 4]
Theory into practice: national initiatives

14 Validity challenges in a high-stakes context: National Curriculum tests in England

Marian Sainsbury and Andrew Watts

Since 1991, England has had a formal and centralised national testing system whose major purpose is accountability, in the public and political sense. Tests of reading have a central place within this system. All children[1] are formally assessed at the ages of 7, 11 and 14, at the end of the phases of education known as key stages 1, 2 and 3 respectively. Results are reported nationally, and are regarded in public discourse as evidence of the success or failure of the education system, and of the education policies of the government of the day. Each year's national results are the subject of news reports, media comment and political debate.

The English National Curriculum testing system has a number of positive strengths, but its high-stakes purpose also introduces tensions. Although there has been evolution since 1991, the present-day system is the same, in its essential features, as the one introduced then. At that time, both curriculum and assessment arrangements were introduced together. The curriculum was defined by means of programmes of study, and associated attainment targets laid out what was to be assessed. This alignment of curriculum and assessment is taken for granted in England, but it should be noted that it is not inevitable, and is in fact a major strength of the system. In the USA, by contrast, there are numerous examples of states where a compulsory assessment has been introduced independently of a pre-existing curriculum, and the task of alignment forms a major research and administrative burden.

The nature of the construct of reading in the National Curriculum can therefore be inferred from the attainment target, which sets out eight levels of attainment, each of them defined by a description consisting of a short paragraph of prose. These eight levels apply to all pupils from the ages of five to 14 years: children progress up the scale from level to level. Most 7-year-olds are at level 2; most 11-year-olds at level 4 and most 14-year-olds at level 5 or 6. As an example, level 4 is defined thus:

> *In responding to a range of texts, pupils show understanding of significant ideas, themes, events and characters, beginning to use inference and deduction. They refer to the text when explaining their views. They locate and use ideas and information.*

The level descriptions are brief and for a fuller explanation of the construct of reading they need to be read alongside the programmes of study. These are divided according to the three key stages. The first category of requirements details the 'knowledge, skills and understanding' to be taught. For example, for key stage 2, the knowledge, skills and understanding section includes lists headed: reading strategies; understanding texts; reading for information; literature; non-fiction and non-literary texts; language structure and variation. The other main category within the programmes of study for reading is entitled 'breadth of study'. In this section is set out the range of literary and non-literary texts that pupils should be taught to read. Thus the curriculum documents define in general terms the range of reading material that children should encounter. In addition, at key stage 3 only, there is a requirement to teach literature drawn from specific lists of novelists and poets.

Since 1998, the teaching of reading and writing in England has been structured by the National Literacy Strategy. This provides a much longer, more detailed and more specific set of guidance. For each term of each year, text types and reading skills are specified. The National Literacy Strategy is a well-resourced government initiative, with a wide range of training and support materials and sets out one way in which the National Curriculum for reading and writing can be taught. However, these are guidelines rather than requirements: it is the programmes of study, much less detailed documents, which constitute the legal requirement for schools, and the basis for test development.

The brief description above should give an indication of the breadth and depth of the construct of reading embodied in the National Curriculum. A very wide range of reading material is required, both literary and non-literary. The skills and understandings go far beyond the mere recognition of words to include appropriate strategies for information handling and literary appreciation. The list of skills presented above as an illustration can be seen to draw upon different perspectives on the nature of reading. 'Reading strategies' and 'understanding of texts' concern decoding and straightforward comprehension and are related to a cognitive psychology perspective. 'Reading for information' and 'literature' and the associated list of approaches to text describe purposeful, responsive and analytic reading and can be traced to theories of literature and information handling. The final element of the list, 'language structure and variation' is an explicit requirement for a linguistic perspective in analysing what is read. All four of the 'layers' of reading in the Sainsbury diagram (see page 17) can be discerned in the programmes of study. As well as these skills and understandings, there is also the suggestion of an attitudinal component. The general requirements include 'interest and pleasure' and 'enthusiastically', in addition to the ability to read independently.

Although this list was drawn from the key stage 2 curriculum, the same is true even for the youngest children: at key stage 1 there is a long list of reading strategies for accurate decoding and understanding, but also the requirement to describe characters and settings, and to respond imaginatively to literature. Children are taught to use reference skills in reading for information, and to begin to analyse texts linguistically, distinguishing between the characteristics of fiction and non-fiction texts. For older students at key stage 3, there is more emphasis on analytic reading, described here as 'understanding the author's craft'.

A further reference document in defining what is assessed in the key stage reading tests is a list of assessment focuses (AFs) that form part of the test specification.

- Assessment focus 1: use a range of strategies, including accurate decoding of text, to read for meaning.

- Assessment focus 2: understand, describe, select or retrieve information, events or ideas from texts and use quotation and reference to text.

- Assessment focus 3: deduce, infer or interpret information, events or ideas from texts.

- Assessment focus 4: identify and comment on the structure and organisation of texts, including grammatical and presentational features at text level.

- Assessment focus 5: explain and comment on writers' use of language, including grammatical and literary features at word and sentence level.

- Assessment focus 6: identify and comment on writers' purposes and viewpoints and the effect of the text on the reader.

- Assessment focus 7: relate texts to their social, cultural and historical contexts and literary traditions.

These apply across all three key stages, although the balance between them varies considerably to reflect the age of the children. Most of them appear in most National Curriculum reading tests, but there is no absolute requirement to cover all of them in any one test; the exact coverage and balance reflects the nature of the texts. This list, too, demonstrates the complex interplay between different theories and definitions of reading in the National Curriculum.

The assessment of this broad and rich construct of reading in a high-stakes context gives rise to significant challenges. Since teachers and schools are held accountable for their test results, they could be motivated to teach only what is tested. Thus there is a need to avoid construct under-representation as this could threaten validity, both in terms of the inferences to be drawn from the results, and of any consequential narrowing of the curriculum. The test developer has the dilemma of including a wide enough range of literature in each year's test to reflect the curriculum 'breadth of study' requirements adequately. At the same time, though, there is a curricular requirement for responsive reading and analysis which rules out the use of several short passages to cover the range. The texts need to be lengthy and weighty enough for pupils to engage meaningfully with the content.

At the seminars that formed the basis for this book, the England national reading tests for 2003 were examined both from an external perspective, by participants from the USA and in relation to the underlying theories that were being discussed. These same tests will be described and discussed in the later parts of this chapter, to illustrate in detail how the challenges are met in practice. A number of general principles can be distinguished at all three key stages.

First, it is accepted that any one year's test cannot cover the whole range of texts and skills required by the curriculum. Instead, each year's test includes a more limited range of reading skills and of text types. But over the years, the tests gradually broaden the range that has been included. To address the requirement for engaged, responsive and analytic reading, there is a principle that full-length texts or extended extracts should be used, and that these are well written and interest or entertain the students as readers. Further, since students' responses to texts will draw on their own experiences and understandings, and will therefore be varied in their content and expression, most questions in any test are open, allowing the student to give his or her own view, explanation or opinion in response to the text.

Key stage 1

Children at key stage 1 range from non-readers to those who are well advanced in reading and understanding simple texts. The assessments to cover this range of ability are the most complex in structure of any National Curriculum reading tests, with four separate instruments addressing levels 1–3 of the attainment target. Teachers decide which of these instruments are most appropriate for each individual child, based on their ongoing assessments.

Beginner readers have either attained or are working towards level 1, and their assessment consists of an individual read-aloud task in which their early understandings of reading are demonstrated with support from the teacher. An overall judgement is made of their ability to recognise words and letters, to use some decoding strategies and to talk in simple terms about the content of their reading. A similar reading task applies at level 2, where the emphasis is upon the teacher's observations of the child's independence, accuracy, understanding and ability to apply strategies in reading unknown words. This task is described in more detail in Whetton (see chapter 8). For both level 1 and level 2, the children read from real books, chosen from a list of comparable difficulty which represent lively and engaging literature. Thus the vocabulary encountered by the young reader is age-appropriate, but is not strictly controlled. These tasks combine an assessment of decoding, comprehending, responding and some simple analysis in a single informal interview in which the overall assessment outcome is decided by the teacher on the basis of observation.

Children who attain level 2 may also take a written test, the form of which will be illustrated by the 2003 test, *Sunflowers*, which is a typical example. Texts and questions are presented in a full-colour booklet. There are three texts: a story, *Billy's Sunflower* by Nicola Moon, in which a little boy learns that flowers die in autumn but can grow again from seeds; information about the artist Van Gogh; and instructions for making a paper sunflower. The questions are presented on the lower half of each page and refer only to the text on that page (see Figure 14.1).

Figure 14.1 Example reading test, *Sunflowers* (reproduced with permissions from QCA)

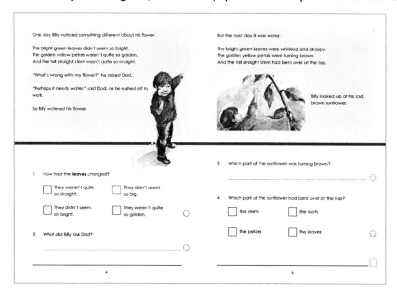

There are 28 questions in this test, around half of them four-option multiple-choice and the rest requiring simple constructed responses. Two of them are two-part questions for which a partial credit is possible, so the total number of marks available is 30. In terms of the assessment focuses listed above, retrieval of information (AF2) accounts for over half of the marks. A typical question of this type is:

Which part of the sunflower had bent over at the top?

☐ the stem   ☐ the roots

☐ the petals   ☐ the leaves

A further quarter of the marks are awarded for questions requiring simple inference (AF3), for example:

How did Mum help Billy?
Write 2 things.

In this case, the text recounts how Billy's Mum dried his tears and then presents in dialogue a conversation in which she explains about plants dying in winter. Typically children find it easy to identify the first of these ways of helping Billy, but some inference is necessary in order to understand that the conversation was also a way of offering help.

One two-part question explicitly asks for a personal response to what has been read (AF6):

The story is both sad and happy. Explain why.

It is sad because …
It is happy because …

This requires an overview of the whole story, and some empathy with the character of Billy, bringing together the ideas that plants die but that they grow again.

Three of the marks are available for answers that demonstrate the beginnings of an ability to analyse presentational features of text (AF4) and the author's choice of language (AF5). Two questions ask about the presentation of the instructions: the list of what is needed; and the reason for numbering each instruction. The language question asks what the words *brown, sad* and *drooping* express about the sunflower.

In this test, unlike the level 2 task, the ability to decode text is not assessed directly but by means of comprehension questions. Even at this very early level the insistence on a highly complex construct of reading in the England National Curriculum assessments is fully apparent.

The final instrument involved in testing reading at key stage 1 is a written test for level 3, for those children who are above average for their age and already reading quite fluently. Entitled *Memories*, the 2003 test includes two texts, presented as separate full-colour documents. The first is a story, *Grandfather's Pencil* by Michael Foreman. The second, contrasting, text is a leaflet, invented but presented authentically, about a children's programme at a local history museum (see Figure 14.2).

For level 3, the questions are presented in a separate booklet so that the children can more easily skim and scan the texts to find their answers. Question formats are more varied than at level 2, and only eight of the 26 marks are for multiple-choice answers. In this test, the number of retrieval (AF2) questions is almost the same as those requiring inference and deduction (AF3). One of the latter type can be used to demonstrate the variety of responses that can be judged acceptable.

Figure 14.2 Example written test for level 3 (reproduced with permissions from QCA)

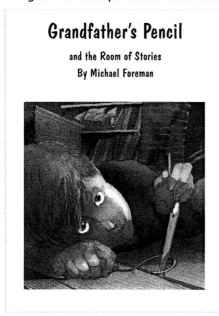

Why would *Journeys* be a good, different title for this story?
Explain as fully as you can.

The story tells how the various objects in a boy's bedroom – pencil, paper, door, floor-boards – have made journeys from their original forest homes. Intertwined with this is the story of the boy himself and his travels around the world as a sailor when he grows up. This question requires children to show some understanding of this theme of journeying and how it is worked out in the book. The acceptable answers are varied. Children could show this understanding by making a generalisation about the objects in the story:

> *The things had all made journeys from the forest to the boy's room.*

> *The paper made a journey back to the forest.*

Alternatively, they could focus on the boy and his travels:

> *The boy who grew up to be a sailor made sea journeys.*

> *Jack was starting out on his own journey of life.*

This is an example of a question where children can be seen responding in different ways to what they have read, using their own experience to select evidence from the text to demonstrate their understanding of the theme. For questions like this, only a skeleton mark scheme is devised before the question is trialled, and children's actual responses have a strong influence in formulating the limits of acceptable and unacceptable answers.

These tests and tasks for the youngest children already show the hallmarks of the England National Curriculum reading tests. Although most of the questions require children to show a basic understanding of what they have read using retrieval and simple inference, there is nevertheless a role for responding to and analysing texts.

Key stage 2

At key stage 2, the national tests cover levels 3–5 and thus apply to all children who have mastered the basics of reading – around 93 per cent of the population. Children below these levels are not included in testing but are assessed by their teachers.

The 2003 reading test is a lively, magazine-style reading booklet entitled *To the Rescue*, together with a separate question booklet. This booklet deals with the theme of heroes and superheroes. It includes several texts of types that have appeared in previous tests: a narrative extract, from Katherine Paterson's *Lyddie*, information listing the characteristics of superheroes and information about special effects in films. Alongside these, there is a text type that has not previously appeared in a key stage 2 test, a short cartoon strip presenting a humorous subversion of the superhero genre (see Figure 14.3). This is an example of the principle of broadening the range of text types year on year whenever possible.

The test has 30 questions yielding one, two or three marks each, and the total number of marks available is 50. Most of the questions are open response, but a number of

Figure 14.3 Example cartoon strip used in reading test (reproduced with permission from QCA)

different closed-response formats are also included. In terms of the classification by assessment focus, a noticeable characteristic of this test is the predominance of inference and deduction, with AF3 accounting for 27 of the 50 marks. The development of this skill is seen as crucial for the age and levels addressed by this test. These inference and deduction questions vary quite considerably in the demands they make of the children, however. On the one hand, there are some requiring a relatively straightforward deduction where the information is found close together in the text:

How helpful are computers in creating special effects?
Use the information on pages 10 and 11 to explain your answer.

To gain full credit for this item, pupils have to bring together the information, stated in different parts of the double page, that computers are helpful for some special effects such as 'morphing' and some sound effects, but in cases such as flying and other sound effects they are unhelpful. Partial credit is available for explaining just one of these points.

Other AF3 questions require an extended response that takes an overview of the text and explains a view with some subtlety or complexity:

In what ways did Lyddie show herself to be a good leader?
Explain fully, using the text to help you.

For full credit of three marks, children need to give an answer that takes into account the calm, bravery, intelligence and practicality of the character:

Even though Lyddie was just a child she did not panic and she knew what to do to control the bear, she got the rest of the family out of harm's way and only thought of saving herself when she knew the others were saved.

Answers that made some relevant points, without the completeness of this example, were awarded partial credit. Here again, the different ways in which pupils interpret their reading and apply to it their ideas about leadership are highly personal, and the mark scheme could only be devised in the light of analysing many answers from children in the trials.

Questions requiring some appreciation of authorial techniques and choices, AFs 4–6, are more frequent at key stage 2 than at key stage 1, though they still account for only around a quarter of the marks. Some address organisational and presentational features (AF4):

Page 11 is clear because it is divided into **questions** and **answers**.
How does this layout help the reader?

Others focus upon the author's use of language (AF5):

Individual ... unique
What do these words on page 8 tell you about superheroes?

Unusually, the use of the very specific superhero genre as the focus of the reading booklet made it possible to ask some questions about this literary tradition (AF7). Such questions appear only rarely in tests for this key stage.

Souperkid flies and wears a special costume.

In what other way is Souperkid like a superhero?

In what way is Souperkid **not** like the superheroes described on page 9?

In one of the final questions of the test, the pupils are asked to bring together their understanding of all the texts they have read, and to give their own opinion, backed up by textual evidence.

'I think Lyddie is a real hero but not a superhero.'

Do you agree with this opinion?

Explain your own opinion fully, using the texts to help you.

In this question can be seen several of the typical characteristics of National Curriculum reading tests as their authors attempt to blend an ambitious construct of reading with the constraints of a high-stakes national system. Children can have any opinion on this question; it is not necessary to agree with the quotation, and some children in the trials showed themselves distinctly unimpressed by Lyddie's achievement when set against superhero exploits. The mark scheme allows a variety of views on this, and in this way the test can genuinely be said to recognise the potential for personal response, and even, to some extent, for different readings in the postmodern sense. But ultimately, this is a test where marks have to be awarded consistently because its major purpose is to award a nationally recognised level for reading. The variety of pupil opinions which are allowed in response to this question must be backed up clearly by reference to textual evidence in order to be creditworthy. The national tests are full of examples such as this one, where many real pupil responses are carefully evaluated in order to devise a mark scheme that respects individual response and opinion whilst at the same time identifying the specific elements that will lead to consistent marking.

Key stage 3

The tests at the end of key stage 3 are taken by pupils at the end of the third year of secondary school, when they are on average 14 years old. About 90 per cent of the pupils in a cohort take the tests, for which the average result is that pupils attain level 5 in English overall. Pupils whose teachers judge their performance to be below level 4 are encouraged not to take the set tests, but to complete some classroom-based tasks instead.

The construct of reading which is evident at this key stage shows the same characteristics as have already been described. The test is based on the same Levels of Attainment statements that are used to underpin the reading curriculum and therefore, where levels of achievement overlap both key stages 2 and 3, at levels 4 and 5 for example, the criteria for judgement are the same. In addition, the Assessment Focuses which underlie the reading test are the same at each key stage, which again reflects a consistent view of the construct of reading which is being assessed.

Though this is true, there is one significant addition to the tests at this stage: a paper which tests the pupils' study of a Shakespeare play. Thus at key stage 3 there are three papers, with the Reading paper scoring 32 marks and the reading section of the Shakespeare paper scoring 18. (The third paper is the Writing paper.) The inclusion of the Shakespeare study reflects the cultural importance attributed to the study of literature, and in particular to the study of Shakespeare. The proportion of reading marks allocated to Shakespeare study is high, but an attempt in 1992 by the Qualifications and Curriculum Authority (QCA) to reduce it by a few marks was rejected by the government after a press campaign about the 'dumbing down' of the English curriculum.

The Shakespeare paper thus adds the study of a work of literature to the construct of reading already described. This study usually takes place in the six months before the tests, with the guidance of the teacher. The pupils are supposed to read the whole play, but they are tested on two short portions of it, selected because they are of dramatic significance to the plot and also are of a manageable length for a test. The pupils can thus get to know those scenes in detail and they must in the test answer one, essay-length question, which asks them to refer to both scenes in their answer.

The mark schemes for the tests claim that the Shakespeare paper 'tests the same set of skills as are assessed on the unseen texts in the Reading paper'. However, the assessment focuses for reading do not underlie the assessment for this paper because, 'The emphasis is on pupils' ability to orchestrate those skills and demonstrate their understanding of and response to the Shakespeare test they have studied...'. Instead of the assessment focuses, the tasks set in the paper are based on one of the following areas related to the study of a Shakespeare play:

- character and motivation
- ideas, themes and issues
- the language of the text
- the text in performance.

  (All references above taken from the KS3 English test mark scheme, QCA, 2004, p.21).

The criteria in the mark scheme state that pupils can gain credit by demonstrating understanding of the set scenes and showing the ability to interpret them in the light of the specific task they have been set. In addition, pupils must show the ability to comment on the language Shakespeare uses to create his dramatic effects. Finally, they must demonstrate that they can use quotations and references to the scenes to back up the points they are making.

The following is taken from the mark scheme for a task on 'Twelfth Night' in the 2004 test. The criteria were used to mark responses to the task:

> Explain whether you think Malvolio deserves sympathy in these extracts, and why.

The marking criteria for the second highest level of performance, gaining a mark of between 13 and 15 out of 18, included the requirements to demonstrate:

> Clear focus on whether Malvolio deserves sympathy at different points and why ... Clear understanding of the effects of some features of language which Malvolio and other characters use ... Well-chosen references to the text [to] justify comments as part of an overall argument.

> (Mark scheme for 2004, p.42).

In terms of the construct described at the beginning of this chapter, therefore, the addition of the Shakespeare paper at key stage 3 represents a significant increase in emphasis on the reading of literary material, and on the skills of responding to literature. It is also argued that the inclusion of the Shakespeare play in the tests can be justified as a way of encouraging involvement in drama. In 2004 the task set on Henry Vth was one in which the pupils had to discuss the play in performance:

> What advice would you give to help the actor playing Henry to convey his different moods before and after battle?

> (Mark scheme for 2004, p.23)

This takes the assessment in the Shakespeare paper well beyond merely the ability to read, since the study of drama requires in addition imaginative and practical skills which have little to do with reading.

If we remember that the pupils know they will have to write on the two set scenes and that teachers know the task could be one about performing the scenes, we can imagine that pupils who have taken part in a classroom performance of the scenes, would not find the drama task above too onerous. However, the skills they would be demonstrating would be a considerable distance from the reading skills we have been discussing so far. It is the case in the national tests in England that the inclusion of Shakespeare paper in the tests puts pressure on the assessment of reading, which for reasons of testing time and style of questioning only has 50 marks allocated to it. Since some at least of these marks are awarded for skills other than those of reading, a great deal is being asked of the remaining marks if they are expected to lead to reliable conclusions about an individual pupil's attainment in reading.

The format of the Reading paper at key stage 3 will be familiar from the descriptions already given of the papers at key stage 2, and even at key stage 1. Three passages are presented in an attractively produced, magazine-style booklet in colour. In 2004 the booklet was entitled *Save It* and it focused on protecting the environment. The selection of different types of text aimed to reflect the National Curriculum's requirement for a range of reading. The passages were:

- a newspaper article about waste collection and disposal

- a survey of the effects of tourism on a beauty spot

- pages from the web-site of the Eden Project, a visitor centre about plants in the environment.

It is interesting to note that in this year there was no literary text on the Reading paper, though this is not the case in every year. In this way the curriculum's requirement that a range of genres and styles should be covered is emphasised in the KS3 tests.

The same AFs, which have already been described, again underpin the construction of the test questions. However, the differentiation between levels in the use of AFs, which has been noted at KS1 and KS2 above, is also seen here. In comparison to the KS2 paper the proportions of questions based on AF2 (understanding and retrieving information) and AF3 (deducing and inferring) were only 3 and 16 per cent. Most of the marks were awarded for commenting on the structure and organisation of texts, 22 per cent; on the writers' use of language, 31 per cent; and on the writers' purposes and view-points, 28 per cent. The construct of reading tested here, therefore, goes well beyond simple decoding and comprehension. Over 80 per cent of the marks are awarded for pupils' ability to comment on the writers' craft in constructing their texts.

A variety of question types is used in the key stage 3 tests, but generally they are open-ended and require more than objective marking. Of the 13 questions in the 2004 test only three, with five marks in total, could be marked objectively. Of the other question types there were those that required the giving of reasons, comment on phrases, extended response (for five marks), and explanation of the writers' style. Two of the questions gave some support to the structuring of answers by providing a table which had to be completed. Even if a first sub-question was a fairly straightforward demand for a word or phrase, the next one required an explanation or comment.

We have noted above that the key stage 3 Reading paper puts a greater emphasis on Assessment Focuses 4, 5 and 6. In 2004, for example, AF4 – comment on text structure – was tested by a question which asked pupils to identify whether the paragraphs in the text about waste disposal were describing personal experiences or giving facts and statistics. The following sub-question asked for an explanation of why the writer had organised the paragraphs in the piece with this combination of experience and statistics.

The questions based on AF5 – comment on the writers' use of language – range from short, direct questions about interpreting meaning, to open questions requiring more extended responses for a mark of 5. Question 6 about the effect of tourism on the beauty spot asked:

What does the phrase *moving relentlessly* suggest about the people?

The final, 5-mark question on the paper focused on the way the Eden web-site tried to win support for the project:

How is language used to convey a positive image of the Eden Project?

It is worth noting here that as the longer, essay-style questions come at the end of a section, after the pupils have focused more closely on the issues and the language in the text, they can use their experience of answering the earlier questions to create their longer, more discursive answers.

A similar variety is used to assess the pupils' ability to comment on the writers' purposes and viewpoints (AF6). One of the questions on the Eden Project web-site asks:

How does paragraph 2 make the reader think the Eden Project is exciting but also has a serious purpose?
Choose two different words or phrases and explain how they create this effect on the reader.

The above question is one of those which gives the pupils some support in answering by providing an answer frame. In comparison, the other 5-mark question on the paper, also addressing AF6, asked:

How does the article try to make the reader feel some responsibility for the problem of waste disposal?

The key stage 3 tests described above have, like those at key stages 1 and 2, attempted to assess a broad definition of what reading is. The AFs lead well beyond mere comprehension, to questions requiring commentary, some of it extended, on the writers' techniques. The curriculum requirement for breadth of reading has led to three texts of different genres being presented in each test, and at key stage 3 a classic literary text is also set for prior study. In addition, the tests are valuing personal responses to reading by giving credit for pupils' opinions and possibly idiosyncratic interpretations. The introduction to the mark scheme (p.5) states that though the mark scheme is designed to be comprehensive

... there will be times when markers need to use their professional judgement as to whether a particular response matches one of the specified answers to the marking key. In such cases, markers will check whether what a pupil has written:

- *answers the question*

- *meets the assessment focus for the question*

- *is relevant in the context of the text it is referring to.*

Such openness to what the pupils want to say is laudable, but it can be imagined that there are disagreements about the markers' interpretation of their brief and schools still appeal more about their key stage 3 English marking than about any other subject or key stage. It is also true that the model for the English test at key stage 3 is pushing the issue of manageability of the test to its limits. The marking task is complex and in 2004 an attempt to alleviate this by having different markers to mark reading and writing, led to an administrative breakdown and significant numbers of results were sent to schools either incorrect or late.

We come back to the challenge of assessing a broad and rich construct of reading in a high-stakes context. In reflecting on this we must ask what the implications are for a time-limited test which aims to assess a construct as broad as reading. Clearly valid reading tests can be successfully constructed: the advantages of standardisation will give it value, even if some of the breadth of the reading curriculum cannot be captured. Perhaps, though, the national reading tests at key stage 3 in England are trying to do too much, by attempting to assess the study of a literary text, commentary on writers' language, and the pupils' personal responses, as well as their ability to comprehend and explain what they have understood in their reading. We must ask whether some parts of what is now assessed by the key stage 3 national reading test should not be assessed in some other way.

Note

1   Children in private schools are not required to be assessed by the national tests, although quite large numbers of these schools choose to use them. Some children with special educational needs may be disapplied from aspects of the National Curriculum and its assessment, but this is infrequent.

15 New perspectives on accountability: statutory assessment of reading of English in Wales

Roger Palmer and David Watcyn Jones

In Wales, the national assessment arrangements are in the process of change. A fundamental shift is taking place from formal testing to much greater reliance on teachers' own assessments. This chapter will describe the background to the changes and illustrate the approach to assessing reading in the tests and in supporting teachers' development as assessors.

Background

Pupils in Wales currently are statutorily assessed at the end of key stages 1, 2 and 3 – at approximately the ages of 7, 11 and 14. The assessment outcomes are reported to parents and a summary of the information is published by the Welsh Assembly Government.

Until recently, attainment has been assessed by both teacher assessment and the outcomes of statutory tasks and tests taken by all pupils in Wales near the end of the final year of the key stage. The tasks and tests provide a standard 'snapshot' of attainment at the end of the key stage, while statutory teacher assessment covers the full range and scope of the programmes of study.

It is the balance between the tasks and tests on the one hand and teacher assessment on the other that is changing. Since 2002, at the end of key stage 1, pupils' attainment has been assessed only by teacher assessment – teachers' professional judgement about pupils' attainment based on the programmes of study they have followed – with no required tasks or tests. From 2005, the same will apply to key stage 2, and from 2006 to key stage 3.

These changes are the result of policy decisions taken by the Welsh Assembly Government. In 2001, it published *The Learning Country* (National Assembly for Wales, 2001), a long term strategic statement setting out a vision for education and training in Wales over ten years. This document initiated a process of change and also led to the appointment of Professor Richard Daugherty to lead a group that reviewed assessment arrangements in Wales for key stages 2 and 3, which reported early in 2004. The conclusions of this group (Daugherty Assessment Review Group, 2004) proposed a staged process of change over the years 2004–08, which has now been accepted as policy by the

Welsh Assembly Government. Testing is largely being replaced by teachers' own judgements, which are to be supported to ensure that they become more robust and consistent.

At the time of writing this chapter, the assessment of reading involves tests alongside teacher assessment at key stages 2 and 3, but teacher assessment alone at key stage 1. The detailed discussion of the assessment of reading that follows will consider the features of both, in relation to the construct of reading.

The reading tests

English statutory tasks/tests have been Wales-only materials since 1998 for key stage 3 and since 2000 for key stage 2. Prior to this, assessment materials were developed jointly for Wales and England. The tests have a rigorous development process, including review by expert committees, informal trialling, and two large-scale formal pre-tests. The assessments are required to meet a number of quality criteria. They should be motivating and challenging for pupils, provide a valid assessment of the related programmes of study and be manageable for teachers to administer. They must reflect the diversity of pupils for whom they are intended, including those with special educational needs. They should take account of the Welsh Assembly Government's cross-cutting themes of sustainable development, social inclusion and equal opportunities and be relevant to pupils in Wales, taking account of the Curriculum Cymreig.

The construct of reading embodied in the tasks and tests is derived from the programmes of study for Reading as specified in *English in the National Curriculum in Wales* (National Assembly for Wales and ACCAC, 2000). For each key stage, the programme of study describes in some detail the range of texts to be read, the skills to be taught and the aspects of language development to be included.

Key stage 2 tasks and tests

Overview

The assessment of reading at key stage 2 takes account of pupils' developing ability to read with understanding and to respond to literature of increasing complexity. Real texts are used with questions ranging from literal comprehension to those which are more thought provoking and for which more than one answer may be acceptable. The four main processes of reading identified by Sainsbury (this volume), namely decoding, comprehending, responding and analysing, are to be found in the tests, with a greater emphasis on the first two at this key stage.

There is a Reading task for level 2 which is based on a range of texts which are manageable by a level 2 reader and which are read aloud to the teacher. The range reflects

materials described in the programme of study. Assessment is made against performance descriptions based on the National Curriculum level descriptions. Teachers are
required to make a rounded judgement in relation to these descriptions to determine if
the pupil has achieved level 2.

The test of Reading for levels 3–5 is based upon a small number of stimulus texts
which are manageable for a level 3 reader. These texts are a selection from the range of
reading material described in the programme of study and are presented in a magazine
format with illustrations added. Selection of texts takes account of the types of text
selected in previous years and provides variety for pupils. The test carries a total of 50
marks and includes a range of types of questions, including those which require an
extended response to reading material. The paper is designed to ensure a balance of
marks across levels 3–5.

In the 2004 Reading test, there were eight different answer formats: short answers,
several line answers, longer answers, multiple-choice answers, tick box answers, table
completion, sequencing and ringing/underlining. Up to 3 marks may be awarded to
those questions and answers which require a more detailed explanation of the pupil's
opinion, supported by reference to the text. Two mark questions generally require
answers which include several sentences or phrases. One mark answers require a word
or phrase, or require a pupil to circle or tick a response.

The mark scheme contains examples of some frequently occurring correct answers
given in the trials. Many pupils will, however, have different ways of wording an acceptable answer. In assessing each answer, markers focus on the content of what has been
written and not on the quality of the writing, expression, grammatical construction and so
on. The mark scheme indicates the criteria on which judgements should be made. In
areas of uncertainty, however, markers are required to exercise professional judgement.

Accountabilities and uses of information

The overall test level for English, made up of Reading and Writing, forms one part of
the statutory end of key stage assessment. A teacher assessment level that carries equal
status to the test is also awarded, and both are reported to parents at the end of key stage
2. These results form part of the data collected by the Welsh Assembly Government.

With tests of this nature and purpose, the primary accountability is what Sainsbury
(this volume) has described as the requirement of the government and society for information about the attainment and progress of 11-year-old pupils at the end of key stage 2.
There is also an element of accountability to the test users, the students and teachers,
who can make use of information derived from the test.

The tests are designed to support teaching and learning and to provide students with an
accessible and manageable means of demonstrating the range of reading skills they have
acquired by this stage of their education. To recognise and support these functions ACCAC
produces annually a report for schools on pupils' performance in the tests. Significantly this
publication is entitled *Implications for Teaching and Learning* (ACCAC, 2003a).

From 2005 onwards, teacher assessment will form the sole statutory end of the key stage assessment. National Curriculum tests will be optional in 2005 and 2006, but will not be produced beyond that date.

An example: the construct of reading in the 2004 key stage 2 test in Wales

The 2004 Reading test (ACCAC, 2004a) was based on a stimulus booklet, *Antarctica*, which contained information and a series of e-mails sent by an explorer, Kym Newbery, during his stay in Antarctica. The booklet contained: a contents page, sections based on 'An introduction to Antarctica', 'The Weather', 'Explorers', 'Expeditions', 'Communication', 'Meet Kym' and five of the e-mails he sent while working in Antarctica. The booklet was attractively illustrated with photographs, maps and diagrams. Additional information was presented in a fact box and glossary. The e-mails sent by Kym Newbery were presented in an e-mail format with the accompanying attachment of a photograph depicting an aspect of the content to support readers. The meaning of subject specific vocabulary, such as 'crevasse', 'rookery' and 'cairn', was presented in explanatory footnotes (see Figure 15.1).

Figure 15.1 2004 Reading test based on a stimulus booklet, *Antarctica* (reproduced with permissions from ACCAC)

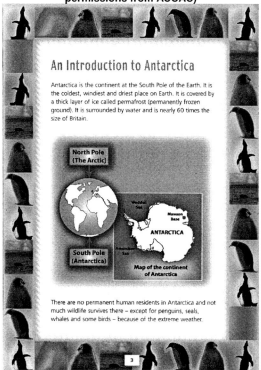

Aspects assessed as part of the processes of decoding, understanding, responding and analysing, include: literal understanding; location of textual evidence; retrieval, synthesis and recasting of information; deduction, inference and interpretation; understanding style, authorial technique and vocabulary choices; understanding presentational and organisational features and personal response.

The focus of multiple-choice questions 1–7 (one mark per question) was pupils' retrieval of information and understanding of simple inference. In Q.1, a simple response identifying the location of Antarctica as being 'near the South pole' was required to earn the available mark. Pupils could locate the relevant information in the first sentence of the introduction. In Q.3, a recognition that the booklet begins with an 'information text' was needed to gain the available mark and concluded the relatively straightforward introduction to the test which gave pupils the opportunity to show they had successfully gained an overview of the material.

A more complex response was required in Q.9 where pupils were asked to consider a series of four statements relating to Antarctica and identify, by means of a tick, whether they were fact or opinion. Up to two marks were available for all statements correctly assigned, with partial credit of one mark available for three correct.

The focus of Q.16 was complex inference. For this two-mark question the first mark was available to pupils who explained why Kym's first e-mail message began with 'Finally' by simply stating he had been waiting a long time before arriving at his destination. References to the length of his wait since first applying for the position or to the lengthy journey he had to undertake were acceptable.

Two marks were awarded to pupils whose response described the emphasis on 'finally' indicating his lengthy wait to get there and also an expression of his feelings about being in Antarctica. The mark scheme successfully discriminates between the more sophisticated and challenging skill of detecting subtle complex inference by awarding the second mark to those pupils who identified this extra layer of meaning from the language and punctuation used.

In Q.31, pupils needed to have gained an overview of the information and be able to give a personal response to the question, 'Do you think you would like to go to Antarctica?'

One mark was available for a simple reason for choice of yes/no/yes and no. Two marks were awarded to pupils who justified their answer with two or more simple reasons or one expanded reason with reference to the text. In order to gain all three available marks pupils needed to provide at least two expanded reasons with textual reference to justify their choice.

Responses referred to various aspects of the reading including the wildlife, scenery, excitement of survival training and the extreme weather conditions. The range of responses seems to indicate pupils had engaged with the subject matter, as in this example:

I would like to go to Antarctica to take in all the incredible views: the craggy mountains and the vast snowy landscapes. To see the glaciers and ice dominating the freezing world, that would be great. At the same time I wouldn't like to go because of the dangers, precautions necessary and the cold. Overall, one day I would like to visit Antarctica because it looks and sounds like a spectacular place.

Key stage 3 test

Overview

The key stage 3 reading test is designed to assess pupils aged 14 working within the range of levels 3–7 inclusive, and, taken together with the writing test result, to give a single level for each pupil at the end of the key stage. As the test targets the expected range of levels for the key stage (3–7), no task is produced at key stage 3.

The reading test assesses aspects of the programme of study including: location of information; inference and deduction; identification of key themes and ideas; expression of responses supported by close reference to the texts and comment on linguistic features. The processes of reading described earlier in this book, namely: decoding, comprehending, responding and analysing, are evident in the test.

The test of reading is based upon a small number of stimulus texts which are accessible to level 3 readers and that present a challenge to level 7 readers. The texts comprise a selection from the categories of text set out in the key stage 3 programme of study. To date, the tests have utilised two passages of broadly comparable length, usually one narrative and one non-narrative (often a media or information text).

Questions on each passage comprise a combination of two relatively low tariff (two and four marks) questions that generally assess information retrieval, inference and deduction, and a higher tariff (eleven marks) question that assesses overall understanding/comprehension of the text, response and appreciation of the writer's use of language, technique and structure. Pupils are given a bullet point framework to guide their reading and preparation of written answers to this high-tariff question on each text.

High tariff questions are marked using criterion referenced performance descriptions (relating to National Curriculum level descriptions), each of which is given a particular mark allocation. The low tariff questions are marked according to individually tailored mark schemes that clearly indicate elements of answers for which marks should be awarded.

The accountability principles and the purposes of testing are the same as outlined above for key stage 2. However, for key stage 3, from 2006 onwards, teacher assessment will form the sole statutory end of the key stage assessment. National Curriculum tests will be optional in 2006 and 2007, but will not be produced beyond that date.

An example: the construct of reading in the 2004 key stage 3 test in Wales

This section explores briefly some of the aspects of reading delineated earlier in this book, notably the main processes of reading: decoding, comprehending, responding and analysing.

The key stage 3 test of reading is designed for use with 14-year-old pupils working within the expected range of levels 3–7. This context largely presumes that pupils appropriately entered for the test will be able to decode effectively. Pupils working below level 3 are statutorily assessed through teacher assessment alone; pupils who have difficulty with decoding are likely to be excluded from taking the test.

The second process, comprehending, features prominently in the test, in terms of basic understanding of written words through questions that invite retrieval of information, and a far more sophisticated awareness of the overall meaning of the test and the writer's purpose and methods.

The opening questions on each passage in the key stage 3 reading test (ACCAC, 2004b) ask pupils to 'write down' or 'list' two points or details from the specified short section near the opening of the passage. Each distinct, appropriate point carries 1 mark.

The second question on each passage carries 4 marks and usually has, as its assessment objectives, location of information and simple inference and deduction. An element of responding is also apparent in this style of questioning, although that is more fully developed in the high tariff questions described later.

An example of a 4 mark question is given below. The text is an article by the Welsh athlete Tanni Grey-Thompson, entitled 'Treat me as a person first, then ask about my disability'. In the question, the term 'list' is again used as described above, while 'explain briefly' invites and encourages pupils to respond and infer, thus moving beyond mere location. One mark is available for each appropriate location and 1 for each linked explanation/inference. The section of the text to which this question refers is reproduced below.

Look again at lines 19–28.

(a) List two things from these lines that shop assistants have said or done which have annoyed Tanni while she was out shopping.

(b) In each case, explain briefly why Tanni was annoyed.

Many people who are disabled experience daily difficulties and discrimination because of the way we are seen. A shop assistant once told me, loudly and slowly: 'Put your change carefully back in your purse, you might lose it.' I have also been in a queue, credit card in hand, waiting to pay for a skirt while the assistant looked everywhere but at me. After five minutes she eventually asked if I would like some help or was waiting for someone. I replied that I was waiting for a bus! With a blank stare, she asked if my carer was coming back. I put the skirt on the counter, said that I no longer wished to purchase it, have never shopped there again and will not be using any other store in the chain.

Marian Sainsbury (chapter 2) has described a holistic view of reading, the four 'layers' of decoding, comprehending, responding and analysing being addressed concurrently. The high tariff reading questions (carrying 11 marks) are clear examples of this approach to the assessment of reading, envisaging 'an active reader, bringing individual world knowledge to build a personal understanding of the text' (Sainsbury, this volume, p.17).

The example from the 2004 reading test given below is representative of this approach, which allows a variety of acceptable responses and interpretations and affords opportunities for pupils to explore the writer's technique; the structure of the text; devices that create interest and tension; choice and use of language and overall impact. The question is based on an edited version of a short story *Neilly and the Fir Tree* by John O'Connor, offering opportunities to demonstrate comprehension of a 'complete' narrative and assess responsive reading of a text written for a real purpose.

This question is about the whole story.

How does the writer create interest and suspense in this story about Neilly?

In your answer you should comment on how the writer:

- makes you feel involved with Neilly at the beginning of the story (lines 1 to 20)

- shows Neilly's changing feelings in lines 21 to 33

- builds suspense in lines 34 to 51

- uses words and phrases to describe Neilly's feelings, and what he can see, at the top of the tree (lines 52 to 60)

- creates interest and suspense in the ending of the story (lines 61 to 82).

Refer to words and phrases from the whole story to support your ideas.

Pupils' responses are marked against a set of performance criteria related directly to the National Curriculum level descriptions for levels 3–7, with two marks available at each level to permit some 'fine tuning' by markers. An award of the full 11 marks available is reserved for responses regarded by markers as being of 'high level 7' standard. The mark scheme provides full exemplification of responses at each level with commentaries, and markers are fully prepared through use of training and standardisation of scripts.

Support for teacher assessment

Teacher assessment covers the full scope of the programmes of study, so that judgements can be made of pupils' attainments across a much wider range of texts, and evidence of reading processes can be obtained in a variety of contexts. At the same time, there is a need to support teachers in developing consistency of judgements, so that the nationally reported teacher assessment levels are dependable. An important element of this is the provision of optional materials exemplifying the expectations related to each National Curriculum level.

Key stage 1

Since 2002 in Wales, teacher assessment has been the only statutory requirement at the end of key stage 1. Teachers use their ongoing records and knowledge of pupils' achievements to make an overall, best fit judgement of the levels attained in oracy, reading and writing.

Optional activities and resources were published in 2003 (ACCAC, 2003b) to aid consistency in making these judgements to supplement ongoing records.

The activities are based around a story book, *Harry and the Bucketful of Dinosaurs* and an information sheet, *Dinosaurs*. Assessments are differentiated so that they can be used with pupils working at Levels 1, 2 and 3. There are a number of activities at word, sentence and text level. The materials can be used at any time of year and can fit into the teacher's own way of working.

Each activity links with a section which provides a range of examples of pupils' work as they engaged in the activity, with commentaries on how teachers used this evidence in making their assessments. These are to be used in conjunction with appropriate exemplar materials and mark schemes already available in school, notably the *Exemplification of Standards* booklets, distributed to schools in 1995, and writing exemplars in previous years' Task handbooks. Occasional references to the level descriptions in the Curriculum Orders have been included in the commentaries. These have been provided in order to help teachers make judgements of pupils' work. They have been used to indicate characteristics of performance and are not intended to be used to level individual pieces of work. Detailed case studies of two children provide additional opportunities for staffroom discussion, intra-school and inter-school moderation and possibly inter-LEA moderation too.

Key stage 2

In 1999, ACCAC developed eight optional assessment units to support the teacher assessment of pupils' Speaking and Listening, Reading and Writing performance from years 3–6 (ACCAC, 1999).

Amongst other principles, the units were designed to:

- provide schools with standard materials that can give evidence of pupils' attainment in English to contribute towards, and enhance the consistency of, teacher assessment throughout the key stage

- provide pupils' responses that may be included in school portfolios designed to exemplify standards in English

- provide examples of assessment criteria linked to the programmes of study and level descriptions for English.

All units provide teaching contexts within which aspects of pupils' performance can be assessed, but they are not end-of-unit tests. By assessing pupils' work against the performance criteria for a unit, aspects of performance characteristics of a level are drawn out, but not as a summative level. As at key stage 1, exemplification and commentary are provided for each unit to identify responses which are characteristic of performance at the different levels.

Whilst the units support the integration of oracy, reading and writing, two units have a specific assessment focus on reading. The nature of the activities and the flexible timescale more easily allows the integration of the processes of decoding, comprehending and responding, with the objective of developing pupils as enthusiastic, independent and reflective readers.

Unit 3, entitled *Finding out about Elephants*, focuses on identifying features of information texts and contrasts with narrative genre. Unit 6, *Fantastic Mr Dahl*, focuses on characteristics of biography and contrasts with other genres.

Key stage 3

In 2000 ACCAC distributed *Optional Assessment Materials for Key Stage 3 English* (ACCAC, 2000), a pack comprising eight units for teachers' optional use in supporting their assessment of pupils' work throughout key stage 3.

Design and preparation of the units was guided by a set of principles, including the following, which are of particular relevance to the assessment of reading.

- Units should integrate the teaching of oracy, reading and writing.

- Assessment opportunities should be built in to as many activities as possible, not just one end-of-unit activity.

- Developing reading skills which lead pupils to appreciate techniques used by writers to achieve effects should be linked explicitly to encouraging pupils to use these techniques in their own writing.

Examination of these principles and the summary of the units should clearly indicate the very different approach to the practice and assessment of reading through the use of the units and assessment by means of end of key stage tests. One of the fundamental differences here is the explicit intention to integrate work on the three attainment targets: Oracy, Reading and Writing. The tests require written answers, though assessment objectives relate solely to reading, and oral responses do not feature in the English tests (although they are utilised in the Welsh test/task arrangements).

In terms of the construct of reading, the units that focus in part on reading adopt again the holistic integration of the processes of decoding, comprehending, responding and analysing. For example, Unit 2, which focuses on pre-1914 poetry, outlines activities that provide opportunities to asses the following skills:

- talking and writing about a range of reading, articulating informed personal opinions

- responding imaginatively and intellectually to the substance and style of what is being read

- reflecting on writers' presentation of ideas, the motivation and behaviour of characters, the development of plot and the overall impact of a text

- analysing and engaging with ideas, themes and language in poetry

- extracting meaning beyond the literal and explaining how choice of language and style affects implied and explicit meanings.

The unit also contains guidance on annotating a text and preparing for and giving, dramatised readings, thus providing assessment opportunities for teachers that cannot be offered in a timed test situation, and covering areas of the programme of study that are not amenable to discrete testing.

Such activities and opportunities, allied to others developed by teachers adapting the units and adopting their principles, provide 'evidence about reading ... evinced through observable performances of one kind or another' (Sainsbury, this volume, p.16). It is a series of such 'performances' and opportunities that provide teachers with a range of evidence, both tangible and more ephemeral, upon which they can base their assessment of pupils' reading (and writing and oral skills).

To help secure teacher judgements, the units provide examples of pupils' work, with commentaries that indicate qualities characteristic of particular levels of attainment, while avoiding any encouragement to level individual pieces of work, or evidence of attainment.

With such different contexts and purposes from the tests, the activities and their related assessment opportunities are far less 'high stakes' and accountability exists primarily in terms of the users: the students and the teachers whose learning and pedagogy they should support. As the activities and outcomes should be used to contribute evidence to end of key stage teacher assessments, there is some element of the more traditional accountability to society and government. However, as the materials are intended for flexible use and as models for adaptation, they should not be regarded as having the same statutory character as the tests. Appropriately, they do not carry the accompanying precise arrangements for timing and administration.

The assessments derived from the activities are, by design, more diagnostic and formative than test outcomes. A key element of the optional assessment materials for key stage 3 is the inclusion of pupil self-assessment sheets that help students recognise what they have achieved and what skills they are demonstrating, but also require them to consider how they will move on and make progress.

Looking ahead

With teacher assessment becoming the sole means of end of key stage assessment in Wales, from 2005 for key stage 2 and 2006 for key stage 3, materials of this nature that support teacher assessment are likely to attract increasing recognition. Concomitantly, their influence is likely to promote in all key stages, but in key stage 3 in particular, an understanding of reading as an interwoven set of processes, in turn integrated with and mutually supported by, speech and writing.

References

Daugherty Assessment Review Group (2004). *Learning Pathways Through Statutory Assessment: Key Stages 2 and 3: Final Report* [online]. Available: http://www.learning wales.gov.uk.

Qualifications, Curriculum and Assessment Authority for Wales (ACCAC) (1999). *Optional Assessment Materials for Key Stage 2 English*. Cardiff: ACCAC.

Qualifications, Curriculum and Assessment Authority for Wales (ACCAC) (2000). *Optional Assessment Materials for Key Stage 3 English*. Cardiff: ACCAC.

Qualifications, Curriculum and Assessment Authority for Wales (ACCAC) (2003a). *Implications for Teaching and Learning at Key Stage 2*. Cardiff: ACCAC.

Qualifications, Curriculum and Assessment Authority for Wales (ACCAC) (2003b). *Optional Assessment Materials for Key Stage 1 English*. Cardiff: ACCAC.

Qualifications, Curriculum and Assessment Authority for Wales (ACCAC) (2004a). *English Tests for Key Stage 2*. Cardiff: ACCAC.

Qualifications, Curriculum and Assessment Authority for Wales (ACCAC) (2004b). *English Tests for Key Stage 3*. Cardiff: ACCAC.

The National Assembly for Wales (2001). *The Learning Country: A Paving Document. A Comprehensive Education and Lifelong Learning Programme to 2010 in Wales*. Cardiff: The National Assembly for Wales.

The National Assembly for Wales and Qualifications, Curriculum and Assessment Authority for Wales (ACCAC) (2000). *English in the National Curriculum in Wales*. Cardiff: ACCAC.

16 There is no alternative … to trusting teachers: reading and assessment in Scotland

Louise Hayward and Ernie Spencer

Construct validity: first know and share what is to be learned

Scotland has an honourable history of approaches that have respected the idea of construct validity in its national assessment systems at 5–14, 14–16 (Standard Grade) and 16–18 (formerly just Higher, now National Qualifications covering a range of levels overlapping with Standard Grade and including Higher). The historical order of events was the development of both Standard Grade and a revised version of Higher in the late 1970s and 1980s, 5–14 in the late 1980s and early 1990s and National Qualifications in the late 1990s. However, despite some marked differences in summative assessment, the validity of all three systems rests on the principle that effective assessment samples a well defined curriculum, a clearly delineated body of knowledge and skills which pupils are to be taught and are expected to learn. The culture has, therefore, given status to clear specification by professional working groups of what matters in learning and teaching a curricular area/subject. Assessment arrangements have been developed with the curriculum firmly in mind.

The designers of the reading curriculum at all three stages were imbued with a philosophy which dates back to Scottish Central Committee on the Curriculum (SCCC) 'Bulletins' of national guidance from the 1960s (see, for example, Scottish Education Department, 1968). These highlighted the value of reading, particularly literature, to growth as a person. The result has been that we have national curricular guidelines for 5–14 (Scottish Office Education Department, 1991) and advice to schools on Standard Grade and National Qualifications that present the study of literature as engaging the reader in thought, stimulating mind and emotions and inevitably involving interaction with and exploration of text. These guidelines and advice promote teaching of all kinds of reading. Reading, in the Scottish curriculum, involves activating pupils' experience of ideas and their imagination in responding to text, as well as their knowledge of how language works. Pursuit of meaning in working out how and why the writer has used language in particular ways is central. At every level, teachers are strongly encouraged to give pupils activities which promote understanding of and engagement in reading as a complex, interactive, reflective, purposeful process. It includes analysis of language and evaluation of and response to both ideas and language use. One example of guidance, related to 'Reading to reflect on the writers' ideas and craft' at 5–14 level D (10–11-year-olds) may serve to illustrate the point.

> *In groups, pupils will discuss: characters, events, conflicts, inter-relationships, content, underlying main ideas and make predictions about them. Teachers will encourage discussion of author's style, in terms of character depiction, descriptions, vocabulary choice. They should compare different writers' treatments of a theme and lead pupils to give opinions, express preferences, comment on aspects of style, identify elements such as bias and accuracy. Written activities may follow from discussions.*

(Scottish Office Education Department, 1991a, p.41)

The construct of reading and assessment in Scotland

The intended model

The model of assessment developed as policy for Standard Grade and Higher English reflected research and theoretical understanding of reading (and other aspects of language use and the assessment of it) at the time. In essence, it was recognised that complex language processes were susceptible to formal testing/examining only to a limited degree and that teachers' professional judgement should have a very significant role in both formative and summative assessment.

The significance given to teachers' professional judgements was to some extent the outcome of debates about how best – or whether it was actually possible – to have a criterion-referenced system at Standard Grade. In 'The assessment of English – what is needed?' (Spencer, 1979), Spencer, surveying current difficulties in defining clear and comprehensive criteria for 'language performance', argued that, since we did not know enough about the nature of both cognitive development and language development, there was a need to concentrate on assessment as a *description of achievement* and of achievement in *specific contexts*. This need had both a theoretical basis and a practical usefulness in motivating pupils, identifying their strengths and needs. Teachers, not examination setters, were those who could know and take account of these specific contexts. Spencer concluded that, 'Some form of individual profile system of assessment is demanded by the state of our knowledge about language development, as well as by the need to "diagnose" strengths and weaknesses in pupils' ability to use language in order to help them improve' (Spencer, 1979, pp.87–8). This conclusion was in harmony with a general interest in descriptive assessment in Scotland at the time. The *Pupils in Profile* project (Scottish Council for Research in Education, 1977), commissioned by the Head-teachers' Association of Scotland, had piloted ways of describing pupils achievements in various secondary subjects and had strongly influenced the Dunning Committee's report (Scottish Education Department, 1977), which proposed the Standard Grade assessment system. This report argued that priority should be given to the introduction of diagnostic assessment procedures into teaching and of criterion-referenced measures into the certification of pupils. It recognised that teachers' professional judgement, suitably moderated, would be an essential component of assessment for certification of abilities that could not be covered in an examination.

Another aspect of the debate about criterion-referencing also guided Scottish thinking. Those developing English courses and assessment rejected the arguments of (mainly American) advocates of domain definition that every learning objective should be specified in detail. They accepted, rather, the viewpoint expressed by Ebel (1972a, 1972b) that teachers need to think hard about their teaching, not atomistically, but rather taking flexible account of many kinds of relationship among things being learned and of learners' interaction with what they are learning. This conception of teaching is very consonant with a rich definition of reading and with the idea that teachers know most about pupils' success in dealing with the tasks and achieving the learning aims they set them.

The traditional Scottish philosophy of reading has much in common with themes emerging from more contemporary research. Harrison (2004), exploring the implications of the post-modern state of our lives for the assessment of reading, argues for approaches to both teaching and assessment that reflect the desirable practice advocated by Scottish curricular policy. These include a local focus for planning the reading experience of pupils, taking account of needs and interests and engaging them in authentic, purposeful tasks; teacher-, peer- and self-assessment; emphasis on the reader's response in interaction with the text and what may be known or guessed of the author's intentions and a portfolio of classwork as the evidence for assessing pupils' success and progress. Harrison presents these approaches as essential if we are to avoid fundamental problems arising from high-stakes testing, which does not validly assess reading development and may actually hamper it. He quotes the American Evaluation Association (AEA) task force's review of all the available evidence on the effects of high-stakes testing, which highlights teacher and administrator deprofessionalisation amongst other unfortunate outcomes.

Teacher professionalism as a critical factor in effective teaching of reading also emerges clearly from the USA National Reading Panel's review of research on teaching comprehension (2000). The review summary argues that teachers need to 'respond flexibly and opportunistically to students' needs for instructive feedback as they read' (p.47) and that teacher education should give more emphasis to ensuring that teachers have the relevant understanding of the nature of reading and of the strategies students need to have explained and demonstrated to them. Similarly, Hoffman and Pearson (2000) argue that teacher *education* for flexible planning, feedback and decision-making is critical, as opposed to mere training to perform a series of routine procedures.

In 'Balancing authenticity and strategy awareness in comprehension instruction', Pearson and Fielding (1998) conclude a review of research relating to the effects of whole books approaches to reading and skills and strategies approaches by advocating the Radical Middle – attention to both authentic, purposeful reading and the direct teaching of specific skills within it. This conclusion of their analysis of the outcomes of a decade of what they describe as war between extremists supporting each side is of particular interest to Scottish teachers. They would claim that they have always been members of the Radical Middle party. The orientation in teaching guidelines and assessment criteria over many years to such aspects of reading as personal motivation, engagement, response and evaluation, analysis of the writer's craft and, in the early years of school, development of phonemic awareness, testifies that neither extreme has ever dominated Scottish thinking about reading.

Pollitt and Taylor, in their contribution to this book (chapter 4), arrive by a different route at the same conclusion as Spencer did in 1979 on the grounds that, at that time, not enough was known about the cognitive processes involved to make effective test design possible (Spencer, 1979). They argue that what we now know about cognitive functioning, for example, the immense speed and complexity of synaptic connections in the brain in bringing schemata of previous knowledge into play to interpret even small amounts of text, confirms that reading is an unobservable process. They refer to Spolsky's (1994) argument that we need to seek rich descriptions of students' understanding, rather than try to measure it.

To what extent have formal assessment arrangements for reading in Scotland, in Higher English (including the new National Qualifications), Standard Grade English and 5–14, taken account of the fact that we are trying to assess pupils' abilities – their strengths and development needs – in a process which is multi-faceted and which involves several types of capacity, not all of which can be demonstrated in a single task/test?

The designers of both Standard Grade and Higher English (both the earlier and the National Qualifications version) devised tasks and assessment criteria that reflect some of the complexity of reading. The reader is expected to construct meaning in texts in terms of both what their authors wrote and the experience, ideas, values and skills that the reader brings to them. The reader is also expected to demonstrate a personal evaluation of or stance towards each text; thorough knowledge of it and ability to relate significant detail to the overall context/theme(s) and analysis and evaluation of the writer's craft, the linguistic and stylistic techniques deployed to convey meaning. In 'close reading' assessment in the examinations, usually using texts that are informative, argumentative or persuasive, rather than literary, questions are included to test ability to analyse and evaluate, as well as to grasp literal and inferential meaning. The combined internal folio plus external examination approach in Standard Grade seeks to ensure that reading and response to literature are assessed in a wide enough range of tasks – three 'critical essays' in the folio of classwork and a detailed 'close reading' test in the examination – to allow reasonably extended sampling of the reflective, analytic and evaluative processes promoted by the curriculum and through teaching. A similar range of tasks, including an extended (1500–1800 word) independent review of personal reading, was set in the Revised Higher English assessment (from 1987) and a version of this remains at the Higher level of the National Qualifications.

An important feature of Standard Grade and Higher assessment of reading has been the requirement for constructed responses, rather than the use of multiple-choice test items. This approach was retained after a debate and a piloting exercise conducted in the 1970s by the then Scottish Certificate of Education Examination Board (now the Scottish Qualifications Agency (SQA)). One determining factor was the difficulty of designing good multiple-choice items to test analysis and evaluation. Another was recognition of the appropriateness of constructed responses in assessing a process which inevitably involves some form of transformation of the message of the text into the reader's perception of its meaning.

Standard Grade and Higher support materials also emphasised the importance of formative assessment and the role of teachers' professional judgement of classwork in teaching and in forming a view about pupils' overall attainment. *Assessment as Part of Teaching*, a Standard Grade paper for all secondary schools provided by HMIE, strongly recommended that teachers should have confidence in their professional judgement and apply it in the ordinary course of teaching to identify pupils' strengths and needs and to find ways of helping each to progress. It argued that discussion with pupils about their understandings and their ways of dealing with tasks was likely to reveal more valuable formative information than a formal test. The paper also advised against frequent summative assessment or frequent practice exam tasks.

When the 5–14 programme was developed in the late 1980s and early 1990s, the National Assessment Guidelines, building on the earlier Standard Grade approaches, went much further to give teachers the central role in all aspects of assessment. Assessment was presented as an essential part of a continuous cycle of planning learning with pupils; teaching and interacting with them; using classroom assessment evidence, mainly informal, though perhaps sometimes from a formal test, both to support learning and to determine (only occasionally) whether they were successfully dealing with the full range of knowledge and skills which constitute achievement of the 5–14 level of attainment relevant for them; and evaluating and modifying teaching and learning activities as a result of reflection on assessment evidence. The idea that most assessment should be an informal aspect of classroom work undertaken by teachers and learners working together was strongly emphasised. A second key idea was the centrality of the teacher's professional judgement (with advice and support) in making a summative assessment of overall attainment. Accordingly, the use of National Assessments in mathematics, reading and writing was subordinated to the teachers' judgement of overall attainment. (National Assessments is the term now used; they were originally National Tests.) Pupils should take a test at a given level of the 5–14 curriculum only when classroom evidence, informal and formal, had already demonstrated their success across the defined strands of reading (or writing) at that level. The function of the test should be simply to confirm the teacher's judgement on the basis of a much more limited range of tasks than could be observed in classwork.

Later publications in Scotland continued to promote formative and diagnostic assessment, called respectively assessment as part of teaching and learning and taking a closer look in the National Guidelines. In particular, a series of booklets offering diagnostic procedures were made freely available to schools. These procedures were *not* tests, but ways of using classroom interaction to identify pupils' strengths and needs as learners in mathematics, science, reading and writing. (Scottish Council for Research in Education, 1995; Hayward and Spencer, 1998). Essentially, *Taking a Closer Look at Reading* provides teachers with exploratory questions and issues to explore with pupils and identifies possible next steps to help pupils to grow as learners. There was a constant emphasis on the importance of the teacher's *own* knowledge of the pupil and on the pupil's own perspective as sources of evidence to inform an analysis of activities and thinking. The exploratory questions and next steps were proposed for four areas of the reading process, which again reinforced the notion of it as rich and complex: Attitude and Motivation; Decoding: Recognising Words and Sentences; Pursuit of Meaning and Awareness of Author's Use of Language. Central to this approach is the idea that a learner is a whole person, whose success and progress in reading depends as much on attitude, motivation and interaction with others as it does on analysis of the construct of reading as decoding, comprehending and responding.

The historical survey of developments in this section shows that there have been significant efforts for a long time in Scotland to promote assessment which reflects as fully a possible a rich construct of the process of reading – so rich that it cannot be encompassed within the format of traditional reading tests. It therefore requires a considerable contribution from the teacher.

The model in practice

What in fact happens in schools? It is not easy to obtain a definitive overall picture of any one scenario. Some sources of evidence, do, however, offer indications. We shall use four of these: Her Majesty's Inspectors of Education (HMIE) Standards and Quality reports; National Assessment results for reading; data from the monitoring programme in Scotland (6th Assessment of Achievement Programme in Reading, 2003) and recent research studies including smaller scale activities where teachers' views have been gathered.

There is evidence that a good deal of work goes on in Scottish classrooms which does indeed develop pupils' reading abilities in the rich way hoped for. There is also evidence that practice in schools and classrooms is variable. There remain issues to be addressed, in relation both to attainment in reading and the classroom experience for many learners. HMIE described very good attainment in a Standards and Quality report (HMIE, 1999), including high quality group discussion on novels and poetry (S1 and S2, ages 12–14); sustained independent comments on demanding literary texts and detailed analysis of writers' craft to support responses and evaluations (S3 and S4, ages 14–16); and mature, independent responses to and analyses of personal reading (S5–S6 pupils, ages 16–18). However, a number of aspects of reading were identified as requiring improvement (HMIE, 1999): in S1–S4 reading for information and appreciation of the writer's craft and, additionally in S1 and S2, reading for meaning and for pleasure. HMI had some significant comments to make about the nature of reading experiences being offered:

> *In almost all departments pupils' essential command of English would be significantly enhanced if, from S1, there were more frequent close reading for analysis of meaning, language awareness and appreciation of the writer's craft.*

(HMIE, 1999, p.15)

The more recent *Improving Achievement in English Language in Primary and Secondary Schools* shows a similar picture across both the primary and the secondary sectors:

> *The evidence about attainment in English Language presents a very mixed and quite complex picture. ... Overall attainment is ... in need of significant improvement from P5–S2.*

(HMIE, 2003, p.8)

The results of the Sixth Survey of English Language (SEED, 2003), undertaken as part of Scotland's national monitoring system, the Assessment of Achievement Programme, are consistent with the findings from HMIE. The AAP reported that the nationally defined 5–14 levels for reading were reached by 63 per cent in P4 (age 8) but by only 41 per cent in P7 (age 11) and 43 per cent in S2 (age 13/14).

It is, however, somewhat surprising to find that, according to National Assessment results reported by schools, there has been a steady annual improvement in levels of attainment in recent years. For 2002–03, these figures indicate that 80.8 per cent of P4, 72.4 per cent of P7 and 60.6 per cent of S2 had been recorded as having achieved the appropriate national level of attainment (SEED, 2004). This evidence sits uneasily with the HMIE reports and the AAP survey. It does, however, resonate with findings reported by Peter Tymms (2004) in relation to the standards data emerging from English primary schools. He argues that national testing has failed to monitor standards over time and cites a number of reasons for this, including the high stakes use of the test data and its impact on classroom practices, the changing curriculum and assessment context, and the ways in which sub-areas of the curriculum have changed differently, e.g. 'Writing has improved much more than reading' (Tymms, 2004, p.492).

So what is really happening in reading in Scottish schools? Commenting on assessment in Scotland, HMIE reports on individual primary and secondary schools suggest that helpful oral or written feedback to pupils on English work, including reading tasks, is fairly common. The Standards and Quality report referred to above (HMIE, 1999) identified only 20 per cent of the schools inspected where such feedback was not provided on most aspects of English. This report also noted that many secondary English departments summarised classwork achievement in individual profiles, sometimes also identifying strengths, development needs and next steps and incorporating an element of pupil self-evaluation. Such feedback and profiles were often based, as far as reading is concerned, on both close-reading/interpretation tasks and extended responses to reading or critical essays. In primary schools' inspection reports, HMIE sometimes note effective formative assessment of reading (and other areas of work) but they do also sometimes consider that judgements about levels of attainment have been made on the basis of too little evidence from classwork (HMIE, 2003, p.26). This comment refers to situations where pupils have been allowed to take a National Assessment before they have had the range of successful experience of various aspects of reading (or writing) necessary to give the teacher evidence of full attainment of the level.

Evidence from teachers in other research projects (Hayward and Hedge, 2005; Hayward *et al.*, 2004) indicates strongly that, despite policy advice to the contrary (Scottish Office Education Department (SOED), 1991b), decisions about levels of attainment have been dominated by National Assessments results, rather than by professional judgement. Despite the positive reactions to the principles of 5–14 Assessment, both originally and when teachers were asked to reconsider them in a national consultation instigated by the Scottish Executive (Hayward *et al.*, 2000), it is clear that many teachers believe that the data from National Assessments are regarded as more important than the evidence from teachers' professional judgement. There is also much anecdotal evidence, for example, from teachers attending Masters' courses in reading in universities, that in many primary schools and for S1/S2 in some secondaries assessment of reading means only 'taking a National Assessment'. Many of these highly-motivated teachers are strongly committed to the principles of 5–14 Assessment, but have not been enabled to live the ideas in practice. They often report that they or their colleagues do not conduct formative assessment of reading in a systematic way. They often say they tend to make decisions about giving pupils a National Assessment on the basis of how far they have progressed through a reading scheme, rather than on evidence of progress across all the strands of the reading programme. Another common view is that a National Assessment at a particular level will be taken if the teacher believes that a pupil has a fighting chance of being successful, rather than when (s)he is sure that all aspects of the level of work specified in the curriculum guidelines have been satisfactorily mastered. National Assessment data were collected nationally in the 1990s and up to 2004. Though there were no published league tables it appears that teachers and schools believe these test results to be an extremely important source of evidence about the quality of their school and of the teachers who work in it.

Recent studies of relations between primary and secondary schools (Hayward *et al.*, 2004; Besley, 2004; Hayward *et al.*, 2002; Baron *et al.*, 2003) indicate a lack of trust in primary assessment by secondary teachers and an awareness of this distrust on the part of primary staff. Secondary teachers regard primary assessment as unreliable: they say that pupils often cannot demonstrate the skills and understandings implied by the National Assessment result provided by the primary school. Primary teachers tend to regard this view as a slight on their professionalism. One reason for this lack of understanding across sectors may be that National Assessment data are being used for essentially different purposes. Primary teachers, in adopting the fighting chance approach to having pupils undertake a National Assessment, may be trying to ensure that as many pupils as possible achieve as high a level as possible. Secondary teachers, on the other hand, may expect that if a pupil is recorded as having attained a particular level then that means that s/he will be able to demonstrate achievement across all the areas of the curriculum at that level.

If, as it appears, we are in a scenario where the only significant assessment activity is taking a National Assessment, perhaps we should cast a critical eye over the tests themselves. To what extent do they assess what they purport to assess and reflect the desirable reading experience promoted by national policy and guidance and good teaching? We address this question in the final section of this chapter, where we consider what is now needed in the assessment of reading in Scotland. But before that, it is important to try to understand the problem a little more deeply. Why, despite the significant efforts to encourage professional judgement in assessment, both formative and summative, are we in the position where many headteachers and teachers rely mainly or solely on the formal National Assessments, about which, when introduced in their original National Test version, there had been much controversy?

Understanding the problem

As part of the national consultation on assessment (Hayward *et al.*, 1999) respondents, including education authorities, teachers and headteachers, teachers' organisations, the Scottish Parent-Teacher Association and university representatives, were asked to identify what might be done to enhance assessment based on teachers' professional judgement. Three areas were identified: a need for practical, professional development activities, specifically opportunities for teachers to work together to consider evidence from pupils and share standards; a reconciliation of assessment to support learning and assessment for wider purposes of accountability; a rationalisation of the bureaucracy associated with assessment. If we reflect on these issues specifically in respect of reading, part of the reason why National Assessments have come to be so dominant may lie in the very complexity of both the reading process and the range of potential evidence related to it. Teachers may have lacked adequate opportunities to help them become confident gatherers and users of classroom assessment information across all the strands of the reading curriculum. Without this and amidst the heavy pressures of planning and teaching, they may have regarded the existence of National Assessments provided by 'experts' as an obvious, easy and safe solution to assessment needs. Schools perceive themselves to be in a scenario where there is pressure from politicians, education authorities and HMIE to improve overall performance. They believe the reputation of the school, in general and in the eyes of inspectors, if they visit, depends heavily on this. In this context, National Assessments have obvious attractions as evidence to justify to HMIE and to one's education authority that, indeed, a school has improved its overall performance.

The original positive attitude of practitioners, researchers and policy makers to the philosophy and principles of the 5–14 Assessment Guidelines identified in the SEED consultation (Hayward et al., 2000) was, therefore, not enough to ensure its translation into practice; nor was the cascade approach to staff development adequate. There was evidence that testing had become dominant because teachers were often less aware of the actual policy and national guidelines than they were of the context of 'performativity' within which they perceived the policy to have emerged (Hayward and Hedge, 2005). Even although there have never been published league tables of Scottish primary schools, the fact that National Assessments data were collected centrally had led people to believe that these results were what really mattered.

The role of HMIE in this process is worthy of consideration, or, more accurately, the role of perceptions of what HMI 'require' and will expect if they visit a school. HMI have in fact strongly supported 5–14 assessment policy on formative assessment and teachers' professional judgement as a key factor in summative assessment. This is clear from their comments and advice in both individual school inspection reports and such national publications as the reports in the 'Standards and Quality' and the 'Improving...' series referred to above. Nevertheless, there is a widespread belief among headteachers (in particular in primary schools) that HMI insist on 'hard evidence', which means a test result.

This belief appears to have been reinforced by the 'target-setting' initiative (now no longer operating at a national level). All education authorities co-operated in this initiative devised by HMI in the 1990s as a significant part of a school's quality assurance. It was based on the principle that effective school improvement action requires clear evidence about many important aspects of a school's life, including attainment and the learning and teaching activities that affect it. Target-setting involved the specification for each school of an agreed measure of improvement in performance – e.g., an additional proportion of pupils attaining level D in P7 or a Credit award at Standard Grade. The intention was that schools, with the support of their education authorities, would achieve the target by improving learning and teaching. In many cases, schools did not interpret this initiative in the way that HMIE intended, with a focus on improving learning and teaching. Sliwka and Spencer (2005) report that many headteachers and classroom teachers hold the view that target-setting encouraged them to focus on summative assessment and that some seem to regard action to develop really effective learning and teaching as separate from, or even inimical to, their need to improve results. Certainly, since both education authorities and HMI were monitoring schools' progress towards their targets, they inevitably became 'high stakes' in the minds of school staff.

HMI may have inadvertently facilitated the predominance of testing over other approaches to assessment in another way, too. Throughout the 1990s, while certainly commenting on and advocating 'assessment as part of teaching' in every inspection, HMI also criticised schools where 5–14 National Assessments were not used 'to confirm teachers' judgements'. They were obliged to do this because it was (and still remains for at least the immediate future) government policy that the tests should be used in this way. The frequent appearance of this criticism in inspection reports proba- bly contributed strongly to the perception that the tests are very important.

To sum up, the problem in Scotland has not been lack of impact from reading research on the national policies and guidance offered to schools. Rather, there have been strong influences on practice from other directions that have led to a narrow, test- dominated view of assessment at 5–14. The critical issue for the future is how to create circumstances where research, policy and practice can grow together to improve chil- dren's experiences as readers in schools. Tackling this issue requires reflection on other kinds of research, on the development of collaborative learning communities.

Current developments

There are current developments in Scotland that seek to improve the situation. Current- ly, the policy context is favourable. In 2003, the partnership agreement between the Scottish Labour Party and the Scottish Liberal Democrats (2003), the parties presently sharing power in the Scottish Parliament, included the following policy statement:

> We will provide more time for learning by simplifying and reducing assessment, end- ing the current national tests for 5–14 year olds. We will promote assessment methods that support learning and teaching. We will measure improvements in overall attain- ment through broad surveys rather than relying on national tests. (2003, p.6)

Should we keep the tests?

The policy commitment just quoted to end the current National Assessments has emerged from a growing concern about the negative effects of such summative assessments on assessment for learning in a culture where 'performativity' has come to dominate think- ing. However, there are other reasons for dissatisfaction with the National Assessments in reading. A preliminary study of the construct validity of the Scottish National Assess- ments in reading (Hayward and Spencer, 2004) demonstrates that even in their most recent form, the National Assessments do not reflect well the construct of reading under- pinning the National Guidelines on 5–14 English Language. Though they were not intended, as simply formal confirmatory tests, to reflect the whole of reading as defined and elaborated in the guidelines, this study suggests that, in fact, they do not even succeed in reflecting as much of the reading process as could be included in a formal test. We analysed the tasks set in National Assessments at levels A (age about 8) to level E (age about 14) using the categorisation of comprehension processes underpinning the Progress in International Reading Literacy Study (Campbell et al., 2001) conducted in 2001 by the International Association for the Evaluation of Educational Achievement (IEA) with chil- dren aged 9–10 in various countries. The PIRLS team defined literacy in terms of active construction of meaning and use of strategies and reflection in reading; reading to learn; participating in communities of readers; and reading for enjoyment. They identified four 'processes of comprehension':

1. focus on and retrieve explicitly stated information

2. make straightforward inferences

3. interpret and integrate ideas and information, including generalising from specifics and drawing on real life experience

4. examine and evaluate content, language and textual elements.

The analysis revealed that at no level did the National Assessments involve any task requiring a constructed response showing personal reaction or evaluation. All tasks were either multiple-choice, true/false/can't tell or cloze completion, of sentences at the lower levels, or summary paragraphs at the higher ones. The proportion of marks allocated to tasks where the answer could be retrieved explicitly from the text was 88 per cent at level A, 79 per cent at B, 80 per cent at C, 64 per cent at D and 86.5 per cent at E. In each case all or almost all of the other tasks involved simple inference. There were very few tasks of PIRLS types 3 and 4. At level D there were two multiple-choice questions requiring recognition of a generalisation based on the text and there were two at level E, again in multiple-choice format, requiring pupils to make a judgement about genre. A 'pass' on the Assessment at any level, widely regarded as guaranteeing attainment of that level in reading, is achieved with 67 per cent of the marks.

By contrast, analysis of the 2003 Standard Grade and NQ Higher examinations showed that, in the close reading (Interpretation) tasks, much larger proportions of marks were obtained in responding to questions of types 3 and 4 in the PIRLS framework: 34 per cent at Standard Grade Foundation (considered to be no more demanding in principle than 5–14 Level E), 64 per cent at both Standard Grade General and Credit and 92 per cent at Higher. In all the Standard Grade and Higher tasks constructed answers are required. In addition to the close reading tasks, pupils produce, at each level of Standard Grade, three extended 'critical essays' on literature studied in class, in which they are expected to demonstrate PIRLS types 3 and 4 processes. At Higher they must achieve criteria matching types 2, 3 and 4 processes in a critical essay and a detailed textual analysis in internal assessment and in two critical essays in the external examination. They also have to pass a close reading test internally (similar in style to the external one analysed).

Standard Grade and the new National Qualifications Higher are not unproblematic. There is, for instance a known tendency for schools to allow pupils in Standard Grade courses to 'polish' pieces of work in their folio for an inordinate amount of time at the expense of a wider range of reading. Because the new National Qualifications at Higher and all other levels include a pass/fail internal summative assessment task (or tasks) for each of three course units, there is a danger of heavily assessment-led teaching. There is a strong case for the view that the present Higher arrangements give too much emphasis to reading. Writing other than critical essays on literature is assessed only internally not on a pass/fail basis in the external examination, which determines the overall grade. Talking is not assessed at all. Nevertheless, it is clear that the message to teachers about the nature of reading from these two assessment systems is that it is indeed rich and complex and requires personal engagement analysis and evaluation. Indeed, the questions in the external close-reading test at Higher are categorised on the paper as U (Understanding), A (Analysis) or E (Evaluation), so that pupils are oriented to the range of types of response expected.

In contrast, the 5–14 National Assessments do not convey this message about the richness of reading. The question types used were selected to reduce marker unreliability, but the result is that the tests have low validity as assessments of reading as it is defined in the 5–14 curriculum. A recent addition to the *writing* test at each level has extended the range of *reading* skills covered by requiring pupils to continue a story or other type of text in the same style/genre as that of the opening paragraphs provided in the test. Nevertheless, overall, the National Assessments provide a poor basis for informing parents, other teachers and those monitoring the schools system about the range and quality of pupils' reading abilities. Perhaps even more significantly, the narrow range of reading skills they cover reinforces a tendency in many schools to give pupils a narrow range of reading experiences, often without expectation of analysis and personal evaluation of ideas and writer's craft. There is in principle a strong case for implementing the policy set out in the political partnership agreement in respect of national testing, that is, to remove it. However, while Circular No.2 to education authorities (SEED, 2005), outlining current government policy on assessment and reporting 3–14, does emphasise the idea of sharing the standard through moderation, it also indicates that National Assessments continue as a means of confirming professional judgement. So our reservations about their validity remain significant.

How should we support teachers as formative and summative assessors?

Irrespective of eventual decisions about testing, a programme to build teachers' confidence and skills in assessment is already in place. Building on the findings of the National Consultation on Assessment (Hayward *et al.*, 1999) the *Assessment is for Learning* initiative was established to try to resolve some of the tensions between the widely endorsed principles of effective assessment, including the centrality of formative assessment and of teachers' professional judgement, and the reality in Scottish classrooms.

The programme initially involved schools representing all the Scottish education authorities in a year of action to develop in their particular circumstances key aspects of assessment that had emerged as critical in the consultation. This development work focused in some schools on formative assessment; in others on pupils' personal learning plans, involving them in collaboration with their teachers in identifying future learning needs; in others on gathering and interpreting assessment evidence for summative assessment and on finding ways of 'sharing the standard' across schools; and in a fourth group on developing parental partnership and reporting to parents. All education authorities are currently engaging all their schools in a planned initiative to promote 'assessment for learning', 'assessment as learning' and 'assessment of learning', using the knowledge about successful practice gained from the schools involved in the first year's work. The aim is to spread widely the strategy employed in the first phase, which was to enable researchers, policy-makers, teachers and pupils to work together in partnership, recognizing that each of these groups brings essential yet different understandings to the development of effective assessment and effective learning and teaching. This work is supported by an on-line resource, available on the LTScotland website, a toolkit, with key principles for different aspects of assessment and exemplars of individual schools' successful practice in the first year of the programme.

We know from the evaluation of the programme conducted by the London Institute of Education (Hallam *et al.*, 2004) of the positive response from teachers involved in the formative assessment programme. They had access through conferences to the work and enthusiasm of researchers such as Dylan Wiliam and Paul Black (1998) and to the experience of teachers elsewhere who had successfully developed formative assessment in their classrooms. They very actively and keenly developed their own approaches through reflection on the research and on the needs of their pupils. They also reported that a crucial aspect of their successful engagement with the programme was the regular opportunity for networking with other teachers also engaged in it, in their own school and more widely at national or regional conferences. The evidence emerging suggests that there are very real, exciting, positive changes in classrooms across Scotland. The spaces for reflection and working out one's own assessment strategy provided within the project enabled teachers to make assessment for learning come alive in their own contexts, sometimes in very different ways. They not only found their involvement professionally fulfilling but they reported positive changes in the quality of pupils' work and in their commitment to learning. Many teachers expressed relief at once again being able to focus on learning and teaching. Some reported that they now understood words they had been using for years, that they were developing a real understanding of what assessment as part of learning actually means. Only a very small number of those involved remained sceptical about the approach (Hayward, Priestly and Young, 2004).

Assessment is for Learning is neither a top down model of change, nor a bottom up model. It recognises that no community, research, policy or practice, can work without the other groups and have any real hope of positive change. It also recognises that old approaches to the growing of new assessment policy and practice will not do. Desforges (2000) argues that if we are to offer better educational opportunities for learners then we need new approaches that transcend traditional practices in research. Influences on the programme come therefore not only from research on assessment as an educational issue but also from research on the development of collaborative learning communities. The aim is to have researchers, policy makers and practitioners work together, taking full account of the many practical factors affecting teaching. The methodology is participative and is consistent with Fullan's admonition that (1993, p.60) any successful innovation will involve '… expanding professional development to include learning while doing and learning from doing'. The *Assessment is for Learning* programme has been heavily influenced by the work of Senge and Scharmer (2001, p.247), who offer a model of collaborative research, arguing that '… knowledge creation is an intensely human, messy process of imagination, invention and learning from mistakes, embedded in a web of human relationships'. This is a model where all involved are learning, pupils, teachers, researchers and policy makers, as they attempt to travel where Fullan (2003) suggests there are not yet roads. Participants in this project must, 'Travel and make the road' (2003, p.106).

The model has regard to what matters for people. Too often we have seen innovation as somehow separate from the people who are an integral part of the process of change. Or we have required change in what teachers and schools must do with little consideration of the implications for change in the policy or research communities. The *Assessment is for Learning* programme offers a more inclusive approach to change that has potential advantage for all the communities involved. Teacher professionalism is enhanced and research, policy and practice begin to move into a closer alignment.

However, if professional judgement is to flourish then the tensions between assessment to support learning and assessment for wider purposes of accountability remain to be addressed. The new approach proposed to monitor national standards will not involve the use of National Assessment data. It will use sample surveys only, in the Scottish Survey of Achievement (SSA), an expanded version of the former Assessment of Achievement Programme (AAP). This is an approach similar to that advocated by Tymms (2004). It is hoped that this approach, combined with improved support for teachers' summative assessment based on professional judgement, should continue to supply the information necessary for schools, education authorities and HMI to monitor the overall attainment of individual schools, without setting one against others in direct competition. Most importantly, it is hoped that it will make it possible to enhance pupils' experiences of and achievements in reading.

We are, therefore, embarking in Scotland on a highly participative general approach to all aspects of assessment, with real emphasis on developing teachers' professional judgement about formative and summative assessment for 5–14. Given this emphasis, the strategy will involve complex resourcing and management challenges. What are the implications for the assessment of *reading*?

In the first phase, teachers involved in the *Assessment is for Learning* programme chose to focus on a wide range of areas of the primary curriculum and secondary subjects. Few, if any, selected reading as their central concern. The *Building Bridges* (across the primary-secondary interface) initiative was initiated, linked to *Assessment is for Learning* and with similar methodology, to focus particularly on literacy. In keeping with the participative approach, participants were invited to identify their own important areas for investigation. About a quarter of the 32 schools initially involved are focused on reading. There is, however, no guarantee that reading will be a focus of attention as education authorities and schools take forward either the general *Assessment is for Learning* or the *Building Bridges* initiatives in the coming years. There is no certainty that reading will feature systematically in the piloting of moderation and standard-sharing that was identified as an issue of concern in the national consultation. The approach to moderation and standard sharing being adopted has been adapted from a model currently in use in Queensland, Australia and will involve this year a large group of schools in Scotland. Is this an opportunity missed? Or would the identification of reading as a particular issue run counter to the philosophy of ownership of priorities? Clearly, there are still aspects of this approach to be worked through amongst the partners of the programme.

What could ensure real attention to reading would be the withdrawal of the National Assessments and the requirement for teachers to use classwork to determine levels of attainment. We have argued earlier in this chapter that there is no alternative to teachers' professional judgement if pupils are to have a rich and deep reading curriculum. Raising the stakes of professional judgement would precipitate a need for the collaboration among the policy, research and teaching communities to address important factors affecting teacher assessment of reading.

Teachers' professional judgement has to be good. The EPPI (2004) review of evidence of reliability and validity of assessment by teachers for summative purposes identifies both validity and reliability weaknesses. However, the research reviewed also suggests several factors that can enhance both the validity and reliability of teachers' summative assessment of classwork. These include: following agreed teacher assessment procedures, including well defined tasks to allow pupils to demonstrate their abilities properly; involving teachers themselves in defining criteria of success on the tasks; use of detailed criteria describing levels of progress in various aspects of achievement; developing teachers' awareness of sources of potential bias in their assessments; and moderation through professional collaboration, which requires protected time for teachers to meet with colleagues and professional advisers. All of these factors need to be given attention specifically in the context of reading.

At the heart of effective formative and summative assessment is a clear understanding of what it is we are trying to find out about – the processes of reading and how pupils engage in them, individually and collectively. The twin themes of Scottish reading and assessment policy of the last thirty years or so are therefore still critical: be clear about what reading aims are (without over-simplifying them) and stimulate and respond to pupils' thinking. But supporting the professional judgement necessary to do this is, we believe, a more complicated business than we had previously thought. What is now clearer is that for professional judgement to thrive, it requires to be situated in a sympathetic educational and political culture. It is now also clearer that for there to be a strong relationship amongst research, policy and practice, there have to be strong, respectful and open partnerships amongst all participants. All of these features are crucial if pupils are to experience reading as a rich, deep and inspiring construct. In Scotland, we are learning as we grow. Researchers, policy makers and practitioners are determined that the current ambitious action to improve assessment and reading in Scotland will succeed. There is no alternative.

References

Baron, S., Hall, S., Martin, M., McCreath, D., Roebuck, M., Schad, D. and Wilkinson, J.E. (2003). *The Learning Communities in Glasgow – Phase 2 Evaluation*. Glasgow: Faculty of Education, University of Glasgow.

Besley, T. (2004). *Quality Audit of Pupil Experience in Primary – Secondary School Transfer in the Eight Integrated Learning Communities of Falkirk Council Education Services*. Glasgow: Faculty of Education, University of Glasgow.

Black, P. and Wiliam, D. (1998). 'Assessment and Classroom Learning', *Assessment in Education*, **5**, 7–36.

Campbell, J., Kelly, D.L., Mullis, I.V., Martin, M.O. and Sainsbury, M. (2001). *Framework and Specifications for the PIRLS Assessment. 2nd edn*. Boston: International Study Centre.

Desforges, C. (2000). 'Familiar challenges and new approaches: necessary advances in theory and methods in research on teaching and learning.' The Desmond Nuttall Memorial Lecture, BERA Annual Conference, Cardiff.

Ebel, R.L. (1972a). *Essentials of Educational Measurement*. New Jersey: Prentice-Hall.

Ebel, R.L. (1972b). 'Some limitations of criterion-referenced measurement.' In: Bracht, G. (Ed) *Perspectives in Educational and Psychological Measurement*. New Jersey: Prentice-Hall.

Evidence for Policy and Practice Information Co-ordinating Centre (EPPI-Centre) (2004). 'A systematic review of the evidence of reliability and validity in assessment by teachers used for summative purposes' [online]. Available: http://eppi.ioe.ac.uk [28 August, 2004].

Fullan, M. (2003). *Change Forces with a Vengeance*. London, Routledge Falmer.

Hallam, S., Kirkton, A., Pfeffers, J., Robertson, P. and Stobart, G. (2004). *Report of the Evaluation of Programme One of the Assessment Development Programme: Support for Professional Practice in Formative Assessment*. London: Institute of Education, University of London.

Harrison, C. (2004). 'Postmodern Principles for Responsive Reading Assessment', *Journal of Research in Reading*, **27**, 2, 163–73.

Hayward, L., Spencer, E., Hedge, N. Arthur, L. and Hollander, R. (2004). *Closing the Gap: Primary-Secondary Liaison in South Lanarkshire. Research Report*, Glasgow: Faculty of Education, University of Glasgow.

Hayward, L., Priestly, M. and Young, M. (2004). 'Ruffling the calm of the ocean floor: merging, policy, practice and research in Scotland', *Oxford Review of Education*, **30**, 3, 397–415.

Hayward, L. and Hedge, N. (2005). 'Travelling towards change in assessment: policy, practice and research in education', *Assessment in Education*, **12**, 1, 55–75.

Hayward, L., Hedge, N. and Bunney, L. (2002). 'Consultation on the review of assessment within New National Qualifications' [online]. Available: at http://www.scotland.gov.uk/library5/cnnqa 00.asp [15 August, 2004].

Hayward, L., Kane, J. and Cogan, N. (2000). *Improving Assessment in Scotland. Research Report to the Scottish Executive Education Department*. University of Glasgow.

Hayward, L. and Spencer, E. (2004). 'The construct of reading in 5–14 National Assessments and in examinations in Scotland' (draft journal paper).

Her Majesty's Inspectorate of Education (HMIE) (1999). *Standards and Quality in Secondary Schools 1994–97*. Edinburgh: Scottish Executive Education Department.

Her Majesty's Inspectorate of Education (HMIE) (2003). *Improving Achievement in English Language in Primary and Secondary Schools*. Edinburgh: Scottish Executive Education Department.

Hoffman, J. and Pearson, P.D. (2000). 'Reading teacher education in the next millennium: what your grandmother's teacher didn't know that your granddaughter's teacher should', *Reading Research Quarterly*, **35**, 1, 28–44.

National Reading Panel (2000). 'Chapter 4, Comprehension.' In: Reports of the Sub-groups [online]. Available: http://www.nationalreadingpanel.org/Publications/publications.htm [15 August, 2004].

Pearson, P.D. and Fielding, L. (1994). Balancing authenticity and strategy awareness in comprehension instruction. Unpublished article adapted from the same authors' 'Synthesis of reading research: reading comprehension: what works?', *Educational Leadership*, **51**, 5, 62–7.

Scottish Council for Research in Education (1977). *Pupils in Profile: Making the Most of Teachers' Knowledge of Pupils*. Edinburgh: Hodder and Stoughton.

Scottish Council for Research in Education (1995). *Taking a Closer Look: Key Ideas in Diagnostic Assessment*. Edinburgh: Scottish Council for Research in Education.

Scottish Education Department (1968). *The Teaching of Literature*. Edinburgh: Scottish Education Department/HMSO.

Scottish Education Department (1977). *Assessment for All (The Dunning Report)*. Edinburgh: Scottish Education Department/HMSO.

Scottish Executive Education Department (2003). *The Report of the Sixth Survey of English Language 2001; Assessment of Achievement Programme*. Edinburgh: Scottish Executive Education Department.

Scottish Executive Education Department (2004). *5–14 Attainment in Publicly Funded Schools, 2002–03*. Edinburgh: Scottish Executive Publications [online]. Available: http:www.scotland.gov.uk/stats/bulletins/00305-03.asp [1 September, 2004].

Scottish Executive Education Department (2005). *Circular No.02 June 2006. Assessment and Reporting 3–14*. Available: http://www.scotland.gov.uk/Resource/Doc/54357/0013630.pdf

Scottish Office Education Department (1991a). *Curriculum and Assessment in Scotland: National Guidelines: English Language 5–14*. Edinburgh: Scottish Office Education Department/HMSO.

Scottish Office Education Department (1991b). *Curriculum and Assessment in Scotland: National Guidelines: Assessment 5–14* . Edinburgh: Scottish Office Education Department/HMSO.

Scottish Labour Party and Scottish Liberal Democrats (2003). 'A Partnership for a Better Scotland: Partnership Agreement' [online]. Available: http://www.scotland.gov.uk/library5/government/pfbs 00.asp [15 August, 2004].

Senge, P. and Scharmer, O. (2001). 'Community action research: learning as a community of practitioners.' In: Reason, P. & Bradbury, H. (Eds) *Handbook of Action Research: Participative Inquiry and Practice.* London, Sage: 238–49.

Sliwka, A. and Spencer, E. (2005). *Scotland: 'Developing a Coherent System of Assessment' in Formative Assessment – Improving Learning in Secondary Classrooms.* Paris: Organisation for Economic Co-operation and Development (OECD).

Spencer, E. (1979). 'The assessment of English – what is needed?' In: Jeffrey, A.W. (Ed) *Issues in Educational Assessment.* Edinburgh: Scottish Education Department/HMSO.

Spolsky, B. (1994). 'Comprehension testing, or can understanding be measured?' In: Brown, G., Malmkjaer, K., Pollitt, A. and Williams, J. (Eds) *Language and Understanding.* Oxford: OUP.

Tymms, P. (2004). 'Are standards rising in English primary schools?', *British Educational Research Journal*, **30**, 4, 477–94.

17 Low-stakes national assessment: national evaluations in France

Martine Rémond

In France, there are some distinct differences from the assessments of reading in the English-speaking world which make up most of this volume. These differences apply both to the definition of reading and to the purposes for testing. The national evaluations of reading in French, which are described in this chapter, are formal national tests intended for formative and diagnostic use.

Background

All schools in France for children aged from 2- or 3-years-old to 18 are required to follow the National Curricula, which apply to primary schools (ages 3–11), *collèges* (ages 12–14) and *lycées* (ages 15–18). This chapter mainly focuses on primary schools, where the National Curriculum currently includes: French, mathematics, science, history, geography, art and design, music and physical education. The national evaluations on entering Grades 3 and 6 (ages 8 and 11 respectively) are devoted to mathematics and French.

The National Curriculum consists of two aspects: programmes of study, which define what is to be taught and goals, which define expected performance at the end of the cycle. French primary schooling is composed of three cycles, each cycle lasting three years. Cycle 1 is entitled 'First acquisitions' and applies to children aged from three to five. Cycle 2, 'Basic acquisitions' covers 5- to 8-year-olds and is followed by Cycle 3, 'Consolidation of acquisitions' for ages 8 to 11. The competences assessed by the national evaluation at the end of Cycle 2 and at the end of Cycle 3 are determined according to the National Curriculum and to the goals fixed for each cycle.

These tests take place at the beginning of the final year of the cycle. The objective is not to summarise or certify the attainments of the cycle that is coming to an end, but to proceed to a diagnostic and formative assessment. The part of the tests which is devoted to French assesses both reading and writing, but writing will not form part of this discussion.

The close relationship between the National Curriculum and the goals provides the basis for the definition of the construct of reading that underlies the national tests.

The reading curriculum

The programmes of study for French are called: *Mastery of Language* and *French Language*. They are divided into the three cycles described above and each is presented as a few pages of text. The first category of requirements indicates the objectives and time which must be devoted to this activity. The second details the knowledge, skills and understandings to be taught. Finally, 'goals for performance at the end of the cycle' are stated. These are listed under the following headings: mastery of oral language, reading and writing, which are divided into: reading comprehension, word recognition, handwriting and spelling, production of text.

In 2002, a new National Curriculum was published. It gives an increased importance to Cycle 3 for reading instruction and it is explicitly stated that teachers must teach literature. A document which is separate from the National Curriculum presents the literary approach and a list of 100 books from which teachers must choose. The aim of this is to teach some common literary heritage.

The goals for Cycle 3 consist of a long list which is divided into general competencies and specific competencies (literature, grammar, spelling, vocabulary, conjugation).

The purpose of assessment

The tests are national diagnostic evaluations with a formative purpose. Two perspectives can be distinguished: one centred on pupils individually, the other centred on the overall population to draw conclusions on the way the system operates.

Within this overall purpose, the test items are constructed to give information about two levels of competence:

- attainments necessary for children to have full access to teaching and learning in the phase of education they are beginning (understanding written instructions, locating explicit information, etc.)

- attainments that are still being acquired (presentation of a text, following complex instructions).

For the individual pupil, the results of the evaluations have an important function in identifying attainment, strengths, weaknesses and difficulties in relation to objectives they should master or to the goals of the phase they are entering. These evaluations are intended to analyse each pupil's performances and difficulties at a given moment of his or her schooling, in order to constitute a summary assessment of attainment. This is expected to have an effect on the regulation of learning for that student through school teaching practices and learning objectives.

For the education system, the national evaluations provide a 'snapshot' of performance each year, giving an indication of percentages of students nationally in relation to the curriculum goals.

In order to fulfil these two main functions, individual and national, two applications can be distinguished. The entire age group carry out the tests, but only a national representative sample is analysed to provide information to policy makers. The procedure takes place under standard conditions as a large-scale evaluation exercise. Tests are administered collectively within a limited time, following extremely precise procedures supervised by the teacher in charge of the class. The students are assessed as a group rather than individually. The overall exercise is implemented by the DPD (Direction of Planning and Development of Education, Ministry of Education).

At the individual level, the teacher can make an analysis of student responses using the codes described in the next section, in order to gain diagnostic information about each pupil. For this purpose, the two levels of competence mentioned above take on a particular importance. The guidance for teachers identifies those skills and understandings that are regarded as essential for pupils to benefit fully from the current curriculum. If students are having difficulty with these basic skills, focused teaching is recommended.

At the national level, the results of the representative sample are analysed and publicised as a summary of the national picture. They provide the content for a publication produced in the form of a brochure and also made available on the internet. National yearly evaluations in France are not used to rank schools or to inform funding decisions. This is an example of a required national assessment system that is low stakes. It is intended to contribute to teaching and learning, and to give information to monitor the system nationally, but it is not used for accountability purposes, either for students or teachers.

The nature of the tests and the construct of reading

The national assessments in France for French have as their basis tables of assessed competences which are built each year according to the National Curriculum and to the goals fixed for each cycle. Any one year's test cannot cover the whole range of knowledge, skills and understandings included in the national references (curriculum and goals). Over the years, the tests must include as wide a variety as possible of skills and text types.

The goals are presented as a table divided into two fields: reading and writing, but only reading will be discussed here. *Reading* is itself divided into two skills: understanding a text (reading comprehension); and mastery of tools of language. This general schema applies to both levels of evaluation (grades 3 and 6). In the first column of the table, we find the list of competences which will be assessed, then the nature of the assessment task. Table 17.1 presents as an example the structure of the 2002 assessment for grade 3 students, and outlines the construct of reading assessed in that year. In other years, the table is slightly different, reflecting the broader construct of reading represented by the National Curriculum programmes of study and the associated goals.

Table 17.1 Structure of competencies and tasks for reading

Reading comprehension

Competencies	Tasks
Understand and apply written instructions for school work	Apply a simple written instruction
	Apply a complex written instruction
Identify types and functions of texts using external indications	Match a work to its cover
Understand the chronology of events in different types of text	Identify chronological indicators in a realistic narrative
	Deduce chronological information from a realistic narrative
Understand spatial relationships and settings in different types of text	Identify an image
	Take a relative spatial point of view
	Trace movements from information given orally
Demonstrate understanding of a text: • after reading, give precise information contained implicitly or explicitly in the text • in a narrative, identify and follow the characters whatever the narrative structure • find the overall significance of a text	Retrieve information from a text (realistic narrative)
	Identify characters using deduction
	Select the sentence that best summarises the narrative
	Retrieve information from a document with both text and images (poster)
	Retrieve information from a text (tale)
	Choose the title of a text (tale)

Tools for language

Competencies	Tasks
Recognise written words from familiar vocabulary Decode unfamiliar words	Cross out the written word when it does not match the picture
Identify common typographical devices and follow the structure of the written page	Understand the organisation of a printed page
	Understand typographical devices
Use context, word families and dictionaries to understand the words of a text	Distinguish the particular sense of a word from its context
Identify agreement, time markers, pronouns and connectives in understanding text	Identify agreement between subject and verb, noun and adjective, using number and gender
	Identify time markers that structure the coherence of a text

The tests consist of open and closed questions, for which marking guidance is provided for teachers.

Because of the formative purpose of the national tests in France, the mark schemes allow more differentiation than simply correct/incorrect: right answers; interesting mistakes (in terms of interpretation); others. This is structured as a scale rather than a long mark scheme (see Figure 17.1). The means of recording errors gives the teacher a detailed picture of pupils' difficulties and the degree to which they have mastered the skills assessed.

Figure 17.1 Example mark scheme

> 1 – Exact answer
>
> 2 – Other correct answer showing mastery of skill
>
> 3 – Partially correct answer, no incorrect element
>
> 4 – Partially correct, partially incorrect answer
>
> 5 – Answer showing misunderstanding of the question
>
> 9 – Incorrect answer
>
> 0 – No answer

The score obtained for each skill (i.e. *Reading comprehension, Tools for Language*), is the percentage of correct answers and makes possible an overall estimation of national performance. In recent years, around two-thirds of the national population at grade 3 were found to have reached the expected standard in reading.

Teachers are involved in the assessment procedures; for they supervise the data collection, process and code these data. They have at their disposal materials which enable them to interpret their pupils' results, from which they can draw pedagogical conclusions. Their analyses are facilitated by easy-to-use software. Interpretation of the national evaluation outcomes plays a part in the training of teachers.

The 2002 tests provide an example of how these principles are translated into practice. For the Reading field, the tests include 7 exercises and 41 items at grade 3 level; 10 exercises and 36 items at grade 6 level.

At grade 3 level, we shall consider the competence *Demonstrate understanding of a text*. In 2002, three exercises were included for assessing this competence, with a time limit of 23 minutes for completion. The texts were a poster, a tale and a short narrative. The longest one of these consists of about 220 words.

The total number of items was 16, ten of them multiple-choice and six constructed response. The open questions only required short answers: one word, a few words (the name of three characters), a sentence or phrase. Figure 17.2 shows an example of the short tale entitled *The Heron*.

Figure 17.2 Text and questions *The Heron*

Read this story, then answer the questions.

A long time ago, there was a poor young man called Wan.

Every day, Wan used to go for a cup of tea close to his home. He never had change to pay for it, but often gave the inn-keeper a drawing to thank him.

One day in spring, Wan told the inn-keeper:

'I am going on a journey. You have always been kind to me. So, I want to give something to you.'

Wan took a paint-brush and ink from his pocket. Then, he drew a big bird, a splendid heron on the wall of the inn.

The inn-keeper and his customers were astonished: it really looked like a real bird ready to fly away.

And Wan added:

'When you clap your hands three times, the heron will come down from the wall and it will dance on the floor.'

Ann Rocard, *Le grand livre des petites histoires*

1 Where did Wan use to have a cup of tea?
    Put a cross in the correct box.
    ☐ at home
    ☐ at the inn
    ☐ at friend's home
    ☐ at customer's home

2 With what did Wan make his drawings?
    Put a cross in the correct box.
    ☐ with a pen and China ink
    ☐ with a paint-brush and painting
    ☐ with a paint-brush and China ink
    ☐ with a pen and a paint-brush

3 Why did he never have coins to pay?
    _____

    What will the inn-keeper have to do to get the heron dancing?
    _____

5 Which of these titles suits the story best?
    Put a cross in the correct box.
    ☐ The Heron
    ☐ The Bird Seller
    ☐ The Magic Picture
    ☐ The Good Inn

Questions 1 and 4, one of them multiple-choice and the other open, each require retrieval of a single piece of information that is expressed as one sentence in the text.

The multiple-choice question 2 is an example of the distinction in the coding frame between answers which are exact or which are partially correct, with or without incorrect elements. The correct answer to this question has two elements. Whilst the third, correct, option includes both, the second is partially correct but omits one element, whereas the first and third include incorrect elements.

As an example of the mark schemes for open responses, question 3 can be considered. For this question, it is necessary to explain: 'Why did he never have coins to pay?'. For a completely correct response, two pieces of information from different parts of the text must be linked, and this link must be inferred. The right answer should 'refer to poverty'. In the text, it says 'a poor young man'. If the answer refers to 'Wan says thank you with his drawings', this mistake receives a special code.

Question 5 requires students to show that they have grasped the main point of the text by selecting an appropriate title.

The second main reading skill assessed, *Tools for Language*, is more difficult to exemplify as it addresses grammatical and vocabulary issues that are mostly specific to French. For example, the exercise that requires distinguishing the sense of words in context is not translatable into English, as the some of the translated words would differ according to the context. However, Figure 17.3 shows an example of an exercise that assesses knowledge of the organisation of the printed page and understanding of typographical devices.

This type of exercise complements and contrasts with the Reading comprehension items, and provides information of a different kind for teachers to use.

Based on its content, each item is attributed to one of the two levels of competence described above: those necessary for pupils to benefit fully from current teaching; or those still being acquired. A large proportion of those items addressing 'necessary' competencies belong to the categories *Recognise written words from familiar vocabulary* and *Understand and apply written instructions for school work*. Software for analysing the results of the tests allows each teacher to identify those pupils who have not acquired these essential competencies. Pupils who fail 75 per cent of the items of this type are considered to be in difficulty. This accounts for about 10 per cent of pupils, who are supported by means of an individual education plan – the PPAP, or *Programme Personnalisé d'Aide et de Progrès*. The specific difficulties that each child is experiencing are identified, and a remedial programme that corresponds to these difficulties is offered to him or her.

The positive result is that nine out of ten pupils are in a position to benefit from the teaching delivered at the beginning of Cycle 3. For the easiest tasks, those requiring location and retrieval of information, the success rates are between 70 and 95 per cent. For understanding the main point of a text (giving the general setting, identifying the main character ...) success rates are between 55 and 65 per cent. Reasoning about a text and bringing information together gives rise to success rates of between 50 and 75 per cent. Finally, the implicit understanding revealed, for example, in inferential questions is only successful in 50 per cent of cases.

Figure 17.3 Text and questions, *Wolves*

Wolves

Wolves are animals that are similar to dogs. They have gradually disappeared from our region because of hunting. They are very good at communicating amongst themselves by means of howls and body language.

In the spring, pairs of wolves look for a quiet place to raise their young. Most often, they settle beneath a rock, a fallen tree or in an old fox's den. The parents are not the only ones responsible for the young: the whole family group shares in looking after the cubs.

Going up-stream, wolves push fish into shallow water and there they catch them in their jaws. They even know how to turn over stones with their paws to look for shrimps. They also hunt mammals such as rabbits or mules. A wolf's stomach can contain four kilos of meat. What an appetite!

1. How many paragraphs are there in this text?

2. Circle the first paragraph.

3. Copy a sentence from the text – whichever you choose.

4. Circle the six commas in the text.

5. The punctuation mark used at the end of the text ! is called:

    Circle the correct answer

    – question mark

    – semicolon

    – exclamation mark

    – speech marks

At the beginning of Cycle 3, and within the limitations of the test exercises, the elaboration of inferences remains difficult for a large number of pupils; amongst these inferences is the understanding of anaphoric references, which is still a cause of difficulty at 12–13 years of age. Spelling in the context of a dictation exercise remains poorly done. Pupils are fairly good at understanding the chronology of a story, but they have difficulty in maintaining a coherent thread of narration in stories that they write. In exercises that require them to select connectives, those which represent logical relationships are still difficult to find.

Thus there are a number of competencies that are quite well mastered by the end of Cycle 2, 'Basic acquisitions', whilst others are still being learned. This reflects the complexity of the operations at work in comprehending text, and the differing requirements of the tasks.

Conclusion

The national tests say something about what children should read and sometimes about how they should read it. They are not based upon predetermined proportions of questions or texts of each type. Texts are chosen for their merit and interest, and the proportion of question types varies in direct relation to the features of the texts selected.

Each pupil's acquisitions and failures can be revealed by an analysis of answers to each item for each test.

Yet diagnostic assessment cannot be expected to deal with everything. It does not allow the identification of all possible difficulties, because not all the competencies related to the goals for the cycle are included in any one test. Results are not comparable from one year to the other since they are not the outcome of strictly comparable tests.

In some cases, it will be necessary to interpret why this child has produced such poor performances and keep exploring his/her difficulties with other tools. Nevertheless, this national evaluation can be seen as a useful tool for detecting problems and gaps in the pupils' knowledge.

The great originality of the French procedure is that it takes place at the beginning of the school year. A diagnostic assessment of every pupil is performed, and it is hoped that teachers change their pedagogy according to their pupils' identified difficulties.

18 The National Assessment of Educational Progress in the USA

Patricia Donahue

General overview

The National Assessment of Educational Progress (NAEP) began to measure student achievement in 1969. It was at the time a radically new idea to assess the knowledge and skills of American youth as a group and to measure the progress of education nationally. This was NAEP's original charge as authorized by congressional legislation. NAEP, also known as The Nation's Report Card, remains, 35 years later, the only federally mandated, nationwide survey of student achievement in the USA, collecting data and reporting on what students know and can do in various subject areas. Subjects assessed regularly by NAEP include US history, civics, science and writing, mathematics and reading.

As a federally mandated program, NAEP is under the direction of the National Center for Education Statistics, which is part of the Federal Department of Education. In 1988, federal legislation established The National Assessment Governing Board (NAGB) to provide bipartisan and independent policy oversight. The board members include teachers, state governors, state legislators, testing experts, school principals and parents. NAGB decides which subjects are to be assessed by NAEP and directs the development of the subject area frameworks and specifications that provide the blueprint for NAEP assessments. In addition, NAGB's charge includes the development of appropriate performance standards, referred to as achievement levels, that are used in reporting NAEP results.

To implement the charge of measuring and reporting student performance, NAEP uses a multi-stage, complex sampling procedure designed to ensure that the schools selected to participate in the assessment represent the broad populations of US students, both on the national and state level as well as in terms of racial/ethnic backgrounds, gender, economic status and instructional experiences. The sampling is crucial to ensure that NAEP provide information on aggregate student achievement and to report the relationship between achievement and background variables.

NAEP assesses representative national samples of 4th, 8th and 12th grade students but, it being by design a survey, students who participate in the assessment do not receive individual scores. That students do not receive individual scores is essential to the nature and purpose of NAEP: the nature being a sampled population and the purpose being to survey and report the knowledge, skills and, to a degree, instructional experiences, for the USA. All students in the country do not take the NAEP assessment and the sampled populations take different parts of the test. Using a procedure called matrix item sampling to reduce individual student burden, no student at a particular grade takes the entire assessment for that grade. For example, thirteen distinct reading blocks are administered at grade 8, but each 8th grader participating in the assessment only takes two blocks. Individual scores would be for different performances on different tests. Instead, NAEP results are reported in aggregate for the country as a whole, for participating states and jurisdictions and for major demographic subgroups. Originally and for the period from 1969 to 1990, NAEP assessments reported results solely for the nation and for major demographic subgroups. Then, in 1990, NAEP's goal was augmented to include the tracking and reporting of academic achievement in individual states. The first NAEP Trial State Assessment was mathematics in 1990. State by state reading assessment followed close upon this in 1992. Most recently, in 2002 and 2003, NAEP for the first time reported results at the district level for those localities that participated in the Trial Urban District Assessment. In little more than a decade since the first Trial State Assessment, the potential exists for a further expansion of NAEP's role.

Results of the NAEP assessment are reported in terms of an average score on the NAEP reading 0–500 scale and in terms of the percentages of students who attain each of three achievement levels, *Basic, Proficient* and *Advanced*. The scale scores indicate what students know and can do as measured by their performance on the assessment. The achievement levels indicate the degree to which student performance meet the standards set for what they should know and be able to do.

The frequency of NAEP assessments varies by subject area. With the exception of the mathematics and reading assessments, which are administered every two years, most of the subject areas are administered every four years.

The NAEP Reading Assessment

Since 1992 the NAEP reading assessment has been developed under a framework reflecting research that views reading as an interactive and constructive process involving the reader, the text and the context of the reading experience. The NAEP *Reading Framework* views reading as a dynamic interplay in which readers bring prior knowledge and previous reading experiences to the text and use various skills and strategies in their transactions with texts. Recognising that readers vary their approach to reading according to the demands of particular texts and situations, the framework specifies the assessment of three 'reading contexts': Reading for Literary Experience, Reading for Information and Reading to Perform a Task. All three purposes are assessed at grades 8 and 12; however, Reading to Perform a Task is not assessed at grade 4. The reading contexts, as presented in the Framework, attempt to codify the types of real world reading situations to be represented in the assessment, as shown in Table 18.1.

Table 18.1 The reading contexts

Context for reading	Description
Reading for literary experience	Readers explore events, characters, themes settings, plots, actions and the language of literary works by reading novels, short stories, poems, plays, legends, biographies, myths and folktales.
Reading for information	Readers gain information to understand the world by reading materials such as magazines, newspapers, textbooks, essays and speeches.
Reading to perform a task	Readers apply what they learn from reading materials such as bus or train schedules, directions for repairs or games, classroom procedures, tax forms (grade 12), maps and so on.

Source: National Assessment Governing Board (2002)

While it could be argued that in a large-scale assessment such as NAEP, the context is essentially the assessment situation, the Contexts for Reading are an attempt to replicate major types of real life reading experiences. The Reading for Literary Experience passages and items allow students to interpret and discuss such literary elements as theme, character motivation, or the importance of the setting to the action of a story. The texts within this context have been primarily narratives: short stories or folktales. Poetry, to a much lesser degree, has been used at grades 8 and 12; however, the poems have had a strong narrative element so as to assess reading comprehension and not poetic skills or knowledge of rhyme and meter. The Reading for Information passages mainly comprise expository texts such as articles about nature or biographical pieces from magazines that students might encounter at school or at home, but speeches have been included at grade 12. Items based on informative passages ask students to consider the major and supporting ideas, the relations between them and the overall message or point of the text. When Reading to Perform a Task, students are asked to read schedules, directions, or documents and to respond to questions aimed at both the information itself and also at how to apply or use the information in the text. Across the three contexts, the NAEP assessment tries to reflect a variety of the reading experiences that students are likely to encounter in real life.

Within these contexts, which broadly define the type of texts used in the assessment, the framework also delineates four Reading Aspects to characterise ways readers may construct meaning from the written word: forming a general understanding, developing interpretation, examining content and structure and making reader–text connections. The Reading Aspects are meant to reflect the different approaches that readers may take in their engagement with a text. For test development purposes, they are meant to ensure ways of tapping different features of the text by encouraging a variety of items that elicit different ways of thinking about texts. In short, the Reading Contexts determine the type of texts used on the assessment and the Reading Aspects determine the type of comprehension questions asked of students (see Table 18.2).

Table 18.2 Reading aspects

Aspect of reading	Description
Forming a general understanding	The reader considers the text in its entirety and provides a global understanding of it.
Developing interpretation	The reader extends initial impressions to develop a more complete understanding. This may involve focusing on specific parts of the text or linking information across the text.
Making reader– text connections	The reader connects information in the text with knowledge and experience. This may include applying ideas in the text to the real world.
Examining content and structure	The reader critically evaluates, compares and contrasts and considers the effects of language features or style in relation to author's purpose.

Source: National Assessment Governing Board (2002)

All items in the NAEP reading assessment are classified as one of these four aspects. Items that ask students to identify the main topic of a passage or to summarise the main events of a story are classified as 'general understanding'. Items that ask students to explain the relationship between two pieces of textual information or to provide evidence from a story to explain a character's action are classified as 'developing interpretation'. The items classified under the aspect 'making reader–text connections' ask the reader to connect information in the text with their prior knowledge or sense of a real-world situation. These items do not demand or assume any prior knowledge about the topic of the passage, nor do they ask about personal feelings. The emphasis is on the making of a connection between text-based ideas and something outside the text. Items that ask students to focus on not just what the text says but also how the text says it are classified as 'examining content and structure'.

The other main features of the NAEP reading assessment are the use of authentic, full-length texts – that is, texts that were written and published for real world purposes, not texts that were written or abridged for the purpose of assessment – and the use of both multiple-choice and constructed-response questions. In the NAEP reading assessment, constructed-response questions are those that require students to write out their answer. Constructed-response questions are used when more than one possible answer would be acceptable and thus allow for a range of interpretations.

The passages used in the NAEP reading assessment vary in length by grade level. As prescribed by the NAEP Reading Framework, 4th grade passages may range from 250 to 800 words; 8th grade passages may range from 400 to 1000 words; and at 12th grade, passages may range from 500 to 1500 words. In addition to length, passages used in the assessment must meet criteria for student interest, developmental and topic appropriateness, style and structure, as well as being considered fair for all groups of students taking the assessment. Meeting all these criteria makes finding suitable passages for the assessment a challenging task indeed.

It is difficult from the vantage of 2004 to realize what an innovation the use of full-length, authentic texts was for a large-scale assessment such as NAEP. Prior to 1992, when the assessment framework that has served as the basis for the current NAEP reading assessment was created, the NAEP test resembled most other tests of reading comprehension. That is, the NAEP test asked students to read a number of short passages and to respond to a few questions about each passage. Even then, however, the NAEP test did not rely solely on multiple-choice questions, but included some constructed-response questions – approximately 6 per cent of the total assessment items. With the marked increase in the length of passages called for by the 1992 Reading Framework came an increase in the number of constructed-response questions. Longer texts allowed for a larger range of interpretations, so in consequence constructed-response was the proper format to accommodate the range of responses. From 1992 onward, about 50 to 60 per cent of the NAEP reading assessment was composed of constructed-response questions. The preponderance of constructed-response questions was a natural outgrowth of the view of reading as a dynamic interplay between reader and text and of the framework's recognition that readers bring various experiences and their own schema to their engagement with text even in an assessment situation.

Development of constructed-response items cannot occur without simultaneously considering how the item will be scored and composing the scoring guide. Every item in the NAEP reading assessment has its own unique scoring guide. Constructed-response items are of two types: short constructed-response items that are scored with either a two-level or a three-level scoring guide and extended constructed-response items that are scored with a four-level scoring guide. The initial iteration of the scoring guide written in conjunction with the item by the test developer anticipates the possible levels of comprehension that the item might elicit. These levels are revisited in light of student responses from the pilot test administration and the guides are revised accordingly.

Multiple-choice and constructed response items are configured into blocks. A block consists of a reading passage and the accompanying items about the passage. Typically, each block has approximately ten items. Students taking the assessment receive a booklet containing two blocks and have 25 minutes to complete each block in their booklet. Total assessment time is 60 minutes, as students also answer some background questions about their educational experiences. From 1992 to 2002 the assessment comprised 23 blocks; it was expanded for 2003 and now comprises a total of 28 blocks.

Inevitably, the scoring of the NAEP reading assessment is an intense occasion for all involved. Test booklets are sent from the administration to the scoring contractor in Iowa City, where the booklets are taken apart and all the items are scanned. While multiple-choice items are machine scored, student responses to the constructed-response items are scanned and images of the responses are presented via computer to teams of trained scorers. A team of ten to 12 individual scorers scores all the responses to a single item, before they go on to the next item. This item-by-item method allows for a more focused scoring than would occur if the all the responses in a block or booklet were presented and the scorers went back and forth among different items. In the 2003 reading assessment, a total of nearly 4 million student responses to constructed-response items were scored (Donahue *et al.*, 2005).

Two types of quality control for the reliability of the scoring are necessary: the monitoring of the scoring of current year responses to ensure that the individual scorers on the team are applying the scoring criteria consistently and the monitoring of across-year scoring in the case of items that have a trend measure. As NAEP is concerned with reporting change in student performance over time, the majority of items in the assessment have a trend measure. For current year inter-rater reliability, a percentage of current year papers receive a second score. For across-year trend reliability, a set of trend papers that reflect the previous year's scoring are scored by the current year team. If the inter-rater reliability for current year falls below a certain standard, or if the trend monitor indicates a shift from how the item was previously scored, the item is retrained and re-scored. Considering that the number of current-year responses for a single item can be as high as 35,000–50,000, a very close eye is kept on the monitoring to ensure that scoring proceeds in an acceptable manner and with the highest standard in mind. The score of every student response is important, for these scores become the raw data from which analysis procedures will produce the NAEP scale scores and achievement level percentages from which the trends in progress will be reported.

It could be said that the reporting of results is the *raison d'être* of the NAEP program. All aspects of the program – test development, sampling, administration and scoring – occur so that student achievement can be captured and student progress can be reported. Having to report on the progress of education was what put the idea of what has become NAEP into the mind of then Commissioner of Education, Francis Keppel. It was the early 1960s and Keppel was obliged to report to Congress on the educational progress of each of the states; however, all the data available to him had to do with such variables as per pupil expenditure, student attendance and teacher salaries. No data of that time captured what students could actually do as a result of their time in school. There were standardized tests, but their purpose was to rank individual students by identifying differences between them, not to measure and report what groups of students could do. Keppel got the national assessment ball rolling in 1963 when he contacted Ralph Tyler at Stanford, who conceived of a new measurement instrument designed to measure set objectives and track changes in performance over time. Six years later the first NAEP assessments were administered in citizenship, science and writing. The first NAEP assessment of reading was administered in 1971 (Jones and Olkin, 2004, pp.25–28).

Concluding remarks

Reading is an elusive construct, because the processes that readers' minds engage in and employ when interacting with texts are invisible – multi-faceted and complex certainly and therefore difficult to capture. Outside of an assessment situation, this elusiveness and complexity is no problem for the reader, but part of the joy of reading and getting lost in a text – for in everyday life we are allowed to read without having to demonstrate our understanding immediately, upon demand, within a time frame. Ideas can germinate for hours, days and weeks; be discussed with others, reframed, reconfigured and rethought at leisure.

It would be costly indeed to assess reading comprehension at the site of its most active occurrence; the reader alone in a room or a public library, book in hand or eyes fixed on the computer screen, at that moment when the self is lost in a fiction or finding the facts that the mind has sought, those moments that transpire when the book rests in the lap or the eyes from the computer and the gaze goes out the window, but doesn't totally register the sun or snow, for the eyes have turned inward to what the mind is doing with the text just read. This is not to suggest that reading is a trance and that testing situations are entirely artificial, for they resemble important types of reading that occur in children's and adult's lives: reading situations that require a response in a limited amount of time, finishing the book for English class, the reviewing of books for publication, the letter that must be written by a certain date. And it is well known that a deadline can jolt the mind into activity and even incite it to perform.

These distinctions between real-life reading and reading in an assessment situation must be acknowledged so the awareness consciously attends and informs the making of tests that aspire to engaging students – as much as is possible in a large-scale assessment situation – in thoughtful reading activity. This is the challenge, the platonic ideal so to speak, of developing a reading assessment that necessarily aims to elicit the best possible performance from students during 60 minutes of testing time. For all those involved in the development of the NAEP test, however, the 4th, 8th and 12th grade students who participate are nameless and faceless; they sit in many different classrooms across the country and they come from widely disparate cultural and economic backgrounds. To capture such a nation of readers is a daunting task and it would be foolhardy to think that we have truly engaged all these students and elicited their highest level of performance. And yet, considering the constraints, I always marvel during scoring sessions at the engagement evident in student responses – the way they use or exceed the five lines provided for short constructed-responses. These are students who have been told that their performance will not affect their grade in any way, told that they are participating in a national survey, told that their performance will contribute to a picture of what students in their grade are capable of doing. There are no stakes for the sampled students themselves. Yet the depth of their responses suggests something about the power of texts. Even in a constrained assessment time of 60 minutes, when they are given the latitude allowed by constructed-response questions students respond to unfamiliar texts and express their ideas; and while responses are scored only for reading comprehension, not writing ability, it is gratifying when students express their ideas eloquently and one dares to hope that an assessment passage has been an occasion for a student to discover an author who they will go on to read or a topic that they will go on to explore. While not within the purview and purpose of the NAEP reading assessment, which by its nature is far from formative, it can be hoped that some of the students who participate are provided with a reading experience not too unlike their actual encounters with texts.

References

Donahue, P.L., Daane, M.C. and Jin, Y. (2005). *The Nation's Report Card: Reading 2003* (NCES 2005–453). US Department of Education, Institute of Education Sciences, National Center for Education Statistics. Washington, DC: US Government Printing Office.

Jones, L.V. and Olkin, I. (Eds) (2004). *The Nation's Report Card: Evolution and Perspectives*. Bloomington: Phi Delta Kappa Educational Foundation, American Educational Research Association.

National Assessment Governing Board (2002). *Reading Framework for the 2003 National Assessment of Educational Progress*. Washington, DC: Author.

19 Concluding reflections: from theories to classrooms

Marian Sainsbury

At the beginning of this book, I outlined the interaction between different views of reading and different views of assessment which makes this such a complex subject. The intervening chapters have done little to simplify this complexity. Somehow, competing theories of reading and competing theories of assessment jostle for position, and out of this jostling emerges classroom practice. The route from theory to classroom is neither simple nor predictable.

This is because both reading and assessment have many different stakeholders. Children, parents, researchers, teachers, employers, governments, ordinary citizens: all are entitled to have expectations of what reading tests can and should deliver. In response to this, the authors have brought together their diverse experiences, knowledge and beliefs, constructing a partial map of an ever-changing territory.

Researchers have been given a clear field to set out their visions. Beech, Pollitt and Taylor have offered perspectives on reading that highlight cognitive processes. Fisher has mapped out the relationship between literacy as social practice, school literacy and test literacy. Harrison has highlighted the uncertainty of meaning in the relationship between writer, reader and text. Stobart has set out a vision of assessment that is fit for a truly formative purpose.

In the later sections of the book, all of these theoretical positions remain evident. The historical overview by Pearson and Hamm specifically links reading assessment to the dominance of particular theoretical frameworks, as does Whetton's account of influential assessments in the UK. In the early 20th century, the emergence of psychology as a scientific discipline led to optimism about its potential both for explicating the reading process and designing precise and accurate tests. This gave rise to examples of assessments linked to specific theories of reading and some such tests are still current, including published tests in the UK and the French national tests described by Rémond. They are mainly characterised by a definition of reading as word recognition and literal comprehension.

Not until the later 20th century did theories of social literacies and postmodern approaches to text become influential, through the study of literature, in defining school literacy. Thompson's chapter describes how the reader's active construction of text was first integrated into high-stakes assessment in the UK. These theories survive, albeit diluted, in many of the most recent tests – for example the national assessments described by Watts and Sainsbury, Palmer and Watcyn Jones, and Donahue. All of these admit of the possibility that differing responses may nevertheless be creditworthy, whilst also retaining something of psychological notions of literal comprehension. Computer-based assessment, as described in the Harrison and Leacock chapters, introduces yet another layer of controversy about the degree of determinacy that can be expected of reading test questions and answers.

Interwoven with this is the evolution of theories of assessment, moving from the early psychologists' assumption of the test-taker as experimental object through to the active metacognitive monitoring by the learner described in the chapters by Stobart, Pepper, Siddiqui and Watts, Hayward and Spencer.

Thus the influence of researchers can be traced in a long line through to contemporary assessments. Alongside this, however, in a point powerfully made in the Whetton chapter, can be seen the influence of another set of stakeholders – the population in general, represented in particular by governments. Their views can be seen especially in the determination of assessment purposes, often requiring reliable national monitoring that reduces the scope for flexibility and student participation in testing reading. Governments also have a say in defining reading itself, reflecting the influence of the non-specialist population, tending to favour determinacy over postmodernism and the literary canon over lesser-known works. Yet again, though, there is no unanimity in the direction of this influence, with government policy in France, Scotland and Wales favouring formative purposes and flexible assessments that diverge from the strong accountability agenda of the USA and England.

On the receiving end of all these influences are perhaps the most important stakeholders of all, those in the classroom – students and their teachers. Fisher makes a strong plea for these groups to have greater influence, arguing for the centrality of learning over performance and for the integration of a broad definition of literacy into learners' experiences.

So we conclude this book very far from any initial aspiration of overarching theoretical structures, or even bridge-building between different approaches. Tests and assessments have proved a useful lens through which to view different definitions of reading. But the tests and assessments themselves are subject to a set of influences just as varied and demanding as those defining reading. And far from reflecting the findings of a pure and progressive research programme, the influences on both derive from a range of stakeholders whose requirements are often incompatible one with another.

At the end of this exploration, then, the picture of reading and its assessment remains messy and confused, with conflicting demands and inconsistent arguments. Theories and values continue to compete, with shifting patterns of ascendancy. Yet perhaps this should be seen as inevitable and even positive. It reflects that fact that in contemporary society the role of literacy is central, a powerful and versatile skill underpinning advanced human understanding and mass communication no less than individual growth and fulfilment.

Index

Entries in *italics* denote publications and specific initiatives.

5–14 programme (Scotland) 226–7, 229, 231–4
'100 per cent coursework' option 122–38

A, E, I, O, U model of purpose 46
AAP *see* Assessment of Achievement Programme
ACCAC reports 212, 218, 219
accountability 3, 135
    APU tests 115
    comprehension assessment 76, 90
    Education Reform Act 122
    key stage 2 assessments 212–13
    National Curriculum 117, 196
    Welsh statutory assessments 210–21
achievement constructs 16
ACT theory of cognition 39–40
activity theory 127–31
adaptive online assessment 140–3
adult readers 18
AEA *see* American Evaluation Association
AFs *see* assessment focuses
age criteria 25
Ahmed, A. 39
algebra questions 164–6
American Evaluation Association (AEA) 224
analytic reading 17, 197–9, 202
Anderson, J.R. 39–40
Anderson, N. 39
answer formats 212
Antarctica booklet (Wales) 213–14
antonyms 161
APU *see* Assessment of Performance Unit
artificial intelligence *see* Intelligent Online Reading Assessment
aspects of reading (NAEP) 252–3
assessment
    conservatism 50–1
    historical contexts 4–5

paradigm competition 2–3
psychological principles 24–32
    see also individual assessment types
Assessment of Achievement Programme (AAP) 228, 236
assessment focuses (AFs) 172, 198
    categorisations 181–3
    feedback 179–93
    key stage 1 200–1
    key stage 3 204–8
    procedure 180–1
    usefulness 184–9
Assessment is for Learning 234–6
'Assessment for Learning' movement 5, 123
Assessment of Performance Unit (APU) 113–15
Assessment Reform Group 189
assessors' focus 190
attainment targets
    France 242
    National Curriculum 196, 199, 205
    Wales 210, 219, 220
'attenuation paradox' 31
authenticity 60, 87, 117
author's authority 60–2
author's techniques *see* writers' techniques
automated marking 158–67
'autonomous' model of literacy 72
Awaida, M. 24

Bakhtin, Mikhail 52–3
basal readers 86, 89
Beech, John R. v, 3–4, 22–37
behaviourism 78–9
behaviours
    good readers 141–2
    online reading 144–8
Billy's Sunflower (Moon) 199–201
Black, Paul 13–14, 64, 127–8, 235
Bradley, L. 28
brain activity 40–1
Brookhart, S.M. 179, 189
Bryant, P. 28

Building Bridges initiative 236
Bullock committee 113, 116
Burt Word Reading Test 104–5

c-rater 158–64
California Learning Assessment System
    (CLAS) 90
Callaghan, James 51, 113
'can do' statements 67
cartoon strips 202–3
case studies
        c-rater 162–3
        online assessment 140–57
Center for the Study of Reading 87
certification 3
children
        central position 64
        performance 66–8
        requirements 68–73
        see also student...
choices 176
Clarke, Kenneth 102–3
CLAS *see* California Learning Assessment
    System
classical test theory 31
classroom assessment 88, 135, 174, 258–9
        see also informal assessment
classroom relationships 127–31
close reading assessment 225, 233–4
cloze procedure 83–4, 109–11
coded responses 175–6
cognitive assessment 79, 86–9
cognitive psychology 38–49, 85–6
College Board tests 91
communication 2, 13
competency assessment 241–5, 247–8
comprehension 17, 38, 41–2
        APU tests 114
        assessment focuses 181–3
        c-rater 158–9, 162–3, 164–6
        France 244, 247–8
        historical foundations 77–81
        infrastructure 82–3
        key stage 1 201
        meaning concept 59
        online assessment 144–6
        Scottish National Assessment 233
        top-down approaches 29

UK history 109–11
US 76–101, 256
WORD test 25–6
computer-based assessment 5, 140–1, 146–7,
    259
        see also online reading assessment
concurrent validity 11
confidence 188–9
consciousness 15
consensus marking 131
consequential validity 10–11, 13, 168, 172
conservatism 50–1
consistency 131–2
consortia 131, 134
construct of reading 8–21
        France 241, 243–8
        National Curriculum 196–8
        Scotland 223–30
        Wales 213–14, 215–17, 219–20
construct validity 8–21, 39, 118, 222–3
constructed responses 158–67, 253–4, 256
constructivist approaches 86–7
content-based responses 158–67
content validity 9, 11
contexts for reading (NAEP) 251–2
contextual information 29, 46
control groups 30
controlled conditions 124, 132
convergent assessment 72
convergent validity 10
correlation statistical analysis 152–3
coursework 55, 122–38
Cox proposals 115
criterion-related validity 11
critical essays 233–4
cross tabulation (c-rater) 164–5
cultural capital 65
cultural transmission 125
Cunningham, A. 29
curricula
        funnel effect 70
        see also National Curriculum...

DARTs *see* Directed Activities Related to
    Texts
data capture online 148–53
Daugherty Assessment Review Group 170
Daugherty, Richard 210

Davis, Frederick 82–3
decoding 2, 16, 29, 199, 201, 216
deconstruction theory 53
deduction skills 201–3
deep learning 170–1
DeNisi, A. 173–4
Department for Education and Science (DES) 102–3
Derrida, Jacques 52, 53
DES see Department for Education and Science
descriptive assessment 223–4
'desired performance' standard 173–5
deviation quotients 112
diagnostic assessment 3
    Edinburgh Reading Tests 111–12
    France 241, 242–3, 249
    Neale Analysis 109
    psychological perspective 22–37
    Scotland 111–12, 227
diagnostic feedback 191
'dialogic' text 52–3
'differentiation by outcome' 124–5
Directed Activities Related to Texts (DARTs) 125
discipline 130
discrete skills 179
discriminant validity 10
divergent assessment 72
division of labour 129
document files online 150
domain restrictions (c-rater) 162
Donahue, Patricia v, 5–6, 250–7
drama tasks 205–6
drivers of theory 76–138
Dual Award GCSE English 124–5
dual route theory 26–7
Dunning Committee report 224
dynamic assessment 89
dyslexia 25–7, 28

e-mails 213–14
Edinburgh Reading Tests 111–12
education definitions 102–3
Education Reform Act (1988) 122
educational constructs 16
Educational Testing Service (ETS) 158
effect sizes 22–3, 30
ego-level feedback 174

emotions 45
empathy 133–4
Engelhard, G. 25, 31–2
Engestrom, Y. 127–9
England 196–209
    see also UK
English as a Second Language (ESL) assessments 83, 84
English GCSE 122–38
English language reading 210–21
EPPI review 237
error analysis in oral reading 81, 108
error detection paradigms 80
error sources
    c-rater 163–4
    test scores 31
ESL assessments see English as a Second Language (ESL) assessments
ETS see Educational Testing Service
evidence methodologies 56–8
examination boards 50–1, 54–5, 62
examination limitations 135
examination modes 56
exemplars 175, 218
experimental online assessment 148–53
expository texts 85
external assessment 135, 136
Eysenck, Hans 25

factor analysis 82–3
familiarity of subject-matter 10
fan fiction sites 61–2
feedback
    assessment focuses 179–93
    c-rater 164–6
    formative assessments 2–3, 13–14, 168, 172–6
films 127
Fisher, Ros v, 4, 64–74
focusing concept 190
    see also assessment focuses
Foreman, Michael 201–2
formal assessment 2–3
formative assessments
    activity theory 127–8
    AFs 179, 189
    construct validity 39
    definition 168–9
    feedback 2–3, 13–14, 168, 172–6

France 241, 242–3, 245
key stage 3 123
learning processes 72–3
role 168–78
Scotland 226–7, 231, 234–8
summative relationship 169–70
validity 168, 172–6
France 5, 241–9
Frith, U. 25
funnel effect 70–1

Gap/Gapadol Reading Comprehension Test 109–11
GCSE English 122–38
gender 23–4, 68, 188
generalisability 60, 90, 91
Gernsbacher, M.A. 41
Gipps, Caroline 135–6
global accountability 135
global system solutions 54–5
goals (French evaluations) 241–2, 243
good readers' behaviours 141–2
Goodman, K.S. 81
Gordon, C. 43
Gorey, K. 27
governments 3, 135, 259
grade descriptions 132
Graded Word Reading Test (Schonell) 106
grammatical expectation 110
Grandfather's Pencil (Foreman) 201–2
Grey-Thompson, Tanni 216
group reading tests 107–8
guild knowledge 71

Haertel, E. 8, 16
Hamm, Diane Nicole v, 60, 76–101
Hanauer, D. 43
Harlen, W. 170, 173
Harrison, Colin v–vi, 4, 5, 50–63, 140–57, 224
Havnes, A. 127
Hayward, Louise vi, 5, 222–40
'Heisenberg' problem 43
Her Majesty's Inspectorate of Schools (HMIS) 102–3, 113
Her Majesty's Inspectors of Education (HMIE) (Scotland) 227–9, 231
hermeneutic tradition 13, 14
The Heron story 245–7

Higgins, Colin vi, 140–57
Higher assessment (Scotland) 225–6, 233–4
higher order reading skills 38
high-stakes assessment 122–3, 135, 196–209
historical contexts 4–5, 76–138
HMIE *see* Her Majesty's Inspectors of Education
HMIS *see* Her Majesty's Inspectorate of Schools

IBM scoring procedures 81
incredulity toward metanarrative 52–62
Indiana 2003 case study 162–3
indices (comprehension) 77–80
individual assessment
comprehension 91
differences 45–6
France 242–3, 247
National Curriculum 204
inference skills 200–3, 214, 247–8
inferred reading process 144
informal assessment 2–3, 5, 13–14, 18
information use 212–14
input, online reading 144, 146
in-service education and training networks 131
INSET networks *see* in-service education and training networks
Inside the Black Box (Black/Wiliam) 64
integration
assessment and training 27–30
language modes 132
theory and assessment 24–7
intelligence 25–6, 79
Intelligent Online Reading Assessment (IORA) 140–3
interactive model 90
internal validity 10
internet 61–2
see also online...
interpretative tradition 12–14, 53
intersentential comprehension 84
IORA *see* Intelligent Online Reading Assessment
IQ tests 25–6
Iser, Wolfgang 52, 53

James, M. 170, 173
Johnson, John 129–30

Johnson-Laird, P.N. 41
Joy, R. 67
juxtaposition 58, 59

Keppel, Francis 255
key stage 1 115–17, 197–202, 217–18
key stage 2 197–8, 202–4, 211–14, 218–19
key stage 3 123, 179–93, 197–8, 204–9,
    215–17, 219–20
King's, Medway and Oxfordshire Formative
    Assessment Project 128
Kintsch, W. 59
Kluger, A.V. 173–4
KS... see key stage...
Kuhn, T. 32

Labour Party 51
language
    AFs 181–4, 186, 188, 191–2
    key stage 1–3 201, 204, 208
    modes 124, 132
    Scottish construct of reading 223
language games theory 52
Language Steering Group (UK) 113
Latent Semantic Analysis (LSA) 143, 147–8,
    151–3
'layers' of reading 216–17
Leacock, Claudia vi, 5, 158–67
league tables 122, 135
The Learning Country 210–11
learning difficulties 26
learning goals 67–8, 70–1
learning process 64–74, 168–76
    see also teaching and learning
learning theories/models 130, 135–6
LEAs see local education authorities
Lewin, Kurt 23
lexical skills 26–7
lexical substitution (c-rater) 161
literacy strategies 66–7, 71–2, 113, 197
literary theory 17, 52, 85, 89–90
literature 50–63, 124, 126, 130–1
local education authorities (LEAs) 108
local system solutions 54–5
London Institute of Education 235
low-stakes national assessment 241–9
LSA see Latent Semantic Analysis
Luke, C. 72

Lyddie (Paterson) 202–4
Lyotard, Jean-François 51, 52

MacLure, M. 132
'magic bullet' approaches 28
mark schemes
    France 245, 247
    National Curriculum 208–9
    Wales 212
    see also scoring procedures
markers/marking 122, 158–67
    see also assessors...
matrix item sampling 251
'Matthew effect' 29
meaning
    communication 2
    construction 41, 125
    individual interpretations 47–8
    polysemic concept 58–9
    postmodernism 52–3
measurement theory 30–2, 45
MEG see Midlands Examining Group
Memories test 201–2
memorising texts 77
memory 43–4, 85–6, 130
    see also recall
mental processes 9, 16
mental representations 38, 41–2, 44
Mental and Scholastic Tests (Burt) 104–5
Messick, Samuel 8–10, 30–1, 172
metacognition 68–9, 87, 88
metanarratives 52–62
methodology range 56–8
Midlands Examining Group (MEG) 131
miscue analysis 66, 69, 81, 116
mixed ability teaching 124–5, 129
modelling 175, 223–30
moderation 131, 134, 237
Moon, Nicola 199–201
Moss, G. 68
Moss, P.A. 13–14
multiple-choice assessments
    mental representations 43
    NAEP 92, 253–4
    online 141, 143
    Reading Test AD 107–8
    scoring procedures 81
    subjectivity 83

NAEP *see* National Assessment of Education-
al Progress
NAGB *see* National Assessment Governing
Board
National Assessment of Educational Progress
(NAEP) 6, 92, 159, 250–7
National Assessment Governing Board
(NAGB) 250
National Assessment (Scotland) 228–34,
236–7
national boards 54–5
National Curriculum (France) 241–9
National Curriculum (UK) 102–3, 107–8,
115–17, 196–209
    see also statutory assessment
national initiatives in practice 196–259
National Literacy Strategy (NLS) 66–7, 71,
197
National Oracy Project (NOP) 129–30
National Qualifications Higher (Scotland) 233
    see also Higher assessment (Scotland)
national surveys (APU) 113–15
native speakers qualification 110
natural language processing (NLP) 158
navigational goals online 150–2
Neale Analysis of Reading Ability 108–9
New Criticism 89
NLP *see* natural language processing
NLS *see* National Literacy Strategy
NOP *see* National Oracy Project
normalisation (*c*-rater) 159–60

objectivity 52, 55–6, 207
observed reading process 144–7
Omar, Nasiroh vi, 140–57
online reading assessment 140–57, 162–3
open-ended questions 158, 163–4, 199, 207
'oracy movement' 129
oral reading 77–8, 81, 108–9, 132–3
    see also reading-aloud tests
O'Sullivan, J. 67
output, online reading 144, 146, 147
Owen, Wilfred 57–8

Palmer, Roger vi–vii, 5, 210–21
paradigm competition 2–3, 7–75
passage dependency 84, 87
Paterson, Katherine 202–4

Pearson, P. David vii, 5, 60, 76–101
peer assessment 55, 56, 71, 175
peer support 184, 186–7
Pepper, Lorna vii, 5, 179–93
performance
    assessment focuses 184
    children 66–8
    comprehension assessment 91
    formative assessment feedback 173–6
    France 242–3
    Scotland 230–2
    Wales 218
performance goals 67–8
Perry Preschool Project (USA) 28
personal constructs 15
phonics 16
phonological dyslexia 27
phonological skills 26–7, 28–30
pilot tests, *c*-rater 163, 165
PIRLS *see* Progress in International Reading
Literacy Study
plagiarism detection 143, 153
poetry 252
policy contexts 232, 234, 237, 259
Pollitt, Alastair vii, 4, 38–49, 225
polysemic concept of meaning 58–9
portfolio-based assessment 60
postmodernism 4, 50–63, 140–57, 258
PowerPoint presentations 57–8
practical applications 140–93, 196–259
predictive validity 11
preschool training 27–8
presentation of texts 201, 203
primary schools 170, 229–30, 241–9
    see also key stage 1; key stage 2
prior knowledge 87
priorities 22–37
process, online reading 144, 146
product of reading 67
professional development, teachers' 223–4,
226, 230, 236–7
programmes of study 196–7, 241–2
Progress in International Reading Literacy
Study (PIRLS) 232–3
pronoun resolution (*c*-rater) 160
prose reading tests 106
psychology 3–4, 22–49, 78, 85–9, 104–5,
258–9

psychometric assessment 79, 81–4
pupils' perceptions 181–7, 190–2
    see also children; student...
Pupils in Profile project 223
purposes
    assessment 18–19, 126–7, 168–9, 242–3
    reading 18–19, 46–7, 126–7

quality control 255
question summaries 47
question wordings 183–4, 188
    see also open-ended questions
questionnaires 180–1

Radical Middle party 225
randomised control designs 30
Rasch measurement model 32
RDC *see* Real-time Data Collection
reader response theories 89–90
    see also responsive reading
reader's role 53, 59–60, 61
reading
    construct validity 8–21
    definitions 102–3, 114, 144
    teaching and learning 65–73
    traditional models 25
reading age assignment 66
reading-aloud tests 117
    see also oral reading
Reading Test AD 107–8
reading theory 30–2
'real books' 102, 103
real-life reading 256
Real-time Data Collection (RDC) 152–3
reasoning 82–3
recall 79–80, 88
    see also memory
reception theory (Iser) 53
redundancy factor 110
regional consortia 54–5
reliability 31–2
    '100 per cent coursework' 122, 134–6
    comprehension assessments 90
    formative assessments 172
    NAEP scoring 255
    National Curriculum Assessment 117
    Scotland 236–7
    student-led assessment 60
Rémond, Martine vii, 5, 241–9

reproduction 58–9
research-based assessment 30
research programs 87
resource allocation 22–3
'response to literature' movement 113
responsive reading
    assessment focuses 183–4
    automated marking 158–67
    GCSE English 126, 133
    National Curriculum 197–9, 202
    postmodern principles 140–57
    validity 9, 17, 18
    Wales 214, 217
    see also reader response theories
responsiveness of assessment system 62
retellings 88
    see also recall
retrieval of information 200, 201
revising answers 184–7
Rosenblatt, Louise 90

Sadler, D.R. 174–6, 189–92
Sainsbury, Marian vii–viii, 1–6, 8–21,
    196–209, 216, 258–9
sampling procedures 250–1
SATs *see* standard assessment tasks
Save It booklet 207–8
Scharmer, O. 236
schemas 41–5, 85–6
Scholastic Aptitude Test 81
Schonell Reading Tests 65, 105–6
schooling in USA 78
Schools' Examination and Assessment Coun-
    cil (SEAC) 102–3
scientific approaches 52, 78–9
scoring procedures 81, 254–5
    see also mark schemes
Scotland 5, 222–40
    see also UK
Scottish Survey of Achievement (SSA) 236
screen captures online 149
SEAC *see* Schools' Examination and Assess-
    ment Council
search tasks online 145–6, 150–2
secondary schools 229–30
    see also key stage 3
self-assessments 55–6, 71, 131, 175
self-generated text activities 59–60
self-perception 174

semantics 143, 147–8
Senge, P. 236
sentence-completion tests 107–8
set texts 124–5
Shakespeare study 205–6
Siddiqui, Rifat viii, 5, 179–93
silent reading 78–9, 106
social nature of assessments 91
socio-cultural contexts 69, 72
sociolinguistics 85, 89, 90
Spear-Swerling, L. 29–30
Spearman, Charles 31
speed criterion, comprehension 80
spelling corrections 161–2, 163–4
Spencer, Ernie viii, 5, 222–40
SSA see Scottish Survey of Achievement
stakeholders 258–9
standard assessment tasks (SATs) 102–3
Standard Grade (Scotland) 225–6, 233
standard-sharing 237
standards, understanding 174–5
Standards and Quality report (HMIE) 227–9
Stanovich, K. 29
statutory assessment (Wales) 210–21
Sternberg, R.J. 29–30
Stobart, Gordon viii, 5, 168–78
story grammars 85
strategic activities 69
Structure Building Framework (Gernsbacher) 41
student-centred assessment 51, 56–7, 60
students
        c-rater feedback 164–6
        formative assessments 170
        see also children
subjectivity 55–6, 83
summary tasks 44–5, 47
summative assessments
        assessment focuses 189
        definition 168
        formative relationship 123, 169–70
        learning processes 73
        Scotland 231, 234–7
        validity 173
Sunflowers test 199–201
superhero genre 202–4
surface dyslexia 22, 27, 28
surface learning 170–1
Survey of English Language 228–9

synapses 40
syntactic variations (c-rater) 160

TAAS see Texas Assessment of Academic
        Skills
Taking a Closer Look at Reading 227
target-setting initiatives 231
task-level feedback 174
tasks
        French national evaluations 244
        generalisability 91
        Welsh statutory assessments 210–14
Taylor, Lynda viii, 4, 38–49, 225
Taylor, Wilson L. 83–4, 109–10
teacher-led assessment 50–1, 55–6, 60–1
teachers
        assessment focuses 187–9
        central position 64
        formative assessments 169, 170
        France 245
        requirements 68–73
        Scotland 222–40
        Wales 210, 215, 217–18, 220
teaching and learning 2–3, 5, 13–14, 65–73,
        127–31
teaching objectives (NLS) 71
test theory 31
tests
        assessment focuses 179
        France 241–9
        funnel effect 70–1
        high-stakes contexts 196–209
        learning relationship 171
        learning to do 64–74
        Scotland 231–4, 236
        UK history 102–21
        validation 8–12
        Wales 210–17, 220
Texas Assessment of Academic Skills (TAAS)
        171
text files online 150
texts
        authority diminution 60–2
        cognitive psychology 85–6
        comprehension process 76
        France 249
        memorisation 77
        NAEP 253–4
        National Curriculum 197–9, 208

texts *contd*
    removing 44, 47
    semantic representation 147–8
    Wales 212, 215
    see also literature
theme park activities 58
theories
    drivers 76–138
    in practice 140–93, 196–259
theory-based assessment 24–7
think-alouds 88
Thomas, P. 125, 134
Thompson, Paul viii, 5, 122–38
Thorndike, E.L. 32, 80
timing of assessments 169–70
To the Rescue booklet 202–4
top-down approaches 29
traditional approaches 25, 125, 129–30
training 27–30
transactive model 90
transformation 58–9
Trial State Assessment (NAEP) 251
truth theories 58–9
Tyler, Ralph 255
Tymms, Peter 228

UK
    examinations system 50–1
    formative/summative assessments 170
    historical contexts 102–21
    teacher trust 222–40
    validation theory 12
    validity challenges 196–209
understanding 43–4
uniform resource locators (URLs) 150
United Kingdom *see* UK
United States *see* USA
unseen texts 124
URLs *see* uniform resource locators
USA 76–101, 196, 250–7

validity 8–21, 31–2
    '100 per cent coursework' 134–6

comprehension assessments 90
    formative assessments 168, 172–6
    National Curriculum 117, 196–209
    Scotland 222–3, 237
    summative assessments 173
    UK reading tests 118
vector-based approaches (LSA) 147–8
verbatim detection 143, 153

Wales 5, 170, 210–21
    see also UK
Warner, L. 134
Watcyn Jones, David viii–ix, 5, 210–21
Watts, A.F. 107–8
Watts, Andrew ix, 5, 179–93, 196–209
Watts-Vernon test 107–8
websites 151, 235
    see also internet
Weschler Objective Reading Dimensions
    (WORD) test 25–6
Whetton, Chris ix, 5, 102–21
whole-language approaches 29, 124
Wiliam, Dylan 64, 127–8, 235
WISC-IV 25–26
Wolves exercise 248
Woodstock Reading Mastery Test 32
WORD *see* Weschler Objective Reading
    Dimensions
word knowledge 82–3
word reading tests 104–5, 106
word similarity matrices 161
workload 136–7
worldwide web *see* internet; online...; web-
    sites
Worthen, J. 125, 130
Wright, Paul 122–3
write-along tasks 88
writers' techniques 201, 203–4, 207–8, 217
writing activities 71
written assessment 133

Young's Group Reading Test 65–6, 108
Yule, W. 26